Heaven's Gates

Paperback Version

This book is a work of non-fiction. Unless otherwise noted, the author and the publisher make no explicit guarantees as to the accuracy of the information contained in this book.

© 2012 Ernest Johnson. All rights reserved.

No part of this book may be reproduced, stored in a retrieval system, or transmitted by any means without the written permission of the author.

First published 2012
Electronically published 2012 by Karah Kious-McJoslin, KarahbarkDesigns.com

Cover art by Karah Kious-McJoslin and Schad McJoslin

ISBN: 978-0-9882803-4-2

Heaven's Gates 1
The Christian Life – 15 Course Study 6
  MASTER OUTLINE NUMBER ONE 6
    THE BIBLE- THE WORD OF GOD 6
    THE BIBLE CLAIMS TO BE THE INSPIRED WORD
    OF GOD: 7
    THE BIBLE IS A DIFFICULT BOOK: 7
    THE BIBLE IS A BOOK OF ONENESS 8
    THE BIBLE CLAIMS SPECIAL POWER: 9
    THE BIBLE COMMANDS THE BELIEVER TO STUDY
    THE SCRIPTURES 11
  MASTER OUTLINE NUMBER TWO 14
    GOD - THE EXISTENCE OF GOD 14
    THE PERSONALITY OF GOD 15
    THE NATURE OF GOD 16
    THE GRACE OF GOD 17
    THE TRINITY OF GOD 19
  MASTER OUTLINE NUMBER THREE 22
    JESUS CHRIST THE SON OF GOD 22
    THE DIETY OF JESUS CHRIST 22
    THE HUMANITY OF JESUS CHRIST 25
    THE VIRGIN BIRTH OF JESUS CHRIST 26
    THE DEATH OF JESUS CHRIST 28
    THE RESURRECTION OF JESUS CHRIST 30
    THE ACENSION AND SECOND COMING OF JESUS
    CHRIST 41
  MASTER OUTLINE NUMBER FOUR 45
    THE HOLY SPIRIT 45
    THE DIETY OF THE HOLY SPIRIT 45
    THE EMBLEMS OF THE HOLY SPIRIT 47
    SINS AGAINST THE HOLY SPIRIT 49
    THE WORK OF THE HOLY SPIRIT 51
    THE FRUIT OF THE HOLY SPIRIT 54
  MASTER OUTLINE NUMBER FIVE 56

- SIN 56
  - THE ORIGIN OF SIN 57
  - WHAT IS SIN 59
  - HOW SIN ENTERED THE WORLD 60
  - THE RESULTS OF SIN 62
  - GOD'S REMEDY FOR SIN 65
- MASTER OUTLINE NUMBER SIX 67
  - JUDGMENTS 67
  - THE JUDGMENT OF THE BELIEVERS SINS 67
  - THE JUDGMENT OF THE BELIEVERS SELF 69
  - THE JUDGEMENT OF THE BELIEVERS WORKS 71
  - THE JUDGMENT OF THE NATIONS 73
  - THE JUDGMENT OF THE WICKED 77
- MASTER OUTLINE NUMBER SEVEN 81
  - REWARDS 81
  - THE CROWN OF LIFE 83
  - THE WREATH IMPERISHABLE 84
  - THE CROWN OF EXALTATION 86
  - THE CROWN OF RIGHTEOUSNESS 88
  - THE CROWN OF GLORY 90
- MASTER OUTLINE NUMBER EIGHT 93
  - THE CHURCH 93
  - THE CHURCH: IT'S FOUDATION 97
  - THE CHURCH: ITS HEAD 99
  - THE CHURCH: ITS ORGANIZATION 102
  - THE CHURCH: ITS DISCIPLINE 107
  - THE CHURCH: ITS WORSHIP AND WORK 110
  - THE CHURCH; ITS POWER 114
  - THE CHURCH: ITS FUTURE 117
- MASTER OUTLINE NUMBER NINE 122
  - PRAYER 122
  - WHAT IS PRAYER 123
  - WHY PRAY 125
  - HOW TO PRAY 126
  - WHERE TO PRAY 129
  - HINDRANCES TO PRAYER 131

DOES GOD ANSWER ALL PRAYERS	132
MASTER STUDY OUTLINE NUMBER TEN	138
FAITH	138
WHAT IS FAITH	140
THE IMPORTANCE OF FAITH	142
LITTLE FAITH	144
THREE KINDS OF FAITH	146
THE HALL OF FAITH	148
MASTER OUTLINE NUMBER ELEVEN	151
THE ABUNDANT LIFE	151
THE ABUNDANT LIFE IS A YIELDED LIFE	152
THE ABUNDANT LIFE IS A SERVICE LIFE	153
THE ABUNDANT LIFE IS A SEPERATED LIFE	156
THE ABUNDANT LIFE IS A SPIRIT-FILLED LIFE	157
THE ABUNDANT LIFE IS A MUTURE LIFE	161
MASTER OUTLINE NUMBER TWELVE	165
REPENTANCE	165
REPENTANCE DEFINED	167
REPENTANCE PREACHED	171
REPENT FROM DEAD WORKS	173
REPENTANCE AND GOD	177
REPENTANCE, IMPOSSIBLE TO RENEW	178
REPENTANCE THE IMPORTANTCE OF	185
REPENTANCE, EVIDENCE OF	186
MASTER OUTLINE NUMBER THIRTEEN	193
THE NEW BIRTH	193
JESUS AND THE TWO BIRTHS	194
THE NEW BIRTH ISSUES A NEW, SINLESS NATURE	197
THE NEW BIRTH IS IMPERISHABLE	198
THE NEW BIRTH-ITS MEANS	200
THE NEW BIRTH-ITS THREEFOLD PROOF	204
MASTER OUTLINE NUMBER FOURTEEN	206
GOD'S PLAN OF SALVATION	206
IT IS A FACT THAT GOD LOVES YOU	207
IT IS A FACT THAT YOU ARE A SINNER	207

   IT IS A FACT THAT YOU ARE DEAD IN SIN 208
   IT IS A FACT THAT CHRIST DIED FOR YOU 209
   IT IS A FACT THAT YOU CAN BE SAVED BY FAITH IN THE LORD JESUS CHRIST 210
   IT IS A FACT YOU CAN BE SAVED AND KNOW IT 212
   IT IS A FACT THAT GOD SAVED YOU TO OBEY HIM 213
  MASTER OUTLINE NUMBER FIFTEEN 216
   HOW TO WITNESS EFFECTIVELY 216
   THE IMPORTANCE OF WITNESSING 218
   THE QUALIFICATIONS OF A WITNESS 227
   THE APPROACH 233
   THE FOLLOW-THROUGH 239
   HOW TO SHARE GOD'S PLAN OF SALVATION 241
   HOW TO GIVE THE INVITATION 242
   HOW TO FOLLOW UP 243

MORAL CHARACTER 245
  MAGNETIC PERSONALITY 249
About the Author 267

The Christian Life – 15 Course Study

In this Master Outline, passages from Scripture are quoted from the New American Standard Bible, and they are shown within brackets { }. The page number preceding these is the page on which the verse is found, when one has a Bible the same as the author's.

Abbreviation: OT = Old Testament.

MASTER OUTLINE NUMBER ONE

THE BIBLE- THE WORD OF GOD

It is so important for a young Christian to start right; therefore, the first lessen is designed to establish your faith in the Bible, for it is the Word of God.

Keep in mind that the Bible is not a book of philosophy, although it is philosophical. Do not go to the Bible for a scientific treatise. However, there is no discrepancy between ascertained facts of science and the Bible. The Bible is not a *book* of history, but is found to be accurate when recording history. The Bible was given to man from God, revealing Jesus Christ, the Son of God, and God the Son, the only Savior.

(Page 1031-John 14:6). {Jesus said to them, "I am the way, and the truth, and the life; no one comes to the father, but through Me."} He is the center and circumference. It is Christ from Genesis to Revelation:

(Page 1019-John 5:39) {You search the Scriptures, because you think that in them you have eternal life; and it is these that bear witness of me.} The Bible is as high above all other books as the heavens are above the earth. Someone has said of the Bible: "Read it to be wise, believe it to be safe, and practice it to be right."

THE BIBLE CLAIMS TO BE THE INSPIRED WORD OF GOD:

(Page 1161, and read 2 Tim 3:16, 17.) {All Scripture is inspired by God and profitable for teaching, for reproof, for correction, for training in righteousness; that the man of God may be adequate, equipped for every good work.}

"All Scripture is inspired by God." By "inspired" we mean that the Holy Spirit exerted His super natural influence upon the writers of the Bible. Therefore, the Scriptures are God inspired word for word. By this we mean that every word, in the original, is fully and equally inspired in all of its teachings. The Bible does not contain the Word of God. It is the Word of God.

The writers of the Bible did not write by natural inspiration, or an act of human will. "Men moved by the Holy Spirit spoke from God": (Page 1195- 2Peter 1:21).for no prophecy was ever made by an act of human will, but men moved by the Holy Spirit of God.

(2 Sam.-23:2 OT). {David said, "The Spirit of the Lord spoke by me, and His word was on my tongue"}

> (1) The Holy Spirit is the author of the Bible: (Page 1195- 2Pet. 1:21).{ For no prophecy was ever made by an act of human will, but men moved by the Holy Spirit spoke from God.}
> (2) Man is the instrument used by the Holy Spirit to write the Bible.
> (3) Results: The infallible Word of God. Therefore, the Bible is free from

error and absolutely trustworthy. (Ps.119:89 OT). {Forever O Lord, Thy word is settled in heaven.} (Page 941-Matt. 24:35). {Heaven and earth will pass away, but My Words shall not pass away}

THE BIBLE IS A DIFFICULT BOOK:

The Bible is a difficult book because it came from the infinite to the finite from the unlimited, all powerful God, to limited man. Therefore, you cannot understand the Bible as you would understand the writings of Plato or Socrates. You can study the great philosophers with the natural mind, and by diligent application, grasp their profound meanings. If the Bible could be understood by natural man, it would be a natural book, and could not be the Word of God. Since the Bible is from God, and therefore spiritual, before you can receive its teachings, you must be born of the Spirit: (Page 1014-John 3:6) and filled with the Spirit: (Page 1134-Eph. 5:18).

Always approach the Bible praying that the Spirit will be your teacher and will guide you to a better understanding of His Holy Word, or it will remain a difficult, closed book: (Page 1033 John 16:12-15)- (John3:6) {That which is born of the flesh is flesh, and that which is born of the Spirit is Spirit.} (Eph. 5:18). {And do not get drunk with wine, for that is dissipation, but be filled with the Spirit}

(John 16:12-15) {Jesus says I have many more things to say to you, but you cannot bear them now. But when He, the Spirit of truth, comes, He will guide you into all the truth; for He will not speak on His own initiative, but whatever He hears, He will speak; and He will disclose to you what is to come. He shall glorify Me; for He shall take of mine, and shall disclose it to you. All things that the father has are Mine; therefore I said, that He takes is Mine, and will disclose it to you.}

THE BIBLE IS A BOOK OF ONENESS

(2 Peter 1:21) {For no prophecy was ever made by an act of human will, but men moved by the Holy Spirit spoke from God.} The oneness or the unity of the Bible is a miracle. It is a library of 66 books, written by over 35 different authors, in a period of approximately 1,500 years. Represented in the authors is a cross section of humanity, educated and uneducated, including kings, fisherman, public officials, farmers, teachers, and physicians. Included in the subjects are religion, history, law, science, poetry, drama, biography, and prophecy. Yet its various parts are harmoniously united as the parts that make up the human body. For 35 authors, with such varied backgrounds,

to write on so many subjects over 1,500 years in absolute harmony is a mathematical impossibility. It could not happen! Then how do we account for the Bible? The only adequate explanation is"....men moved by the Holy Spirit spoke from God.

THE BIBLE CLAIMS SPECIAL POWER:

(Heb.4:12) {For the Word of God is living and active and sharper than any two-edged sword, and piercing as far as the division of soul and spirit of both joints and marrow, and able to judge the thoughts and intentions of the heart.} "For the word of God is living and active…:

(1) The Bible claims dividing power as a sword (above verse). The Bible will separate man from sin: (Ps. 119:11OT), {Thy Word I have treasured in my heart, That I may not sin against Thee.} Or sin will separate man from the Bible: (Is. 59:2OT). {But your iniquities have made a separation between you and your God, And your sins have hidden His face from you, so that He does not hear.}

(2) The Bible claims reflecting power as a mirror: (Page 1185-James 1:22-25). {But prove yourselves doers of the word, and not merely hearers who delude themselves. For if anyone is a hearer of the word and not a doer, he is like a man who looks at his natural face in a mirror, for once he looked at himself and gone away, he has immediately forgotten what kind of person he was. But one who looks intently at the perfect law, the law of liberty, and abides by it, not having become a forgetful hearer but an effectual doer, this man shall be blessed in what he does.} In the Bible we see ourselves as God sees us-as sinners: (Page 1084-Rom. 3:23). {It is a fact that you are a sinner. For all have sinned and fall short of the glory of God.}

(3) The Bible claims cleansing power as water: (Page 1134-Eph. 5:26). {That He might sanctify her, having cleansed her by the washing of the water with the word. David prayed that God would wash him from iniquity and cleans him from sin:} (Ps. 51:2). {Wash me thoroughly from my iniquity, and cleans me from my sin.}

(4) The Bible claims reproductive power as seed: (Page 1190-1Pet. 1:23). The new birth is imperishable. For you have been born again not of seed which is perishable but imperishable, that is, through the living and abiding word of God. We are the children of God, because we have been born into the family of God by the imperishable seed of God. This is the new birth: (Page 1014-John 3:1-7). {Now there was a man of the Pharisees, named Nicodemus, a ruler of the Jews; this man came to him by night, and said to Him "Rabbi, we know that you have come from God as a teacher; for no one can do these signs that You do unless god is with him." Jesus answered and said to him, "Truly, truly, I say to you, unless one is born again, he cannot see the kingdom of God." Nicodemus said to Him, "How can a man be born when he is old? He cannot enter a second time into his mother's womb and be born, can he?" Jesus answered, "Truly, truly, I say to you, unless one is born of water, and the Spirit, he cannot enter the kingdom of God. That which is born of flesh is flesh, and that which is born of Spirit is spirit. Do not marvel that I said to you, 'You must be born again.'"}

(5) The Bible claims nourishing power as food: (Page1190-1Pet.2:2). {Like newborn babes, long for the pure milk of the word, that by it you may grow in respect to salvation.} The Bible is spiritual food for the soul. No Christian can remain strong in the Lord and not study the Word of God.

THE BIBLE COMMANDS THE BELIEVER TO STUDY THE SCRIPTURES

(2 Tim. 2:15) {Be diligent to present yourself approved to God as a workman who does not need to be ashamed, handling accurately the word of truth.}

"Be diligent to present yourself approved to God" is a command. As you study the Bible, you will discover that it does not just contain the word of God-it is the Word of God. You must also keep in mind that the Word of God contains the words of God, as well as the words of Satan, demons, angels, and man- both good and bad. God is truth and cannot lie. Satan"... is a liar, and the father of lies"

(Page 1024-John 8:44). {"You are of your father the devil, and you want to do the desires of your father. He was a murderer from the beginning, and does not stand in the truth, because there is no truth in him. Whenever he speaks a lie, he speaks from his own nature; for he is a liar, and the father of lies.}

Man is natural and therefore limited, and does not always speak the truth. To illustrate: (Page 938-Matt.22:15-46). {Then the Pharisees went and counseled together how they might entrap Him in what He said. And they sent their disciples to Him, along with the Herodians, saying, "Teacher, we know that You are truthful and teach the way of God and truth, and defer to no one; for You are not partial to any. Tell us therefore, what do you think? Is it lawful to give poll-tax to Caesar, or not?" But Jesus perceived their malice, and said, "Why are you testing Me, you hypocrites? Show Me the coin used for the poll-tax." And they brought Him a denarius. And He said to them, "Whose likeness and inscription is this?" They said to Him, "Caesars." Then He said to them, "Then render to Caesar the things that are Caesar's; and to God the things that are God's" and hearing this, they marveled, and leaving Him they went away. On that say some Sadducees (who say there is no resurrection) came to Him and questioned Him, saying, "Teacher, Moses said, 'If a man dies, having no children, his brother as next of kin shall marry his wife, and raise up an offspring to his brother.' Now there were seven brothers with us; and the first married and died, and having no offspring left his wife to his brother; so also the second, and the third, down to the seventh. And last of all, the woman died. In the resurrection therefore whose wife of the seven shall she be? For they all had her." But Jesus answered and said to them. "You are mistaken, not understanding the scriptures, or the power of God. For in the resurrection they neither marry, nor are given in marriage, but are like angels in heaven. But regarding the resurrection of the dead, have you not read that which was spoken to you by God saying, 'I am the God of Abraham, and the god of Isaac, and the God of Jacob?' He is not the God of the dead but of the living." And when the multitudes heard this, they were astonished at His teaching. But when the Pharisees heard that He had put the Sadducees to silence, they gathered themselves together. And one of them, a lawyer, asked him a question, testing Him, "Teacher, which is the great commandment in the law?" And He said to him, "'You shall love the Lord you God with all your heart, and with all your mind.' This is the great and foremost commandant. The second is like it, 'You shall love your neighbor as yourself.' On these two commandants depend the whole law and the Prophets." Now while the Pharisees were gathered together, Jesus asked them a question, saying, "What do you think about the Christ, whose son is He?" They said to Him, The son of David." He said to them, "Then how does David in the Spirit call Him 'Lord' saying, 'The Lord said to my Lord, "Sit at My right hand Until I put Thine enemies beneath thy feet?"' If David then calls Him 'Lord,' how is He his son?" And no one was able to answer Him a word, nor did anyone dare from that day on to ask Him another question.}

  In the above portion of Scripture, we have the words of Jesus, of the Pharisees, of the Herodians, and of the Sadducees. The Pharisees, Herodians, and Sadducees were trying to entangle Jesus in His teachings, that they might accuse Him of breaking God's law. Their words were spoken with evil intent,

revealing the thinking of the natural man, along with the words of God that came from the lips of Jesus. As you study the bible, ask yourself these questions:
   (1) Who is speaking: God, demon, angel, or man?
   (2) To whom is He speaking: to the nation of Israel, to the Gentiles, to the Church, to men in general, or to some individual man or being?
   (3) How can this scripture be applied to my own life to make me a better Christian

MASTER OUTLINE NUMBER TWO

GOD - THE EXISTENCE OF GOD

The Bible reveals God as the only Infinite and Eternal being, no beginning and no ending. He is Creator and Sustainer of all things. He is the Supreme Personal Intelligence, and Righteous Ruler of His universe. He is life, and therefore, the only source of life: (Page1018-John 5:26). {"For just as he Father has life in Himself, even so He gave to the Son also to have life in Himself.}

Man is natural and cannot know God. {"Can you discover the depths of God?" Can you discover the limits of the Almightly:?} (Job11:7 OT). God is a person and can be known only by revelation. In the Old Testament He revealed Himself to and through His prophets. In the New Testament He reveals himself through His Son Jesus Christ: (Page1170-Heb. 1:1-3). { God after He spoke long ago to the fathers in the prophets an many portions and in many ways, in these last says has spoken to us in His Son, shom He appointed heir of all things, through whom also He made the world. And He is radiance of His glory and the exact representation of His nature, and upholds all things by the Word of His power. When He made purification of sins, He sat dawn at the right hand of the Majesty on High;}

(Page 1179-Heb. 11:5,6). The Existence of God. {By faith Enoch was taken up so that he should not see death; And he was not found because God took him up; for he obtained the witness that before his being taken up he was pleasing God. And without faith it is impossible to please Him, for he who comes to God must believe that He is, and that He is a rewarder of those who seek Him.}

The Bible no where attempts to prove to argue the existence of God. "For he who comes to God must believe that He is." The existence of God is a fact taken for granted by the writers of both the old and new testaments.

"In the beginning God": (Gen.1:1OT). The Bible opens by announcing the sublime fact of God and His existence. There are arguments for the existence of God; they not conclusive, but they are food for thought.

(1) Universal belief in God comes from within man. It is innate in man, and comes from rational intuition.

(2) The argument from "cause and effect." Everything that began owes its existence to a cause. We have a watch; we must have a watchmaker. We have a building, we must have a builder. We have a creation; then we must have a creator. This creation could not have come into existence without an intelligent, personal creator anymore than the alphabet could produce a book itself without an author.

(3) The argument from anthropology. Man's moral and intellectual nature argues for a more moral and intellectual creator.

(4) The Bible and the Christ that it reveals, His virgin birth, His sinless life, His vicarious death, and His bodily resurrection-all of this and much more argue for the existence of God.

THE PERSONALITY OF GOD

(1Thes. 1:9) {For they themselves report about us what kind of a reception we had with you, and how you turned to God from idols to serve a living and true God.}

The Bible reveals God as a personality. He is called "…. A living and true God"- One possessing self-consciousness and self-determination. His personality is shown in what He does, such as:

(1) God loves. "God so loved the world": (Page1015- John 3:16). {"For God so loved the world, that He gave His only begotten Son, that whoever believes in Him should not parish, but have eternal life.}

(2) God hates. (Page 558 Prov.6:16 OT). {"There are six things which the Lord hates"}

(3) God cares. "He cares for you ": (Page 1193-1 Pet. 5:7). {Casting all your anxiety upon Him, because He cares for you.}

(4) God grieves. "He was grieved in His heart": (Gen. 6:6 OT). {And the Lord was sorry that He had made man on the earth, and He was grieved in His heart}.

Only a personality can hate, care, and grieve; therefore God must be a living, eternal, and personal being.

THE NATURE OF GOD

There are four definitions of God in the Bible. Since God cannot be defined, they are incomplete. However, they do throw light upon the nature of God. They are:

(1) "God is love." (1 John4:8) {The one who does not love does not know God, for God is love.} This is the nature of God in His divine compassion.

(2) "God is light" (Page1199-1 John 1:5). {And this is the message we have heard from Him and announce to you, that God is light, and in him there is no darkness at all. This is the nature of God in His divine character: In Him there is no darkness.}

(3) "God is a consuming fire": (Page 1182-Heb. 12:29). {For Our God is a consuming fire.} This is the nature of God in His divine holiness.

(4) "God is a spirit": (Page 1016-John 4:24). {"For God is spirit, and those who worship Him must worship Him in spirit and truth. This is the nature of God in His divine essence.}

The attributes of God reveal His nature. Do not think of His attributes as abstract, but as vital mediums through which His holy nature is unveiled- attributes ascribed to Him, such as:

(A) Life is ascribed to God: (Page 1018-John 5:26). {"For just as the Father has life in Himself, even so He gave to the Son also to have life in Himself;}

(B) All knowledge is ascribed to God: (Ps.147:5 OT). Great is our Lord, and abundant in strength; His

understanding in infinite. (Innumerable).
(C) All power is ascribed to God: (Page 1223-Rev. 19:6). {And I heard as it were, the voice of a great multitude and as the sound of many waters and as the sound of mighty peals of thunder, saying, "Hallelujah! For the Lord our God, the Almighty, reigns."}
(D) Filling the universe with His presence is ascribed to God: (Page 557 Ps.139:1-10 OT).{ O Lord, Thou hast searched me and known me. Thou dost know me when I set down and when I rise up; Thou dost understand my thought from afar. Thou dost scrutinize my path and my lying down. And art intimately acquainted with all my ways. Even before there is a word on my tongue. Behold, O Lord Thou dost know it all. Thou hast enclosed me behind and before. And laid Thy hand upon me; Such knowledge is to wonderful for me. It is too high, I cannot attain it. Where can I go from Thy Spirit? Or where can I flee from Thy presence? If I ascend to heaven, Thou art there; If I make my bed in Sheol, behold, Thou art there (The Neither World). If I take the wings of the dawn. If I dwell in the remotest part of the sea. Even there Thy hand will lead me. And Thy right hand will lay hold of me.} God is everywhere present, but He is not in everything. If God were in everything, man could worship any object and he would be worshiping God. God is a spirit being. "And those who worship Him must worship in Spirit and truth."

THE GRACE OF GOD

(Eph. 2:8) {For by grace you have been saved through faith; and that not of yourselves, it is a gift of God;}

Grace is the love and mercy of God in action. Mercy is negative, and love is positive; both together mean grace. To show mercy in love is grace. God showed mercy in love when He sent His Son to bear our sins in His own body on the cross:

(Page1015-John 3:16). {For God so loved the world, that He gave His only begotten Son, that whoever believes in Him should not parish, but have eternal life.}
- (1) The grace of God saves forever: (Page 1089-Rom.8:38.39). {For I am convinced that neither death, nor life, nor angels, nor principalities, nor things present, nor things to come, nor powers, nor height, nor depth, nor any other created thing, shall be able to separate us from the love of God, which is in Christ Jesus our Lord.}
- (2) The grace of God is unconditional; that is we are not saved on the condition that we "hold out unto the end" or that we "fail not" or that we "do our best." We are saved by the grace of God, apart from good works.
- (3) The grace of God is sufficient: (Page 1121- 2Cor. 12:9). {And He has said to me, "My grace is sufficient for you, for power is perfected in weakness." Most gladly, therefore, I will rather boast about my weaknesses, that the power of Christ may dwell in me}
- (4) The grace of God makes no discrimination: (Page 1226-Rev. 22:17). {And the Spirit and the bride say, "Come." And let the one who hears say "Come." And let the one who is thirsty come; let the one who wishes take the water of life without cost.}
- (5) The grace of God justifies: (Page1084-Rom.3:23.24). {For all have sinned and fall short of the glory of God, being justified as a gift by His grace through redemption which is in Christ Jesus;}
- (6) The grace of God makes every believer an heir: (Page 1166-Titus3:7). {That being justified by His grace we might be made heirs according to the hope of eternal life.}
- (7) The grace of God teaches the believer how to live: (Page 1165-Titus 2:11.12). {For the grace of God has appeared, bringing salvation to all men, instructing us to deny ungodliness and worldly desires and to live

sensibly, righteously and godly in the present age.}
The grace of God is nothing less than the unlimited love of God expressed in the gift of His Son, our Savior. It is the undeserved love of God toward sinners.

THE TRINITY OF GOD

(Page 915-Matt. 3:16.17): {And after being baptize Jesus went up immediately from the water, and behold, the heavens were opened, and he saw the Spirit of God descending as a dove, and coming upon Him, and behold, a voice out of the heavens, saying. "This is My beloved Son, in whom I am well-pleased."} Trinity of God we mean His tri-personal existence as Father, Son, and Holy Spirit-three distinct persons in one God.

(1) The Father is recognized as God: (Page 1189-1 Pet. 1:2). { According to the foreknowledge of God the Father, by the sanctifying work of the Spirit, that you may obey Jesus Christ and be sprinkled with his Blood: May grace and peace be yours in the fullest measure.} And is all the fullness of the Godhead invisible: (Page 1012-John 1:18). { No man has seen God at any time; the only begotten God (Son) who is in the bosom of the father, He has explained Him.}

(2) The Son is recognized as God: (Page 1171-Heb. 1:8).{But of the Son He says, Thy throne O God is for ever and ever, And the righteous Scepter is the Scepter of His kingdom.} And is all the fullness of the Godhead manifested in the flesh: (Page 1012-John1:14). {And the word became flesh, and dwelt among us, and we beheld His glory, glory as of the only begotten from the Father, full of grace and truth. Begotten,} (only one of His Kind.)

(3)The Holy Spirit is recognized as God: (Page 1047-Acts 5:3.4). {But Peter said, "Ananias, why has Satan filled your heart to lie to the Holy Spirit, and to keep back some of the price of the land? while it remained unsold, did it not remain your own? And after it was sold, was it not under your control? Why is it that you have conceived this deed in your heart? You have not lied to men, but to God."} And is all the fullness of the Godhead acting upon man, convicting him of sin: (Page 1033- John 16:7-11) {But I tell you the truth, it is to your advantage that I go away; for if I do not go away, the Helper shall not come to you; but if I go I will send Him to you. And He when He comes, will convict the world concerning sin, and righteousness, and judgment; concerning sin, because they do not believe me; and concerning righteousness, because I go to the father, and you no longer behold Me; and concerning judgment, because the ruler of this world has been judged. And guiding the believer into all truth.} (Page1033-John 16: 12-15). {I have many more things to say to you, but you cannot bear them now. But when He, the Spirit of truth, comes, He will guide you into all truth; for He will not speak on His own initiative, but whatever He hears, He will speak' and He will disclose to you what is to come. He shall glorify Me for He shall take of Mine, and shall disclose it to you. All things that the Father has are Mine therefore I said, that He takes of Mine, and will disclose it to you.}

(4) The doctrine of the Trinity is not explicit in the Old Testament, but is rather implied, "Then God said, Let us make man…": (Gen.1:26 OT). Then God said, {"Let us make man in Our image, according to our likeness; and let them rule over the fish of the sea and over the birds of the sky (heavens) and over the cattle and over all the earth, and over every creeping thing that creeps on the earth."}

(5) The doctrine of the Trinity is revealed in the New Testament. In the below Scriptures: (Page 914 Matt. 3:16.17). {And after being baptized, Jesus went up immediately from the water, and behold, the heavens were opened, and he saw the

Spirit of God descending as a dove, and coming upon Him. And behold a voice out of the heavens, saying, "This is My beloved Son, in whom I am well-pleased."} We have Christ being baptized in water, the Father speaking from heaven, and the Holy Spirit descending as a dove. We are to be baptized in the name (not names) of "the Father and the son and the Holy Spirit": Page 949-Matt.28:19). {"Go therefore and make disciples of all the nations, baptizing them in the name of the Father and the Son and the Holy Spirit.}

    (6) Even creation implies the doctrine of the Trinity. In creation, we have space, matter, and time in one creation. In space, we have length, breadth, and height in one space. In matter, we have energy, motion, and phenomenon in one substance. In time we have past, present, and future in one time. In man, we have body, soul, and spirit in one man: (Page 1151-1Thess. 5:23). {Now may the God of peace Himself sanctify you: entirely; and may your spirit and soul and body be preserved complete, without blame at the coming of our Lord Jesus Christ.}

    (7) In the Holy Trinity, we have Father, Son, and Holy Spirit in one God.

MASTER OUTLINE NUMBER THREE

JESUS CHRIST THE SON OF GOD

Christianity differs from all religions-it is the life of the Son of God made living in man. Christ is Christianity, Christianity is Christ. He is the supreme subject of each book in the New Testament, and fulfills all the promises of God in the Old Testament, from His incarnation to His second coming as "Lord of lords and King of kings": Page 1222-Rev. 17:14 says {These will wage war against the Lamb, and the Lamb will overcome them, because He is Lord of lords and King of kings, and those who are with him are the called and chosen and faithful."}

He is the God man Christ Jesus in glory, exalted above all creatures. (Page 948-Matt. 28:18). {Jesus said, "Authority has been given to me in heaven and earth."}

During His earthly ministry, He claimed to be God incarnate (in human flesh). He is all that He claimed to be, or He is less than least: (Page 1210-Rev 1:8). {"I am the Alpha and Omega," says the Lord God. "who is and who was and who is to come, the Almighty."}

Before His claim can be denied, there are some things that must be accounted for:
    A. His virgin birth,
    B. His holy, sinless life,
    C. His many miracles,
    D. His vicarious death and His bodily resurrection.

THE DIETY OF JESUS CHRIST

The deity of Jesus Christ, or His God nature, is well established in the New Testament. Some of the facts are:
    (1) He is called God by the Apostle John in John 1:1: (Page 1011 John 1:1) {In the beginning was the Word, and the Word was with God, And the Word was God.}
    (2) He is called God by the Apostle Thomas: (Page 1038-John 20:28). {Says Thomas answered and said to Him,

"My Lord and my God!"}
(3) He is called God by God the Father: (Page 1171-Heb. 1:8). {But of the Son He says, "Thy Throne, O God, is forever and ever.}
(4) He claimed to be God in that He was the Father before creation: (Page1034-John 17:5). {"And now, glorify Thou Me together with Thy self, Father, with the glory which I had with Thee before the world was.}
(5) He claimed to be God in that He was before Abraham: "Abraham rejoiced to see me say…" (Page 1024-John 8:51-59). {"Truly, truly, I say to you, if anyone keeps My word he never shall see death." The Jews said to Him, "Now we know that You have a demon. Abraham died, and the prophets also; and you say, 'If anyone keeps My word, he shall never taste death.' Surely You are not greater than our father Abraham, who died? The prophets died too; Whom do You make Yourself out to be?" Jesus answered. "If I glorify myself, My glory is nothing; it is My Father who glorifies Me, of whom you say, 'He is our God'; and you have not come to know Him, but I know Him; and if I say that I do not know Him, I shall be a liar like you, but I do know Him, and keep his word. 'Your father Abraham rejoiced to see My day, and he saw it and was glad." Then the Jews therefore said to Him, "You are not yet fifty years old, and have you seen Abraham?" Jesus said to them, "Truly, truly, I say to you, before Abraham was born, I am." Therefore they picked up stones to throw at Him; but Jesus hid Himself, and went out of the temple.}
(6) He received worship, and only God is to be worshiped: (Page 929 Matt. 14:33). {And those in the boat worshiped Him, saying, "You are certainly Gods Son!"} Angels refused worship: (Page 1226-Rev. 22:8.9). {And I, John, am the one who heard and saw these things. And when I heard and saw, I fell down to

worship at the feet of the angel who showed me these things. And he said to me, "Do not do that I am a fellow servant of yours and your brethren the prophets and of those who heed the words of this book; worship God."} Man refused worship: (Page 1055-Acts 10:25.26). {And when it came about that Peter entered, Cornelius met him, and fell at his feet and worshiped him. But Peter raised him up, saying. "Stand up; I too am just a man."}

(7) He forgives sin: (Page 953-Mark 2:5-11). {And Jesus seeing their faith said to the Paralytic, "My son, you sins are forgiven." But there were some scribes sitting there and reasoning in their hearts, "Why does this man speak this way? He is blaspheming; who can forgive sins but God alone?" And immediately Jesus aware in His spirit that they were reasoning that way within themselves, said to them, "Why are you reasoning about these things in your hearts? Which is easier, to say to the paralytic, 'Your sins are forgiven' or to say, 'Arise, and take up your pallet and walk?' But in order that you may know that the Son of Man has authority on earth to forgive sins- He said to the paralytic- 'I say to you rise, take up your pallet and go home.'"}

(8) He is creator and maker of all things: (Page 1142-Col. 1:16). {For by Him all things were created, both in the heavens and on earth, visible and invisible, whether thrones or dominions or rulers or authorities-all things have been created by Him and for Him.}

(9) He is the sustainer of all things: (Page 1170-Heb.1:3). {And He is the radiance of His glory and the exact representation of His nature, and upholds all things by the word of His power. When He had made purification of sins, He sat down at the right hand of the Majesty on High;}

(10) Only God can control the universe: He claimed to have all authority…in heaven and on earth: (Page 948

Matt. 28:18). {And Jesus came up and spoke to them saying, "All authority has been given to me in heaven and on earth."}

(11) God has all authority: He walked upon the blue waters of Galilee. The winds and the waves obeyed His command. He healed the sick and raised the dead. He gave sight to the blind and hearing to the deaf. He cast out demons and made the lame walk. He turned water into wine, and fed five thousand with the lunch of a lad.

THE HUMANITY OF JESUS CHRIST

The humanity of Jesus Christ is seen in His human parentage (Page 913-Matt.2:11).{"Where is He who has been born King of the Jews? For we saw His star in the east, and have come to worship Him "}

(1) He developed as a normal human being: (Page 978-Luke 2:52). {And Jesus kept increasing in wisdom and stature, and in favor with God and men.}

(2) He was subject to all the infirmities of the human nature:

(A) He was hungry: (Page 915-Matt. 4:2). {And after He had fasted forty days and forty nights, He then became hungry.}

(B) He was thirsty: (Page 1037-John 19:28). {After this, Jesus, knowing that all things had already been accomplished, in order that the Scripture might be fulfilled ,said" I am thirsty."}

(C) He was weary: (Page 1016-John 4:6). {And Jacob's well was there. Jesus therefore, being wearied from His journey, was sitting thus by the well. It was about the sixth hour.}

(D) He wept: (Page1027-John 11:35). {Jesus wept}

(E) He was tempted: (Page 1173-Heb. 4:15). {For we do not have a high priest who cannot sympathize with our weaknesses, but one who has been

tempted in all things as we are, yet with out sin.}
Jesus is man, and yet He is more than man. He is not God and man, but God-man. He is God in human flesh. His two natures are bound together in such a way that the two become one, having a single conscious and will.

THE VIRGIN BIRTH OF JESUS CHRIST

(Page 975 Luke 1:26-35). {Now in the sixth month the angel Gabriel was sent from God to a city in Galilee, called Nazareth. To a virgin engaged to a man whose name was Joseph, of the descendants of David; and the virgin's name was Mary. And coming in, he said to her, "Hail, favored one! The Lord is with you." But she was greatly troubled at this statement, and kept pondering what kind of salutation this might be. And the angel said to her, "Do not be afraid, Mary; for you have found favor with God. And behold, you will conceive in your womb, and bear a son, and you shall name Him Jesus. He will be great, and will be called the Son of the Most High; and the Lord God will give Him the throne of His Father David; and He will reign over the house of Jacob forever; and His Kingdom will have no end." And Mary said to the angel, "How can this be, since I am a virgin?" And the angel answered and said to her, "The Holy Spirit will come upon you, and the power of the Most High will over shadow you; and for that reason the holy offspring shall be called the Son of God."}

The virgin birth is without parallel in human history. It was by the virgin birth that God became man, other being that of man--man without sin. (Page 1173-Heb.4:15). {For we do not have a high priest who cannot sympathize with our weaknesses, but one who has been tempted in all things as we are, yet without sin.} The union of the two natures became the God-man Christ Jesus.

> (1) The first of the virgin birth is found in: (Gen.3:15 (OT)). { And I will put enmity between you and the woman, And between your seed and her seed; He shall bruise you on the head, And you shall bruise him on

the heal.} The one to defeat Satan was to be born of the "seed" of the woman. Understand that One was to be born of a woman without a human father. (above verses Luke-34.35).

(2) Isaiah prophesied that a "virgin will be with child and bear a son, and she child will call His name Immanuel (God is with us)"- (Is.7:14). {"Therefore the Lord Himself will give you a sign: Behold, a virgin will be with child and bear a son, and she will call His name Immanuel."}

(3) Again Isaiah prophesied saying, "a child will be born of us, a son will be given us": (Is. 9:6.7). {For a child will be born of us, a son will be given us; And the government will rest on His shoulders; And His name will be called Wonderful Eternal Counselor, Mighty God. There will be no end to the increase of his government or of peace. On the throne of David and over His kingdom, To establish it and uphold it with justice and righteousness from then on and forevermore. The zeal of the Lord of hosts will accomplish this.} This means that God gave His only begotten son who was with Him from eternity, and the child Jesus was born of a virgin. God gave His Son "to us."

(4) According to prophecy, He was to be born in Bethlehem: (Micah 5:2 OT). {"But as for you, Bethlehem Ephrathah, Too little to be among clans of Judah, From you will go forth for Me to be ruler of Israel. His goings forth are from long ago, From the days of eternity."} Joseph with Mary went up to Bethlehem to be taxed, and to fulfill prophecy. (Page 977-Luke 2:1-7). {Now it came about in those days that a decree went out from Caesar Augustus, that a census be taken of all the inhabited earth. This was the first census taken while Quirinius was governor of Syria. And all were proceeding to register for the

census, everyone to his own city. And Joseph also went up from Galilee, from the city of Nazareth, to Judea, to the city of David, which is called Bethlehem, because he was of the house and family of David, in order to register, along with Mary, who was engaged to him, and was with child. And it came about that while they were there, the days were completed for her to give birth. And she gave birth to her first-born son; and she wrapped Him clothe, and laid Him in a manger, (feeding trough) because there was no room for them in the inn.}

THE DEATH OF JESUS CHRIST

(Phil. 2:8) {And being found in appearance as a man, He humbled Himself by becoming obedient to the point of death, even death on a cross.} The death of Jesus Christ is mentioned more than 120 times in the New Testament, and is spoken of many times by the prophets in the Old Testaments.

(1) The death of Jesus Christ was vicarious: (Page 936-Matt.20:28). {Just as the Son of Man did not come to be served, but to serve, and to give His life a ransom for many.} He was God's substitute for sinners: (Page 1116-2Cor. 5:21). {He made Him who knew no sin to be sin on our behalf, that we might become the righteousness of God in Him. On the cross, Christ was made sin for the sinner. By faith in Him the sinner is made righteous with the righteousness of God.}

(2) Death of Jesus was natural: (Page 1037-John 19:31-37). {The Jews therefore, because it was the day of preparation, so that the bodies should not remain on the cross on the Sabbath (for the Sabbath was a high day) asked Pilate that their legs might be broken, and that they might be taken away. The soldiers therefore came, and broke the legs of the first man, and of the other man who was crucified with Him; but coming to Jesus, when they saw that He had already been dead,

they did not break his legs; but one of the soldiers pierced his side with a spear, and immediately there came out blood and water. And he who has seen has born witness, and his witness is true; and he knows that he is telling the truth, so that you also may believe. For these things came to pass, that the Scripture might be fulfilled. Not a bone of Him shall be broken."} And another Scripture says, "They shall look upon Him whom they pierced." By a natural death, we mean that His Spirit and soul were separated from His body.

(3) The death of Jesus Christ was unnatural: (Page 1087-Rom. 6:23). {For the wages of sin is death, but the free gift of God is eternal life in Christ Jesus our Lord.} By an unnatural death, we mean that since He was sinless, in that He "committed no sin: (Page 1116-2Cor. 5:21). {He made Him who knew no sin to be sin on our behalf, that we might become the righteousness of God in Him.} ----before He could die, He had to be "made sin on our behalf." Therefore, His death was unnatural.

(4) The death of Jesus Christ was preternatural: (Page 1219-Rev. 13:8). {And all who dwell on the earth will worship Him, everyone whose name has not been written from the foundation of the world in the book of life of the Lamb who has been slain.} By this, we mean that the death of Jesus Christ was not an afterthought with God; it was the forethought of God.

(5) The death of Jesus Christ was supernatural: (Page 1026-John 10:17.18). {"For this reason, the Father loves Me, because I lay down My life that I may take it again. No one has taken it away from Me, but I lay it down on My own initiative. I have authority to lay it down, and I have authority to take it up again. This commandment I received from My Father."} Jesus said, "no one has taken it away from me." Then He said, "I lay it down on My own initiative (supernaturally)." "I have authority to take it up again

(supernaturally)." This He did on the cross, and three days and three nights later, He took up life again when arose from the dead. Only God in the form of man could die a vicarious, natural, unnatural preternatural, and supernatural death.

THE RESURRECTION OF JESUS CHRIST

(Page 947 Matt. 28:1-20). {Now after the Sabbath, as it began to dawn toward the first day of the week, Mary Magdalene and the other Mary came to look at the grave. And behold, a severe earthquake had occurred, for an angel of the Lord descended from heaved and came and rolled and his away the stone and sat upon it. And his appearance was like lightning, and his garment as white as snow; and the guards shook for fear of him, and became like dead men. And the angel answered and said to the women, "Do not be afraid; I know that you are looking for Jesus who has been crucified. He is not here, for He has risen, just as He said. Come, see the place where He was lying. And go quickly and tell His disciples that He has risen from the dead; and behold, He is going before you. There you will see Him; behold I have told you." And they departed quickly from the tomb with fear and great joy and ran to report it to His disciples. And behold, Jesus met them and greeted them. And they came up and took hold of His feet and worshiped Him. Then Jesus said to them, "Do not be afraid; go and take word to my brethren to leave Galilee, and there they shall see Me." Now while they were on there way, behold, some of the guard came into the city and reported to the chief priest all that had happened. And when they had assembled with the elders and counseled together, they gave a large sum of money to the soldiers, and said, "You are to say, 'His disciples came by night and stole Him away while we were asleep.' And if this could come to the governor's ears, we will win Him over and keep you out of trouble." And they took the money and did as they had been instructed; and this story was widely spread among the Jews, and it is to this day. But the eleven disciples proceeded to Galilee, to the mountain which Jesus had And Jesus designated. And when they saw Him, they worshiped Him; but some were doubtful. And Jesus came up and spoke to them, saying "All authority has been given to me in heaven and on earth. Go therefore and make disciples of all nations, baptizing them in the name of the Father and the Son and the Holy Spirit. Teaching them to observe all that I commanded you; and lo, I am with you always, even to the end of the age."}

Jesus said, "I am the resurrection and the life": (Page 1027-John 11:25). {Jesus said to her, "I am the resurrection and the life; he who believes in Me shall live even if he dies."} The resurrection of Jesus Christ was the doctrine of every disciple, the faith of every believer, the courage of every martyr, the theme of every sermon, and the power of every evangelist. Luke tells us that we have "many convincing proofs" of His resurrection: (Page 1041-Acts 1:3). {To these He also presented Himself alive, after His suffering, by many convincing proofs, appearing to them over a period of forty days, and speaking of the things concerning the kingdom of God.}

Lets us look at some of the "convincing proofs" according to eye witnesses:

(1) After His resurrection He appeared first to Mary Magdalene: (Page 1038-John 20:11-18). {But Mary was standing outside the tomb weeping; and so as she wept, she stooped and looked into the tomb; and she beheld two angels in white sitting one at the head, and one at the feet, where the body of Jesus had been laying. And they said to her, "Woman, why are you weeping?" she said to them, "Because they have taken away my Lord, and I do not know where they have laid Him." When she had said this, she turned around, and beheld Jesus standing there, and did not know that it was Jesus. Jesus said to her, "Woman why are you weeping? Whom are you seeking?" Supposing Him for the gardener, she said to Him, "Sir, if you had carried Him away, tell me where you have laid Him, and I will

take Him away." Jesus said to her, "Mary!" She turned and said to Him in Hebrew, Rabboni" (which means, Teacher) Jesus said to her, "Stop clinging to me, for I have not ascended to the Father; but go to my brethren, and say to them, 'I ascend to My Father and your Father, and My God and your God.'" Mary Magdalene came, announcing to the disciples, "I have seen the Lord," and that He had said these things to her.}

(2) He appeared to the women returning from the grave: (Page 948-Matt. 28:5-10). {And the angel answered and said to the women, "Do not be afraid; for I know that you are looking for Jesus who has been crucified He s not here, for He has risen, just as He said. Come, see the place where He was lying. And go quickly and tell His disciples that He has risen from the dead; and behold, He is going before you into Galilee, there you will see Him; behold, I have told you." And they departed quickly from the tomb with fear and great joy and ran to report it to His disciples. And behold, Jesus met them and greeted them. And they came up and took hold of His feet and worshiped Him. Then Jesus said to them, "Do not be afraid; go and take word to my brethren to leave Galilee, and there they shall see Me."}

(3) Then He appeared to Peter: (Page 1009-Luke 24:34). Saying, {"The Lord has really risen, and has appeared to Simon."}

(4) To the Emmaus disciples: (Page 1008-Luke 24:13-31). {And behold, two of them were going that very day to a village named Emmaus, which was about seven miles from Jerusalem. And they were conversing with each other about all these things which had taken place. And it came about that while they were conversing and discussing, Jesus Himself approached, and began traveling with them. But their eyes were

prevented from recognizing Him. And He said to them, "What are these words that you are exchanging with one another as you are walking?" And they stood still, looking sad. And one of them, named Cleopas , answered and said to Him "Are you the only one visiting Jerusalem and unaware of the things which have happened here these days?" And He said to them, "What things?" And they said to Him, "The things about Jesus the Nazarene, who was a prophet mighty in deed and word in the sight of God and all the people, and how the chief priests and our rulers delivered Him up to the sentence of death, and crucified Him. But we were hoping that it was He who was going to redeem Israel. Indeed, besides all this, it is the third day since these things happened. But also some women among us amazed us. When they were at the tomb early in the morning, and did not find the His body, they came, saying that they had also seen a vision of angels, who said that He was alive. And some of those who were with us went to the tomb and found it just exactly as the women said; but Him they did not see." And He said to them. "O foolish men and slow of heart to believe in all that the prophets have spoken! Was it not necessary for the Christ to suffer these things and to enter into His glory?" And the beginning with Moses and with all the prophets, He explained to them the things concerning Himself in all the scriptures. And they approached the village where they were going, and He acted as though He would go farther. And they urged Him, saying, "Stay with us, for it is getting toward evening, and the day is now nearly over." And He went in to stay with them. And it came about that when He had reclined at the table with them, He took the bread and blessed it, and breaking it, He began giving it to them. And their eyes were opened and they recognized Him; And He

vanished from their sight.}
(5) To the apostles, Thomas not present: (1009 Luke 24: 36-43). {And while they were telling these things, He Himself stood in their midst. But they were startled and frightened and thought they were seeing a spirit. And He said to them "Why are you troubled, and why do doubts arise in your hearts? See My hands and My feet, that it is I Myself; touch Me and see, for a spirit does not have flesh and bones as you see I have." And when He had said this, He showed them His hands and His feet. And while they still could not believe it for joy and marveling. He said to them "Have you anything here to eat?" And they gave Him a piece of a broiled fish; and He took it and ate it before them.}
(6) Again to the apostles, Thomas present: (Page-1038-John 20:24-29). {But Thomas, one of the twelve, called Didymus, was not with them, when Jesus came. The other disciples therefore were saying to him, "We have seen the Lord!" But he said to them, "Unless I shall see in His hands the imprint of the nails, and put my finger into the place of the nails, and put my hand into His side, I will not believe." And after eight days again His disciples were inside, and Thomas with them. Jesus came, the doors having been shut, and stood in their midst, and said, "Peace be with you." Then He said to Thomas, "Reach here your finger, and see my hands; and reach here your hand, and put it into my side; and be not unbelieving, but believing." Thomas answered and said to Him, "My Lord and My God!" Jesus said to him, "Because you have seen me, have you believed? Blessed are they who did not see, and yet believed."}
(7) To the seven by the Sea of Tiberias: (Page 1039-John 21: 1-23). {After there things Jesus manifested Himself again to the disciples at the Sea of Tiberias, and He manifested Himself in this way. They were together

Simon Peter, and Thomas called Didymus, and Nathanael of Cana in Galilee, and the sons of Zebedee, and two others of His disciples. Simon Peter said to them, "I am going fishing." They said to him, "We will also come with you." They went out, and got into the boat; and that night they caught nothing. But when the day was now breaking, Jesus stood on the beach; yet His disciples did not know that it was Jesus. Jesus therefore said to them, "Children, you do not have any fish, do you?" They answered Him, "no." And He said to them, "Cast the net on the right-hand side of the boat, and you will find a catch." They cast therefore, and then they were not able to haul it in because of the great number of fish. That disciple therefore, whom Jesus loved said to Peter, "It is the Lord" And so when Simon Peter heard that it was the Lord, he put his outer garment (for he was stripped for work) and threw himself into the sea. But the other disciples came in the little boat, for they were not far from the land, but about one hundred yards away, dragging the net full of fish. And so when they got out upon the land, they saw a charcoal fire already laid, and fish placed on it, and bread. Jesus said to them, "Bring some of the fish which you have caught." Simon Peter went up, and drew the net to land, full of large fish, a hundred and fifty-three; and although there were so many, the net was not torn. Jesus said to them, "Come and have breakfast" None of the disciples ventured to question Him, "Who are you?" knowing that it was the Lord. Jesus came and took the bread, and gave it to them, and the fish likewise. This is now the third time that Jesus was manifested to the disciples, after He was raised from the dead. So when they had finished breakfast, Jesus said to Simon Peter, "Simon son of John do you love me more than these?" He said to Him, "Yes Lord; You know that I love you." He said to him, "Tend my lambs." He said to him again a second time, "Simon, son of John, do you love me?" He said to Him, "Yes Lord: You know I love you." He said to him, "Shepherd My sheep." He said to him a third time, Simon, son of John, "Do you love me?" Peter was grieved because He said to him a third time, "Do you love me?" And he said to Him, "Lord, You know all things; You know that I love You." Jesus said to him, "Tend My sheep. Truly, truly, I say to you, when you were younger, you used to gird yourself, and walk wherever you wished; but when you grow old, you will stretch out your hands, and someone else will gird you, and bring you where you do not wish to go." Now this He said, signifying by what kind of death he would glorify God. And when He had spoken this, He said to him, "Follow Me!" Peter turning around, saw the disciple whom Jesus loved following them; the one who also had leaned back on His breast at the supper, and said, "Lord, who is the one who betrays you?" Peter therefore seeing him said to Jesus, "Lord, and what about this man?" Jesus said to him, "If I want him to remain until I come, what is that to you? You follow Me!" This saying therefore went out among the brethren that that disciple would not die; yet Jesus did not say to him that he would not die, but only, "If I want him to remain until I come, what is that to you?"}

(8) To over five hundred brethren: (Page 1109-1Cor. 15:6). {After that He appeared to more than five hundred brethren at one time, most of whom remain until now, but some have fallen asleep;}

(9) He was seen of James: (Page 1109-1Cor. 15:7). {Then He appeared to James, then to all the apostles;}

(10) He was seen again by the eleven apostles: (Page948-Matt. 28:16-20). {But the eleven disciples proceeded to Galilee, to the mountain which Jesus had designated.

And when they saw Him, they worshiped Him; but some were doubtful. And Jesus came up and spoke to them saying, "All authority has been given to Me in heaven and on earth. Go therefore and make disciples of the nations, baptizing them in the name of the Father and the Son and the Holy Spirit, teaching them to observe all that I commanded you; and lo, I am with you always, even to the end of the age."} (Page 1041-Acts1:3-12).{To these He presented Himself alive, after His suffering, by many convincing proofs, appearing to them over a period of forty days, and speaking of the things concerning the kingdom of God. And gathering them together, He commanded them not to leave Jerusalem, but to wait for what the Father had promised, "Which," He said, "you heard from Me; for John baptized with water, but you shall be baptized with the Holy Spirit not many days from now." And so when they had come together, they were asking Him saying, "Lord, is it at this time You are restoring the kingdom of Israel?" He said to them, "It is not for you to know times or epochs which the Father has fixed by His own authority; but you shall receive power when the Holy Spirit has come upon you; and you shall be My witnesses both in Jerusalem, and in all Judea and Samaria, and even to the remotest part of the earth." And after He had said these things, He was lifted up while they were looking on and a cloud received Him out of their sight. And as they were gazing intently into the sky while He was departing, behold, two men in white clothing stood beside them; and they also said, "Men of Galilee, why do you stand looking into the sky? This Jesus, who has been taken up from you into heaven, will come in just the same way as you have watched Him go into heaven." Then they returned to Jerusalem from the mount called Olivet, which is near Jerusalem, a Sabbath day's journey away.}

(11) He was seen of Stephen, the first martyr: (Page 1051-Acts7:55). {But being full of the Holy Spirit, he gazed intently into the heaven and saw the glory of God, and Jesus standing at the right hand of God.}

(12) He was seen of Paul on his way to Damascus: (Page 1053-Acts 9:3-6; also Page 1109- 1Cor. 15:8). {And it came about that as he journeyed, he was approaching Damascus, and suddenly a light from heaven flashed around him; and he fell to the ground, and heard a voice saying to him, "Saul, Saul, why are you persecuting Me?" and He said, "I am Jesus whom you are persecuting, but rise, and enter the city, and it shall be told you what you must do."} Also: (Page 1109-1Cor.15:8). { and last of all, as it were to one untimely born, He appeared to me also. }

Many of these eye witnesses martyrs' deaths because they preached the resurrection of Jesus Christ. They were glad to die for a living Christ. They had many "convincing proofs." When Jesus was arrested in the garden of Gethsemane, all if His disciples "left Him and fled": (Page 945-Matt. 26:56). {"But all this has taken place that the Scriptures of the prophets may be fulfilled." Then all the disciples left Him and fled. } From this time until after His resurrection, the disciples lived in fear. They did not believe that He would rise from the dead: (Page 1038-John 20:9). {For as yet they did not understand the Scripture that He must rise again from the dead.} Had Jesus not come from the dead, the cross would have been the end of Christianity.

After the death of Jesus, we see His disciples dejected, discouraged, and defeated. The death of Jesus meant but one thing to them; the end. How do we account for the great change that came into their lives, three days and three nights later? The only logical explanation is they had the "convincing proofs" He had risen from the dead, and was alive forevermore. They saw Him, talked to Him, touched Him, and ate with Him. Now look at some "convincing proofs" according to circumstantial evidence:

(1) The change that came into the lives of the disciples: after the resurrection-from fear to unlimited courage. They rejoiced in persecution: (Page 1049-Acts 5:40-42). {And they took his advice; and after calling the apostles in, they flogged them and ordered them to speak no more in the name of Jesus, and released them. So they went on their way from the presence of the Council, rejoicing that they had been considered worthy to suffer shame for His name. And every day in the temple from house to house, they kept right on teaching and preaching Jesus as the Christ.} They chose death, with faith in the resurrected Christ, rather than to deny that faith and be released. (Page 1181-Heb. 11:35). {Women received back their dead by resurrection; and others were tortured, not accepting their release, in order that they might obtain a better resurrection.}

(2) The early church began to worship on the first day of the week, the day of the resurrection. It was not a law- it was spontaneous: (Page1067-Acts 20:7). {And on the first day of the week, when we were gathered together to break bread, Paul began talking to them, intending to depart the next day, and he prolonged his message until midnight.} For almost two thousand years the church has worshiped on the first day. For the Christian, every Sunday is Easter.

(3) The early Christians went everywhere with the word of the resurrection: (Page1052-Acts 8:1-4). {And Saul was in hearty agreement with putting him to death. And on that day a great persecution arose against the church in Jerusalem; and they were all scattered throughout the regions of Judea and Samaria, except the apostles. And some devout men buried Stephen, and made loud lamentation over him. But Saul began ravaging the church, entering house after house; and dragging off men and women, he would put them in

prison. Therefore, those who had been scattered went about preaching the word.} The empty tomb- for if Jesus is not alive, what happened to His body? The Roman guards were paid to say, "His disciples came by night and stole Him away while we were asleep" First, the disciples lacked the courage. Had the disciples stolen His body, then how do we account for the fact that they all suffered, and most of them died martyrs; deaths? In the face of death, one of them would have revealed the hiding place of the "stolen body" to save his own life. Second, no one was ever arrested or tried for stealing the body of Jesus. It is evident that the governing officials did not believe the story of the guards. Third, the guard could have been put to death for sleeping while on watch.

(4) If they were asleep, how could they have known that it was the disciples who "stole" the body? Fifth, had the enemies of Jesus moved the body, they could have produced it and brought a quick end to Christianity, and they would have!

(5) The linen wrappings found in the empty tomb are proof of the resurrection: (Page 1038 John 20:1-10) {Now on the first day of the week Mary Magdalene came early to the tomb, while it was still dark, and saw the stone already taken away from the tomb. And so she ran and came to Simon Peter, and to the other disciple whom Jesus loved, and said to them, "They have taken away the Lord out of the tomb, and we do not know where they have laid Him." Peter therefore went forth, and the other disciple, and they were going to the tomb. And the two were running together; and the other disciple ran ahead faster than Peter, and came to the tomb first; and stooping and looking in, he saw the linen wrappings lying there; but he did not go in. Simon Peter therefore also came following him, and entered the tomb; and he beheld the linen wrappings

lying there, and the face-cloth, which had been on His head, not lying with the linen wrappings, rolled up in a place by it self. So the other disciple, who had first come to the tomb entered then also, and he saw and believed. For as yet they did not understand the Scripture, that He must rise again from the dead. So the disciples went away again to their homes.} Had friend or foe stolen the body, they would not have removed the linen wrapping; since He had been dead three days and nights. When John saw the linen wrapping and recognized that they were folded the same as when they were wrapped about the body, he knew that a miracle had taken place. Jesus came out of the wrappings, and they collapsed without disturbing the folds. They were left in the empty tomb as "convincing proof"; and when John saw and understood, he believed that Jesus had come from the dead.

THE ACENSION AND SECOND COMING OF JESUS CHRIST

(Page 1042-Acts 1:9-11). {And after He had said these things, He was lifted up while they were looking on, and a cloud received Him out of their sight. And as they were gazing intently into the sky while He was departing, behold, two men in white clothing stood beside them; and they also said, "Men of Galilee, why do you stand looking into the sky? This Jesus, who has been taken up from you into heaven, will come in just the same way as you have watched Him go into heaven."}

After forty days of instructing His disciples, the risen Christ ascended up on high and is seated at the right hand of the Father: (Page 1178-Heb. 10:12). { But He having offered one sacrifice for sins for all times, sat down at the right hand of God,}

Two men have brought the message of His second coming to the apostles: "This Jesus, who has been taken up from you into heaven, will come in just the same way…"

This message of the second coming of Jesus is so important, that it is mentioned over three hundred times in the New Testament.

    (1) He is coming to take His church to be with Him: (Page 1150-1Thess. 4:16.17); also {For the Lord Himself will descend from heaven with a shout, with the voice of the archangel and with the trumpet of God; and the dead in Christ will rise first. Then we who are alive and remain shall be caught up together with them in the clouds to meet the Lord in the air, and thus we shall always be with the Lord.} (Page 1031John 14"1-6). {"Let not your heart be troubled, believe in God, believe also in Me. In My Father's house are many dwelling places; if it were not so, I would have told you; for I go to prepare a place for you, and if I go and prepare a place for you, I will come again, and receive you to Myself; that where I am, there you may be also. And you know the way where I am going." Thomas said to Him, "Lord, we do not know where You are going, how do we know the way?" Jesus said to him, "I am the way, and the truth, and the life; no one comes to the Father, but through Me."}

    (2) He is coming to judge the nations: (Page 942-Matt. 25:31-46). {"But when the Son of Man comes in His Glory, and all the angels with Him, then He will sit on His glorious throne. "And all the nations will be gathered before Him; and He will separate them from one another, as the shepherd separates the sheep from the goats; and He will put the sheep on His right, and the goats on His left. Then the King will say to those on his right, 'Come, you who are blessed of My father, inherit the kingdom prepared for you from the foundation of the world. For I was hungry, and you gave Me something to eat; I was thirsty, and you gave Me drink; I was a stranger, and you invited Me in; naked, and you clothed Me; I was sick, and you visited

Me; I was in prison, and you came to me.' Then the righteous will answer Him, saying, 'Lord, when did we see You hungry, and feed You, or thirsty, and give You drink? And when did we see You a stranger, and invite You in, or naked, and clothe You? And when did we see you sick, or in prison, and come to You?' And the King will answer and say to them, 'Truly, I say to you, to the extent that you did it to one of these brothers of Mine, even the least of them, you did it to Me.' Then He will also say to those on Left, 'Depart from Me, accursed ones, into the eternal fire which has been prepared for the devil and his angels; for I was hungry, and you gave Me nothing to eat; I was thirsty, and you gave Me nothing to drink; I was a stranger, and you did not invite Me in; naked and you did not clothe Me; sick, and in prison, and you did not visit Me.' Then they themselves also will answer, saying, 'Lord, when did we see You hungry, or thirsty, or a stranger, or naked, or sick, or in prison, and did not take care of You?' Then He will answer them, saying, 'Truly I say to you, to the extent that you did not do it to one of the least of these, you did not do it to Me.' And these will go away into eternal punishment, but the righteous into eternal life."}

(3) He is coming to save Israel: (Page 1092-Rom. 11:25.26). {For I do not want you, brethren, to be uninformed of this mystery, lest you be wise in your own estimation, that a partial hardening has happened to Israel until the fullness of the Gentiles has come in; and thus all Israel will be saved; just as it is written, "the deliverer will come from Zion, He will remove ungodliness from Jacob."}

(4) He is coming to set upon the throne of David: (Page 975-Luke1:31-32).{And behold, you will conceive in your womb, and bear a son, and you shall name Him Jesus. He will be great, and will be called the Son of

the Most High; and the Lord God will give Him the throne of His father David.} Also: (Isaiah. Page 635-9:6.7). {For a child will be born to us, a son will be given to us. And the government will rest on His shoulders. And His name will be called Wonderful Counselor, Might God, Eternal Father, Prince of Peace. There will be no end to the increase of His government or of peace, On the throne of David and over His kingdom, To establish it and to uphold it with justice and righteousness From then on and forevermore. The zeal of the Lord of hosts will accomplish this.}

(5) He is coming to bring righteous government to this earth: (Page 1171-Heb. 1:8). {But of the Son He says "Thy throne, O God, is forever and ever, And the righteous scepter is the scepter of His kingdom.}

Jesus Christ is coming back to this earth again. "Come Lord Jesus" (Page 1226-Rev. 22:20). {He who testifies to these things says, "Yes I am coming quickly." Amen, Come, Lord Jesus.}

MASTER OUTLINE NUMBER FOUR

THE HOLY SPIRIT

The Holy Spirit is God, and is equal to the Father and the Son. Don't ever speak of Him as "it" or refer to Him as "an influence." He is God the Holy Spirit, and is set forth in the Bible as being distinct from the Father and the Son. In the Genesis account of creation, He is seen actively engaged in the work of creation, along with the Father and Son. In the Old Testament, He came upon men to empower them for service; but, when they were disobedient, He departed from them. When David sinned against the Lord, he prayed, "Do not take Thy Holy Spirit from me"

(Page 529-Ps. 51:11 OT). {Do not cast me away from Thy presence, And do not take Thy Holy Spirit from me.}

In the New Testament, after Pentecost, we see the Holy Spirit indwelling the believer, never to leave him, filling and empowering him for service. The study of the person and work of the Holy Spirit is of utmost importance. A Scriptural understanding of God the Holy Spirit will make you a better Christian and servant of God.

THE DIETY OF THE HOLY SPIRIT

(Acts 5:3.4). {But Peter said, "Ananias, why has Satan filled your heart to lie to the Holy Spirit, and to keep back some of the price of land? While it remained unsold, did it not remain your own? And after it was sold, was it not under your control? Why is it that you have conceived this deed in your heart? You have not lied to men, but to God."}

In dealing with Ananias, Peter revealed the deity of the Holy Spirit when he said, "Ananias, why has Satan filled your heart to lie to the Holy Spirit…You have not lied to men, but to God." In this Scripture it is very clear that the Holy Spirit is God, and He is co-equal, co-eternal, and coexistent with the Father and the

Son. His deity is also set forth in that He possesses divine attributes:

(1) He is everywhere present in the universe: (Page 557-Ps. 139:7-10 OT). {Where can I go from Thy Spirit? Or where can I flee Thy presence? If I ascend to heaven, Thou art there; If I make my bed in Sheol, (the neither world) behold, Thou art there. If I take the wings of the dawn, If I dwell in the remotest part of the sea, Even there Thy hand will lead me, And Thy right Hand will lay hold of me.}

(2) He has all power: (Page 975-Luke1:35): {And the angel answered and said to her, "The Holy Spirit will come upon you, and the power of the Most High will overshadow you; and for that reason the holy offspring to shall be called the Son of God."}

(3) He has all knowledge: (Page 1099-1Cor. 2:10.11). {For to us God revealed them through the Spirit; for the Spirit searches all things, even the depths of God. For who among men knows the thoughts of a man except the spirit of the man, which is in him? Even so the thoughts of God no one knows except the Spirit of God.}

(4) He is eternal: (Page 1177-Heb.9:14). {how much more will the blood of Christ, who through the eternal Spirit offered Himself without blemish to God, cleanse your conscious from dead works to serve the living God?}

(5) He was raised from the dead by the Power of the Holy Spirit: (Page 1088-Rom. 8:11). { But if the Spirit of Him who raised Jesus from the dead dwells in you, He who raised Christ Jesus from the will also give life to your mortal bodies through His Spirit who indwells in you. }

(6) Jesus gave the commandments to the apostles and the church through the Holy Spirit: (Page 1041-Acts 1:2). {until the day when He was taken up, after He had by

the Holy Spirit given orders to the apostles whom He had chosen. }

If Jesus did depend upon the Holy Spirit during His life and ministry here on the earth, can we afford to do less?

THE EMBLEMS OF THE HOLY SPIRIT

(Luke 3:16): {John answered and said to them all, "As for me, I baptized you with water; but One is coming who is mightier than I, and I am not fit to untie the thongs of His scandals; He will baptize you with the Holy spirit and fire.}

It is often difficult to impart truth by the use of words. Frequently they reveal only a half truth, leaving the other half hidden. The writers of the Bible used certain emblems when unfolding the mysteries of the Holy Spirit, because they illustrate more about Him than volumes can contain.

They are:

(1) Fire as an emblem. Fire speaks of His consuming, purifying power in the life of believer. (Page 1043- Acts 2:3. {And there appeared to them tongues as fire distributing themselves, and they rested on each one of them.}

Also:

(Page 642 Is. 6:1-7).{In the year of King Uzziah's death, I saw the Lord sitting on a throne, lofty and exalted, with the train of His robe filling the temple. Seraphim stood above Him, each having six wings; with two he covered his face, and with two he covered his feet, and with two he flew. And one called out to the other and said, "Holy, Holy, Holy, is the Lord of hosts. The whole earth is filled with His glory." And the foundations of the thresholds trembled at the voice of him who called out, while the temple was filling with smoke. Then I said, "Woe is me, for I am ruined! Because I am a man of unclean lips, And I live among a people of unclean lips; For my eyes have seen the King, the Lord of hosts." Then one of the Seraphim flew to me, with a burning coal in his hand which he had taken from the alter with tongs. And he touched my mouth with it and said, "Behold, this has touched your lips; and your iniquity is taken away, and your sin is forgiven."}

(2) Wind as an emblem: (Page 1014-John3:8). {"The wind blows where it wishes and you hear the sound of it, but do not know where it comes from and where it is going; so is everyone who is born of the Spirit."} Wind speaks of His hidden depth in His mighty regenerating power.

(3) Water as an emblem: (Page 1022-John 7:37-39). {Now on the last day, the great day of the feast, Jesus stood and cried out, saying "If any man is thirsty, let him come to me and drink. He who believes in Me, as the Scriptures said, 'From his (out of his belly) innermost being shall flow rivers of living water.'" But this He spoke of the Spirit, whom those who believed in Him were to receive; for the Spirit was not yet given, because Jesus was not yet glorified.} Water speaks of His power to fill the believer to overflowing with spiritual life.

(4) Seal as an emblem: (Page 1130-Eph. 1:13). { In Him, you also, after listening to the message of truth, the gospel of your salvation-having also believed, you were sealed in Him with the Holy Spirit of promise.} Seal speaks of ownership of the believer; it is a finished, eternal transaction.

(5) Oil as an emblem: (Page 1055-Acts 10:38). { "You know of Jesus of Nazareth, how God anointed Him with the Holy Spirit and with power, and how He went about doing good, and healing all those who were oppressed by the devil; for God was with Him.} Oil speaks of His power to anoint for service.

(6) Dove as an emblem: (Page 952-Mark 1:10). {And immediately coming out of the water, He saw the

heavens opening, and the Spirit like a dove descending upon Him.} The dove speaks of His gentle, tender, peaceful nature. We may know "the peace of God, which surpass all comprehension." (Page 1139-Phil. 4:7). { And the peace of God, which surpasses all comprehension, shall guard your hearts and your minds in Jesus Christ.} Only when fully surrendered to God.

SINS AGAINST THE HOLY SPIRIT

(Page 924 Matt. 12:31.32). {"There fore I say to you, any sin and blasphemy shall be forgiven men, but blasphemy against the Spirit shall not be forgiven. And whoever shall speak a word against the Son of Man, it shall be forgiven him; but whoever shall speak against the Holy Spirit, It shall not be forgiven him, either in this age, or in the age to come."}

This a solemn study, because the Holy Spirit is God, and can be sinned against by both the believer and the unbeliever. May He help you search your heart as you consider:

(1) The sin of blaspheming the Holy Spirit. This sin is committed by unbelievers. It is often called the "unpardonable sin." It has no forgiveness. It was committed by the enemies of Jesus when they accused Him of casting out demons by the power of Satan: (Page 925-Matt. 12:24). {But when the Pharisees heard it, they said, "This man casts out demons only by Beelzebul the ruler of the demons."} When Jesus claimed to cast them out by the "Spirit of God": (Page 925-Matt. 12:28. {"But if I cast out demons by the Spirit of God, then the kingdom of God has come upon you."}

(2) The sin of resisting the Holy Spirit: (Page 1051-Acts 7:51). {"You men who are stiff-necked and uncircumcised in heart and ears are always resisting the Holy Spirit; you are doing just as your fathers did."} This sin is committed by the unbeliever when rejecting Jesus Christ as Savior and Lord.

(3) The sin of grieving the Holy Spirit: (Page 1133-Eph. 4:30-32). {And do not grieve the Holy Spirit of God by whom you were sealed for the say of redemption. Let all bitterness and wrath and anger and clamor and slander be put away from you, along with all malice. And be kind to one another, tender-hearted forgiving each other, just as God in Christ also has forgiven you.} This sin is committed by believers. He is grieved by us unless He controls our lives to the glory of Jesus Christ.

(4) The sin of Quenching the Holy Spirit: (Page 1151-1Thes. 5:19). {Do not quench the Holy Spirit.} This sin is committed by Christians when know sin is allowed to go un-confessed.: (Page 1199-1John 1:9). {If we confess our sins, He is faithful and righteous to forgive us our sins and to cleanse us from all unrighteousness.}
Also:
(Isaiah 58:1.2OT). {Behold the Lords hand is not so short That it cannot save; Neither is His ear so dull That it cannot hear. But your iniquities have made a separation between you and your God And your sins have hidden His face from you, so that He does not hear.}

(5) The sin of lying to the Holy Spirit: (Page 1047-Acts 5:1-11). {But a certain man named Ananias, with his wife Sapphira, sold a piece of property, and kept back some of the price for himself, with his wife's full knowledge, and bringing a portion of it, he laid it at the apostles feet. But Peter said, "Ananias, why has Satan filled your heart to lie to the Holy Spirit, and to keep some of the price of the land? While it remained unsold, did it not remain your own? And after it was sold, was it not under your control? Why is it that you have conceived this deed in your heart You have not lied to men, but to God." And as He heard these

words, Ananias fell down and breathed his last; and great fear came upon all who heard it. And the young men arose and covered him up, and after carrying him out, they buried him. Now there elapsed an interval of about three hours, and his wife came in, not knowing what had happened. And Peter responded to her, "Tell me whether you sold the land for such and such a price?" And she said, "Yes, that was the price." Then Peter said to her, why is it that you have agreed together to put the Spirit of the Lord to the test? Behold the feet of those who have buried your husband are at the door, and they shall carry you out as well." And she fell immediately to his feet, and breathed her last; and the young men came in and found her dead, and they carried her out and buried her beside her husband. And great fear came upon the whole church, and upon all who heard of these things.} The sin of Ananias and Sapphira was deception, born in jealousy. They tried to mock God. (Page 1128-Gal. 6:7). {Do not be deceived, God is not mocked; for whatever a man sows, this he will also reap.}

The Holy Spirit can be sinned against, because He is God.

THE WORK OF THE HOLY SPIRIT

(Page1033-John16:7-14): {"But I tell you the truth, it is to your advantage that I go away; for if I do not go away, the Helper shall not come to you; but if I go, I will send Him to you. And He when He comes, will convict the world concerning sin, and righteousness and judgment; concerning sin, because they do not believe me; and concerning righteousness, because I go to the Father, and you no longer behold Me; and concerning judgment, because the ruler of this world has been judged. I have many more things to say to you, but you cannot bear them now. But when He, the Spirit of truth, comes, He will guide you into all truth; for He will not speak on His own initiative, but whatever He hears, He will speak; and He will disclose to you what is to come. He shall glorify Me; for He shall take of Mine, and shall disclose it to you. All things that the Father has are Mine; therefore I said, that He takes of Mine, and will disclose it to you.}

In instructing His disciples regarding the coming of the Holy Spirit, Jesus said, "…for If I do not go away, the Helper shall not come to you; but if I go, I will send Him to you. And He, when He comes, will.…"

(1) Convict men of the sin of unbelief.
(2) Convict men that Jesus is the righteousness of God: (Page 1090-Rom. 10:3.4). {For not knowing about God's righteousness, and seeking to establish their own, they did not subject themselves to the righteousness of God. For Christ is the end of the law for righteousness to everyone who believes.}
(3) Convict men that the power of Satan has been broken.
(4) Regenerate the believer: (Page 1014 John 3:5). {Jesus answered, "Truly, truly, I say to you, unless one is born of water and the Spirit, he cannot enter into the kingdom of God."} (Page 1166-Titus 3:5).{ He saved us, not on the bases of deeds which we have done in righteousness, but according to His mercy by the washing of regeneration and renewing by the Holy Spirit,}
(5) Indwell the believer: (Page 1102-1Cor. 6:19.20). {Or do you not know that your body is a temple (sanctuary) of the Holy Spirit who is in you, whom you have from God, and that you are not your own? For you have been bought with a price: therefore glorify God in your body.}
(6) Seal the believer: (Page 1130- Eph. 1:13.14). {In Him, you also, after listening to the message of truth, the gospel of your salvation-having also believed, you were sealed in Him with the Holy Spirit of promise, who is given as a pledge of our inheritance, with a view to the redemption of God's own possession, to

the praise of His glory.}

(7) Baptize the believer: (Page 1041-Acta1:5). {for John baptized with water, but you shall be baptized with the Holy Spirit not many days from now."}
Also:
(Page 1107-1Cor.12:13). {For by one Spirit we were all baptized into one body, whether Jews or Greeks, whether slaves or free, and we were all made to drink of one Spirit.}

(8) Infill the believer: (Page 1134-Eph. 5:18). {And do not get drunk with wine, for that is dissipation, but be filled with the Spirit.}

(9) Empower the believer: (Page 1041-Acts 1:8). {but you shall receive power when the Holy Spirit has come upon you; and you shall be my witnesses both in Jerusalem and in all Judea and Samaria, and even to the remotest part of the earth.}

(10) Lead the believer: (Page 1127-Gal. 5:16-18).{ But I say, walk by the Spirit, and you will not carry out the desire of the flesh. For the flesh sets its desire against the Spirit, and the Spirit against the flesh; for these are in opposition to one another, so that you may not do the things that you please. But if you are lead by the Spirit, you are not under the law.}

(11) Administer spiritual gifts to the believer: (Page 1107-1Cor. 12:1-11). {Now concerning spiritual gifts, brethren, I do not want you to be unaware. You know that when you were pagans, you were led astray to the dumb idols, however you were led. Therefore I make known to you, "Jesus is Lord" except by the Holy Spirit. Now there are varieties of gifts, but the same Spirit. And there are varieties of ministries, and the same Lord. And there are varieties of effects, but the same God who works all things in all persons. But to each one is given the manifestation of the Spirit for the common good. For to one is given the word of

wisdom through the Spirit, and to another the word of knowledge according to the same Spirit; to another faith by the same Spirit, and to another gifts of healing by the same Spirit, and to another the effecting of miracles, and to another prophecy, and to another the distinguishing of spirits, to another various kinds of tongues, and to another the interpretation of tongues. But one and the same Spirit works all these things, distributing to each one individually just as He wills.}

The Holy Spirit came on the day of Pentecost, to remain with the church until it is complete and presented to the Lord Jesus at His coming. Just as Jesus Christ finished the work He came to do in the flesh, so the Holy Spirit will finish the work He came to do in the church.

THE FRUIT OF THE HOLY SPIRIT

(Gal. 5:22.23). {But the fruit of the Spirit is love, joy, peace, kindness, goodness, faithfulness, gentleness, self-control,; against such things there is no law.}

The fruit of the Spirit is love. "Only as we live in love can we fulfill the will of God in our lives. The believer must become love-inspired, lovemastered, and love-driven.

(Page 1116-2Cor. 5:14). {For the love of Christ controls us, having concluded this, that one died for all, therefore all died;} Without the fruit of the Spirit (love), we are just a religious noise: (Page1108-1Cor. 13:1). {If I speak with the tongues of men and of angels, but do not have love, I have become a noisy gong or a clanging cymbal.}

The fruit of the Spirit is love, "and is manifested joy, peace, patience, kindness, goodness, faithfulness, gentleness, and self-control:

(1) "Joy is love's strength.
(2) "Peace is love's security.
(3) "Patience is love's endurance.
(4) "Kindness is love's character.
(5) "Goodness is love's character.

(6) "Faithfulness is love's confidence.
(7) "Gentleness is love's humility.
(8) "Self-control is love's victory. Against such things there is no law." A Holy Spirit-controlled man needs no law to cause him to live a righteous life.

The secret of a Spirit controlled life is found in dedication to God: (Page 1092-Rom. 12:1.2). {I urge you therefore, brethren, by the mercies of God, to present your bodies a living sacrifice, acceptable to God, which is your spiritual service of worship. And do not be conformed to this world, but be transformed by the renewing of your mind, that you may prove what the will of God is, that which is good and acceptable and perfect.}

Put your all on the Alter and the Holy Spirit will fill your heart with the love of God: (Page 1085-Rom. 5:5). {And hope does not disappoint, because the love of God has been poured out within our hearts through the Holy Spirit who was given to us.}

MASTER OUTLINE NUMBER FIVE

SIN

In considering the question of sin, we are faced with two startling facts. The first fact is that man makes so little of sin. To some, it is an illusion- a religious mirage- the invention of some fanatic. It is denied, joked about, and laughed at by man. Many who believe sin to be a fact, continue in it with little thought of penalty.

The second fact is that God makes so much of sin, "The person who sins dies": (Page 769-Ezek. 18:20). {"The person who sins will die. The son will not bear the punishment for the father's iniquity, nor will the father bear the punishment for the son's iniquity; the righteousness of the righteous will be upon himself, and the wickedness of the wicked will be upon himself."}

"The wages of sin is death": (Page 1087:-Rom. 6:23).{For the wages of sin is death, but the free gift of God is eternal life in Christ Jesus out Lord.} All sins are an abomination to God: (Prov.6:16-19) {There are six things the Lord hates, Yes, seven which are an abomination to Him: Haughty eyes, a lying tongue, And hands that shed innocent blood, A heart that devises wicked plans, Feet that run rapidly to evil, A false witness who utters lies, and one who spreads strife among brothers.}

God hates those who do iniquity: (Ps. 5:5 OT). {The boastful shall not stand before Thine eyes; Thou dost hate all who do iniquity.}

Moses said, " ...everyone who acts unjustly is an abomination to the Lord": (Duet. 25:16 OT). {"For everyone who does these things, everyone who acts unjustly is an abomination to the Lord your God.}

Sin is an evil force. Its presence cannot be escaped in this life, but it can be overcome by the power of God.

THE ORIGIN OF SIN

(Jude 1207 1:6). {And the angels who did not keep their own domain but abandoned their proper abode, He has kept in eternal bonds under darkness for the judgment of the great day.}

The origin of sin is one of the mysteries of the Bible. "The secret things belong to the Lord our God" (Duet. 29:29 OT): {"The secret things belong to the Lord our God, but the things revealed belong to us and to our sons forever; that we may observe all the words of this law.}

Its origin is one of the "secret things" that will remain wrapped in obscurity.

Sin was first noted in the heart of Satan. "He was created a perfect being,"… (Page 780-Ezek. 28:11-19 OT): {Again the word of the Lord came to me saying, "Son of man, take up a lamentation over the king of Tyre, and say to him, 'Thus says the Lord God, "You had the seal of perfection, Full of wisdom and perfect beauty. You were in Eden, the garden of God; Every precious stone was your covering: The ruby, the topaz, the diamond; the beryl, the onyx, and the jasper; The lapis lazuli, the turquoise, and the emerald; And the gold, the workmanship of your settings and sockets, Was in you. On the day you were created They were prepared."' You were the anointed cherub who covers, And I placed you there. You were on the holy mountain of God ; You walked in the midst of the stones of fire. You were blameless in your ways From the day you were created, Until unrighteousness was found in you. By the abundance of your trade You were internally filled with violence. And you sinned; Therefore I have cast you as profane From the mountain of God. And I have destroyed you, O covering (guardian) cherub, From the midst of the stones of fire. Your heart was lifted up because or your beauty; You corrupted your wisdom by reason of your splendor. I cast you to the ground; I put you before kings, That they may see you. By the multitude of your iniquities, In the unrighteousness of your trade, You profaned your sanctuaries. Therefore I have brought fire from the midst of you. It has consumed you; And I have turned you to ashes on the earth In the eyes of all who see you. All who know you among the peoples Are appalled at you; You have become terrified, And you will be no more."}

Satan fell from perfection when he exerted his will above the will of God. Five times he said, "I will": (Is. 14:12-17) {"How you have fallen from heaven, O star of the morning, son of the dawn! You have been cut down to the earth, You who have weakened the nations! But you said in your heart, 'I will ascend to heaven; I will raise my throne above the stars of God, And I will sit on the mount of assembly In the recesses of the north. I will ascend above the heights of the clouds; I will make my self like the Most High.' Nevertheless you will thrust down to Sheol, To the recess of the pit. Those who see you will gaze at you, They will ponder over you saying, 'Is this the man who made the earth tremble, Who shook kingdoms, Who made the world like the wilderness and overthrew the cities, Who did not allow his prisoners to go home?'"}

It was his will over God's will—this is sin. It is believed that Satan, when first created, was the ruler of this earth: (Gen. 1:1 OT) {In the beginning God created the heavens and the earth} and that he fell through self-will; and at his fall, the earth became "formless and void":

(Gen.. 1:2 OT) {And the earth was formless and void, and darkness was over the surface of the deep; and the Spirit of God was moving over the surface of the waters.}

Isaiah tells us that God created the earth "and did not create it a waste place": (Is. 45:18 OT) {For thus says the Lord, who created the heavens (He is the God who formed the earth and made it, He established it and did not create it a waste place, But formed it to be inhabited), "I am the Lord, and there is none else."}

He did not create it a chaos. The earth was a perfect creation in Genesis 1:1 (OT). Something happened that caused a catastrophe and the earth became "formless and void" (Genesis 1:2 OT), but it was not created thus.

It is believed that some of the angels, along with Satan, sinned by leaving their first estate. This does not provide that Satan was the originator of sin, but is does reveal sin in the heart of Satan before God created man.

WHAT IS SIN

(Page 1201-1 John 3:4.) {Everyone who practices sin also practices lawlessness; and sin is lawlessness.}

It is impossible to deny the existence of sin, when the whole world is in conflict between good and evil. If sin were not a fact, there would be no crime; we would not need jails or prisons. We would need no locks on our doors, or vaults for our valuables. To some, sin is being indiscreet; or it is a weakness of the flesh. To others, it is the absence from good. To the so called scholar, sin is ignorance; and to the evolutionist, it is the nature of the beast. The latest theory is that sin is a disease to be treated by science, because man is not a sinner- he is only sick. To others, sin is a form of selfishness, but to God declares that:

(1) Sin is lawlessness: (above verse 4).
(2) Sin is falling short of the glory of God: (Page 1084-Rom. 3:23): {for all have sinned and fall short of the glory of God.}
(3) Sin is revolting against God: (Is. 1:2 OT) {Listen O heavens, and hear O earth; For the Lord speaks, "Sons I have reared and brought up, But they have revolted against Me."}
(4) Sin is unbelief; it makes God a liar: (Page 1203-1 John 5:10) {The one who believes in the Son of God has the witness in himself; the one who does not believe God has made Him a liar, because he has not believed in the witness that God has borne concerning His Son.}
(5) Sin is going your own way, planning your life according to your own will, without seeking the will of God: (Is. 53:6) {All of us like sheep have gone astray, Each one of us has turned to his own way; But the Lord has caused the iniquity of us all to fall on Him.}

(6) All unrighteousness is sin: (Page 1203-I John5:17) {All unrighteousness is sin, and there is a sin not leading to death.}

Sin is folly to deceive you, a force to destroy you, and a fact to condemn you. Sin is a volitional act of disobedience against the revealed will of God.

HOW SIN ENTERED THE WORLD

(Page 1085-Rom 5:12) {Therefore, just as through one man sin entered into the world, and death through sin, and so death spread to all men, because all sinned.}

"Through one man sin entered the world" (above verse). The fall of man is found in Genesis 3:1-24 (OT) {Now the serpent was more crafty than any beast of the field which the Lord God had made. And he said to the women, "In deed, has God said, 'You shall not eat from any tree of the garden?'" And the women said to the serpent, "But from the fruit of the tree which is in the middle of the garden, God has said, 'You shall not eat from it or touch it, lest you die.'" And the serpent said to the woman, "You surely shall not die! For God knows that in the day you eat from it your eyes will be opened, and you will be like God, knowing good and evil." When the woman saw that the tree was good for food, and that it was a delight to the eyes, and that the tree was desirable to make one wise, she took from its fruit and ate; and she gave also to her husband with her, and he ate. Then the eyes of both of them were opened, and they knew that they were naked; and they sewed fig leaves together and made themselves loin coverings. And they heard the sound of the Lord God walking in the garden in the cool of the day, and the man and his wife hid themselves from the presence of the Lord God among the trees of the garden. Then the Lord God called to the man, and said to him, "Where are you?" And he said, "I heard the sound of Thee in the garden, and I was afraid because I was naked; so I hid myself." And He said, "Who told you that you were naked? Have you eaten from the tree of which I commanded you not to eat?" And the man said, "The woman whom Thou gavest to be with me, she gave me from the tree and I ate." Then the Lord said to the woman, "What is this you have done?" And the woman said, "The serpent deceived me, and I ate." And the Lord said to the serpent, "Because you have done this, Cursed are you more than all cattle, and more than every beast of the field; On your belly shall you go, And dust you and u shall eat All the days of your life; And I will put enmity between you and the woman, And between your seed and her seed; He shall bruise you on the head, And you shall bruise him on the heal." To the woman He said, "I will greatly multiply Your pain in childbirth, In pain you shall bring forth children; Yet your desire shall be for your husband, and he shall rule over you." Then to Adam He said, "Because you have listened to the voice of your wife, and have eaten from the tree about which I commanded you saying, 'You shall not eat from it' Cursed is the ground because of you; in toil you shall eat of it all the days of your life. Both thorns and thistles it shall grow for you; and you shall eat the plants of the field; by the sweat of your face You shall eat bread, till you return to the ground, because from it you were taken; For you are dust, and to dust you shall return." Now the man called his wife's name Eve, because she was the mother of all the living. And the Lord God made garments of skin for Adam and his wife, and clothed both of them. Then the Lord God said, "Behold, the man has become like one of Us, knowing good and evil; and now lest he stretch out his hand, and take also from the tree of life, and eat, and live forever." Therefore the Lord God sent him out from the garden of Eden, to cultivate the ground from which he was taken. So He drove the man out; and at the east of the garden of Eden He stationed the cherubim, and the flaming sword which turned every direction, to the guard the way to the tree of Life}

"Through one man sin entered the world" (above verse). The fall of man is found in (Gen.-3:1-24). When Adam sinned, his seed became perishable. (Page 1190- 1Pet. 1:23). {for you have been born again not of seed which is perishable but imperishable, that is, through the living and abiding word of

God. For "All flesh is like grass, And all its glory like a flower of grass. That withers, And the flower falls off, But the Word of the Lord abides forever."}

Therefore, we are sinners because we are born in sin: (Ps.-51:5 O T). {Behold, I was brought forth in iniquity, And in sin my mother conceived me.}

You do not have to teach children to be bad. But you do have to teach them how to good. You do not have to teach them how to lie, but you do have to teach them how to tell the truth. (Page 1086-Rom. 5:18). {So then through one transgression, there resulted condemnation to all men, even so through one act of righteousness there resulted justification of life to all men.}

According to the Word of God, all men are judged sinners; all are condemned already. (Page 1015-John 3:18). {He who believes in Him is not judged; he who does not believe has been judged already, because he has not believed in the name of the Only begotten Son of God.}

"All have sinned": (Page 1084-Rom 3:23). {for all have sinned and fall short of the glory of God,}

Sin entered the world through our first parents in the Garden of Eden, and "all have sinned" because all are sinners. Man sins by choice, because he is a sinner by nature. Therefore, the dominion sin has over you is according to the delight you have in it.

THE RESULTS OF SIN

(Eph. 2:1) {And you were dead in your trespasses and sins.} "...the wages of sin is death," As a result of man's sin, there are three deaths. Keep in mind that death does not annihilate; it only separates. In the Garden of Eden, it separated man from God spiritually: this is spiritual death. In natural death, it separates the spirit and the soul from the body; this is physical death. In the final death, it separates from the mercy of God forever; this is eternal

    (1) The wages of sin is spiritual death. Just as sin separated man from God spiritually and drove him from the

presence of God out of the Garden, so sin will separate you from God (Isaiah 59:1.2 OT). {Behold, the Lord's hand is not so short That it cannot save; Neither is His ear so dull That it cannot hear. But your iniquities have made a separation between you and your God, And your sins have hidden His face from you, so that He does not hear.} The only way back to God is to confess your sins to Him. (Page 1199-1John 1:9). {If we confess our sins, He is faithful and righteous to forgive us our sins and to cleanse us from all unrighteousness.} And forsake your sins (Isaiah. 55:7 OT). {Let the wicked forsake his way, And the unrighteousness man his thoughts; And let him return to the Lord, And He will have compassion on him; and to our God. For He will abundantly pardon.} That you may be restored to fellowship with God.

(2) The wages of sin is physical death. Physical death is a result of sin. Death had no claim on man until man sinned. Now all die, because all are in sin. Death is universal, and since we have a universal effect, we must have a universal cause, and that cause is universal sin. All men die—the good and the bad—the young and the old—and man will continue to die until death is destroyed by the Lord Jesus Christ: (Page 1110-1Cor. 15:26). {The last enemy that will be abolished is death.} And is swallowed up in victory: (Page 1111-1Cor. 15:54-57). {But when this perishable will have put on the imperishable, and this mortal will have put on immortality, then will come about the saying that is written, Death is swallowed up in victory. "O death, where is your victory? O death, where is your sting?" The sting of death is sin, and the power of sin is the law; but thanks be to God, who gives us the victory through our Lord Jesus Christ.

(3) The wages of sin is eternal death. "The person who sins will die": (Ezek.-18:20 OT). {"The person who sins

will die. The son will not bear the punishment for the fathers iniquity, nor will the father bear the punishment for the sons iniquity; the righteousness of the righteous will be upon himself, and the wickedness of the wicked". will be upon himself.} This is eternal separation from the love of God: (Page-Rev. 20:14). {And death and Hades were throne into the lake of fire. This is the second death, the lake of fire.} Once the soul passes through the portals of Hades he is lost and lost forever. He will continue to exist, but without hope. He is damned and damned to all eternity. Eternal death is eternal separation from God (Page 998- Luke 16:19-31). {Now there was a certain rich man, and he habitually dressed in purple and fine linen, gaily living in splendor every day. And a certain poor man named Lazarus was laid at his gate, covered with sores, and longing to be fed with the crumbs which were falling from the rich man's table; besides, even the dogs were coming and licking his sores. Now it came about that the poor man died and he was carried away by the angels to Abraham's bosom; and the rich man also died and was buried. And in Hades he lifted up his eyes, being in torment, and saw Abraham far away, and Lazarus in his bosom. And he cried, "Father Abraham, have mercy on me, and send Lazarus, that he may dip the tip of his finger in water and cool my tongue; for I am in agony in this flame." But Abraham said, "Child, remember that during your life you received your good things, and likewise Lazarus bad things; but now he is being comforted here, and you are in agony. And besides all this, between us and you there is a great chasm fixed, in order that those who wish to come over here from here to you may not be able , and that none may cross over from there to us." And he said, "Then I beg you, Father, that you send him to my fathers house- for I have five brothers-that he may warn them, lest they also come to this place of torment." But Abraham said, "They have Moses and the Prophets; let them hear them." But he said, "No, Father Abraham, but if someone goes to them from the dead, they will repent!" But he said, "If they do not listen to Moses and the Prophets, neither will they be persuaded if someone rises from the dead.'"

GOD'S REMEDY FOR SIN

(Page 1116-2Cor. 5:21). {He made Him who knew no sin to be sin on our behalf, that we might become the righteous of God in Him.} Man, not willing to accept God's remedy for his sin, strives to bring about his own salvation by human means.

(1) He strives for self-righteousness, when he needs to be made the righteousness of God (Above verse; also Is. 64:6 OT). {For all of us have become like one who is unclean, And all our righteous deeds are like A filthy garment; And all of us wither like a leaf, And our iniquities, like the wind, take us away.}

(2) He strives to reform, when he needs to be regenerated: (Page1166-Titus 3:5). {He saved us, not on the basis of deeds which we have done in righteousness, but according to His mercy, by the washing of regeneration and renewing by the Holy Spirit.}

(3) He strives to turn over a new leaf, when he needs a new life: (Page 1025-John 10:10) {"The thief comes only to steal, and kill, and destroy; I came that they might have life, and might have it more abundantly."}

(4)He strives to be justified by the law when he needs to be justified by faith in the Lord Jesus Christ: (Page 1125-Gal. 2:16) {Nevertheless know that a man is not justified by the works of the law but through faith in Christ Jesus, even we have believed in Christ Jesus, that we may be justified by faith in Christ, and not by works of the law; since by the works of the law shall no flesh be justified.}

(5) He strives to clean up the old man, when he needs to be made a new man in Christ: (Page 1133-Eph. 4:24). {and put on the new self, which in the likeness of God has been created in righteousness and holiness of the truth.}

(6) He strives to be saved by good works, when he needs salvation by the grace of God. The only remedy for the ruin of man is the Son of God, being sin for us on the cross. The only way to receive this remedy is by faith in Him as personal Savior: (Page 1038-John 20:30.31). {Many other signs therefore Jesus also performed in the presence of the disciples, which are not in this book; but these have been written that you may believe that Jesus is the Christ, the Son of God; and that believing you may have life in His name.}

MASTER OUTLINE NUMBER SIX

JUDGMENTS

In the scriptures, we are instructed in how we should be "handling accurately the word of truth." (Page 1160-2Tim 2:15). {Be diligent to present yourself approved to God as a workman who does not need to be ashamed, handling accurately the word of truth.}

This is most essential when studying judgments. Do not endeavor to make all the judgments conform to the theory of one "general judgment." The "general judgment" theory is the invention of religion, and is not taught in the Word of God. There are five separate judgments revealed in the Bible, and they differ as to time, place, and purpose. Yet, they all have one thing in common: the Lord Jesus Christ is the judge: (Page 1018-John 5:22). {"For not even the Father judges anyone, but He has given all judgment to the Son,}

Everyone—from Adam to the last man to be born on this earth—will stand before the Lord Jesus Christ to be judged. In the first judgment, the sins of the believers have already been judged in Christ on the cross. In the second judgment, the believer is to judge self, or be judged by the Lord Jesus Christ and disciplined. In the third judgment, all believers must appear at the "judgment seat of Christ" where their works are to be judged. In the fourth judgment, all nations are to be judged at the second coming of Christ. In the fifth judgment, the wicked dead are to be judged at the great white throne.

THE JUDGMENT OF THE BELIEVERS SINS

(Page 1018_John 5:24). {"True, truly, I say to you, he who hears My word and believes Him who sent Me, has eternal life, and does not come into judgment, but has passed out of death into life.}

In the above verse, our Lord tells us that the believer "does not come into judgment." Our sins were judged in Christ on

Calvary and every believer "has passed out of death into life." This is present salvation. Christ paid for our sins. He was judged in the believer's stead. The believer will not come into judgment because:

> (1) Jesus Christ paid the penalty, and on the grounds of His substitutional death, the believer is separated from his sins forever (Ps.103:12). {As far as the east is from the west, So far He removed our transgression from us.}
>
> (2) The sins of the believer have been wiped out and God has promised that He "will not remember your sins": (Is. 43:25). {"I, even I, am the one who wipes out your transgressions for My own sake.}
>
> (3) Our Lord suffered for our sins, "the just for the unjust" that we might be saved and never come into judgment as sinners: (Page 1192-1 Pet. 3:18). {For Christ also died for sins once for all, the just for the unjust, in order that He might bring us to God, having been put to death in the flesh, but made alive in the spirit.}
>
> (4) The believer will never be condemned with the world, because Christ was made a curse for us on the cross, and on our behalf": (Page 1116-2Cor. 5:21). {He made Him who knew no sin to be sin on our behalf, that we might become the righteousness of God in Him.}

Christ was made a curse for us on the cross, and on our behalf redeemed us from the curse of the law: (Page 1125- Gal. 3:13) {Christ redeemed us from the curse of the law, having become a curse for us- for it is written, "Cursed is everyone who hangs on a tree."}

"He has been manifested to put away sin by the sacrifice of Himself": (Page 1178-Heb. 9:26). {Otherwise, He would have needed to suffer since the foundation of the world: but now once at the consummation of the ages He has been manifested to put away sin by the sacrifices of himself.}

The believer will not come into judgment because his sins have been purified: (Page 1170- Heb. 1:3). And He is the radiance of His glory and the exact representation of His nature, and upholds all things by His power. When He had made purification of sins, He sat down at the right hand of the Majesty on high;}

THE JUDGMENT OF THE BELIEVERS SELF

(Page 1106-1Cor. 11:31.32). {But as we judged ourselves rightly, we should not be judged. But when we are judged, we are disciplined by the Lord in order that we may not be condemned along with the world}

The judgment of the believers self is more than judging things in the believer's life. When the believer judges self, the good and the bad in his life come to light; and he will confess the bad: (Page 1199- 1John 1:9). {If we confess our sins, He is faithful and righteous to forgive us our sins and to cleanse us from all unrighteousness.} And forsake it: (Page Is. 55:7). {Let the wicked forsake his way, And the unrighteous man his thoughts; And let him return to the Lord, And He will have compassion on Him; and to our God,}

However, it is not enough just to judge the believer; he must judge self.

- (1) To judge self is to practice self –abnegation, for when the believer sees self as God sees him, he will renounce self. It is replacing the self-life with the Christ-life: (Page 1145-Col 3:4). {When Christ, who is our life, is revealed, then you also will be revealed with Him in glory.}
- (2) To judge self is to deny self. This is more than self-denial. Self-denial is denying one's self of the gratifications of the flesh. If we practice self-denial only, it is treating the symptom and not the cause, But when we deny self, we are attacking the cause, for in self (that is, in the flesh) "nothing good dwells": (Page 1087-Rom. 7:18). {For I know that nothing good dwells in me, that is in my flesh; for the wishing is present in me, but the doing of the good is not.} To

deny self is to take up our cross and follow Christ: (Page 961-Mark 8:34-38). {And He summoned the multitude with His disciples, and said to them, "If anyone wishes to come after Me, let him deny himself, and take up his cross, and follow Me. For whoever wishes to save his life shall lose it; but whoever loses life for My sake and the gospels shall save it. For what does it profit a man to gain the whole world, and forfeit his soul? For what shall a man give in exchange for his own soul?" For whoever is ashamed of Me and My words in this adulterous and sinful generation, the Son of Man will also be ashamed of him when He comes in the glory of His Father with the holy angels."}

(3) To judge self is to lose the self-life, and to find the Christ-life: (Page 1125-Gal. 2:20) {"I have been crucified with Christ; and it is no longer I who live, but Christ lives in me; and the life which I now live in the flesh I live by faith in the Son of God, who loved me, and delivered Himself up for me.}

(4) To judge self is to no longer be self-conscious, but to become Christ-conscious: (Page 949-Matt. 28:20). {teaching them to observe all that I commanded you; and lo, I am with you always, even to the end of the age.}

(5) To judge self is to no longer be self-controlled, but to become Christ-controlled: (Page 1053-Acts 9:6). {but rise, and enter the city, and it shall be told you what you must do.}

(6) To judge self is to no longer practice self-esteem, but to esteem others better than self: (Page 1137- Phil. 2:3). {Do knowing from selfishness (contentiousness) or empty conceit, but with humility of mind let each of you regard one another as more important than himself;}

THE JUDGEMENT OF THE BELIEVERS WORKS

(Page 1116-2Cor 5:10). {For we must all appear before the judgment seat of Christ, that each one may be recompensed for his deeds in the body, according to what he has done, whether good or bad.} (The things through the body).

The believer's works will be judged at the "judgment seat of Christ," which is referred to many times in the Bible. A careful reading of 2 Cor.- 5:10 with the context reveals that only believers will appear at the "judgment seat of Christ." Their works will be judged, not their sins, for we have already seen that all sins of the believer were judged in Christ on Calvary, and "There is therefore now no condemnation for those who are in Christ Jesus": (Page 1088-Rom.8;1). {There is therefore now no condemnation for those who are in Christ Jesus.}

> (1) This judgment will take place "in the air", following the first resurrection. "The dead in Christ will rise first": (Page 1150-1Thes 4:14-18). {For if we believe that Jesus died and rose again, even so God will bring with Him those who have fallen asleep in Jesus. For this we say to you by the word of the Lord, that we who are alive, and remain until the coming of the Lord, shall not precede those who have fallen asleep. For the Lord Himself will descend with a shout, with the voice of the Archangel, and with trumpet of God; and the dead in Christ will rise first. Then we who are alive and remain shall be caught up together with them in the clouds to meet the Lord in the air, and thus we shall always be with the Lord. Therefore comfort one another with these words.} There will be a thousand years between the resurrection of the saved and the unsaved: (Page 1224-Rev. 20:4.5). {And I saw thrones, and they sat upon them, and judgment was given to them. And I saw the souls of those who had been beheaded because of the testimony of Jesus and because of the Word of God, and those who had not worshiped the beast or his image, and had not received

the mark upon their forehead and upon their hand; and they came to life and reigned with Christ for a thousand years. The rest of the dead did nor come to life until the thousand years were completed. This is the first resurrection.} There will be a thousand years between the "judgment seat of Christ" where only the saved will appear and the "great white throne judgment" where only unsaved will appear.

(2) At the judgment seat of Christ, the believer will give account of himself to God. Therefore, we should look to our own works, and not judge the works of others (Page 1094- Rom. 14:10-13). {But you, why do you judge your brother? Or you again, why do you regard your brother with contempt? For we shall all stand before the judgment seat of God. For it is written, "As I live, says the Lord, every knee shall bow to Me, And every tongue shall give praise to God" So then each one of us shall give account to himself to God. Therefore let us not judge one another anymore, but rather determine this - not to put an obstacle or a stumbling block in a brother's way.}

(3) It is a most humbling thought to know that some day the believer will face all of his works—"good or bad." Some will be ashamed: (Page 1200-1John 2:28). {And now, little children, abide in Him, so that when He appears, we may have confidence and not shrink away from Him in shame at His coming.} And suffer loss- not the loss of salvation, but the loss of rewards: (Page 1100- 1Cor. 3:11-15). {For if man can lay a foundation other then the one which is laid, which is Jesus Christ. Now if any man builds upon the foundation with gold, silver, precious stones, wood, hay, straw, each man's work will become evident; for the day will show it, because it is to be revealed with fire; and fire itself will test the quality of each man's work. If any man's work which he has built upon it remains, he shall receive a

reward. If any man's work is burned up, he shall suffer loss; but he himself shall be saved, yet so as through fire.}

So whatever you do, do it for the glory of God: (Page 1145-Col. 3:17). {And whatever you do in word or deed, do all in the name of the Lord Jesus, giving thanks through Him to God the Father.}

THE JUDGMENT OF THE NATIONS

(Page 942-Matt. 25:31-46). {But when the Son of Man comes in His glory, and all the angels with Him, then He will sit on His glorious throne. And all the nations will be gathered before Him; and He will separate them from one another, as the shepherd separates the sheep from the goats; and He will put the sheep of His right, and the goats on His left. Then the King will say to those on is right, "Come, you who are blessed of My Father, inherit the kingdom prepared for you from the foundation of the world. For I was hungry, and you gave Me something to eat; I was thirsty, and you gave me something to drink; I was a stranger, and you invited me in; naked, and you clothed Me; I was sick, and you visited Me." Then the righteousness will answer Him, saying, "Lord, when did we see You hungry, and feed You, or thirsty, and give You drink? And when did we see You a stranger, and invite You in, of naked, and clothe You? And when did we see You sick, or in prison, and come to You?" And the King will answer and say to them, "Truly I say to you, to the extent that you did it to one of these brothers of Mine, even the least of them, you did it to Me." Then He will say to those on His left, "Depart from Me, accursed ones, into the eternal fire which has been prepared for the devil and his angels; for I was hungry, and you gave Me nothing to eat; I was thirsty, and you gave Me nothing to drink; I was a stranger, and you did not invite Me in; naked, and you did not clothe Me; sick, and in prison and you did not visit Me." Then they themselves also will answer, saying, "Lord, when did we see you hungry, or thirsty, or a stranger, or naked, or sick, or in prison, and did not take care of you?" Then He will answer them, saying, "Truly I say to you, to the extent that you did not do it to one of least of these, you did not do it to Me." And these will go away into eternal punishment, but the righteous into eternal life.}

This judgment is not the judgment of the great white throne: (Page 1224- Rev. 20:11-15). {And I saw a great white throne and Him who sat upon it, from whose presence earth and heaven fled away, and no place was found for them. And I saw the dead, the great and the small, standing before the throne, and books (scrolls) were opened; and another book was opened, which is the book of life; and the dead were judged from the things which were written in the books, according their deeds. And the sea gave up the dead which were in it, and death and Hades gave up the dead which were in them; and they were judged, every one of them according to their deeds. And the death and Hades were thrown into the lake of fire. This is the second death, the lake of fire. And if anyone's name was not found written in the book of life, he was thrown into the lake of fire.}

A careful comparison of the two judgments will establish the following facts:

    (1) The judgment of the nations will take place "when the Son of Man comes in His glory… then He will sit on His glorious throne. "The great white throne is never called "the Throne of His Glory" (Page 1224- Rev.20:11-15).

    (2) At this judgment, He will judge the living nations: (Page 834-Joel 3:11-16 OT). {Hasten and come, all you surrounding nations, And gather yourselves there. Bring down, O Lord, Thy mighty ones. Let the nations be aroused And come up to the valley of Jehoshaphat. For there I will sit to judge All the surrounding nations. Put in the sickle, for the harvest is ripe. Come tread, for the wine press is full; The vats overflow, for their wickedness is great. Multitudes, multitudes in the

valley of decision! For the day of the Lord is near in the valley of decision. The sun and the moon grow dark, And the stars lose their brightness. And the Lord roars from Zion And utters His voice from Jerusalem, And the heavens and the earth tremble. But the Lord is a refuge for His people And a stronghold to the sons of Israel.} At the white throne judgment, He will judge the wicked dead.

(3) At this judgment, there will be no resurrection of the dead. At the great white throne all the wicked dead are raised: (Page 1224-Rev. 20:13). {And the sea gave up the dead which were in it, and death and Hades gave up the dead which were in them; and they were judged, everyone of them; and they were judged, everyone of them according to their deeds.}

(4) At this judgment, the judge is God "the King" judging the living nations in His earthly kingdom. At the great white throne, the judge is God, judging only the wicked dead.

(5) At this judgment, there are no books opened. At the great white throne, the "books were opened."

(6) At this judgment, there are three classes judged: "sheep"--the saved: (Page 1215-Rev. 7:9-17); {And when He broke the fifth seal, I saw underneath the alter the souls of those who had been slain because of the Word of God, and because of the testimony which they had maintained; And they cried out with a loud voice, saying, "How long, O Lord, holy and true, wilt Thou refrain from judging and avenging our blood on those who dwell on the earth?" And there was given to each of them a white robe; and they were told that they should rest for a little while longer, until the number of their fellow servants and their brethren who were to be killed even as they had been, should be completed also. And I looked when he broke the sixth seal, and there was a great earthquake; and the sun became black as

sackcloth made of hair, and the whole moon became like blood; And the stars of the sky fell to the earth, as a fig tree casts its unripe figs when shaken by a great wind. And the sky was split apart like a scroll when it is rolled up; and every mountain and island were moved out of their places. And the kings of the earth and the great men and the commanders (in command of one thousand troops) and the rich and the strong and every slave and free man, hid themselves in the caves and among the rocks of the mountains: and they said to the mountains and to the rocks, "Fall on us and hide us from the presence (face) of Him who sits on the throne, and from the wrath of the Lamb; for the great day of their wrath has come; and who is able to stand?"}

Goats-the unsaved: (Page 1152- 2Thes 1:7-10). {and to give relief to you who are afflicted and to us as well when the Lord Jesus shall be revealed from heaven with His mighty angels in flaming fire. Dealing out retribution to those who do not know God and to those who do not obey the gospel of our Lord Jesus. And these will pay the penalty of eternal destruction, away from the presence of the Lord and from the glory of His power. When He comes to be glorified in His saints (Holy ones) on that day, and to be marveled at among all who have believed-for our testimony to you was believed.}

"Tribes"—the elect of Israel: (Page 1215-Rev. 7:1-8). {After this I saw four angels standing as the four corners of the earth, holding back the four winds of the earth, so that no wind should blow on the earth or on the sea or on any tree. And I saw another angel ascending from the rising of the sun, having the seal of the living God: and He cried out with a loud voice to the four angels to whom it was granted to harm the earth and the sea. Saying, "Do not harm the earth or the sea or the trees, until we have sealed the bond servants of our God on their forehead." And I heard the number of those who were sealed, one hundred and forty four thousand sealed from every tribe of the sons of Israel: from the tribe of Judah, twelve thousand were sealed, from the tribe of Reuben twelve thousand, from the tribe of Gad twelve thousand, from the tribe of Asher twelve thousand, from the tribe of Naphtali twelve thousand, from the tribe of Manasseh twelve thousand, from the tribe of Simeon twelve thousand, from the tribe of Levi twelve thousand, from the tribe of Issachar twelve thousand, from the tribe of Zebulun twelve thousand, from the tribe of Joseph twelve thousand, from the tribe of Benjamin twelve thousand were sealed.}

Also: (Page 1092-Rom. 11:25-28). { For I do not want you, brethren, to be uninformed of this mystery, lest you be wise in your own estimation, that a partial hardening has happened to Israel until the fullness of the Gentiles has come in; and thus all Israel will be saved; just as it is written, "The deliverer will come from Zion, He will remove all ungodliness from Jacob. And this is My covenant with them, when I take away their sins. From the stand point of the gospel they are enemies for your sake, but from the stand point of God's choice they are beloved for the sake of the fathers.} At the great white throne, there is only one class: "the dead."

(7) At this judgment, the King gives the kingdom to those who have eternal life, At the great white throne, there are no saved and no kingdom; they are all "thrown into the lake of fire."

THE JUDGMENT OF THE WICKED

(Page 1224-Rev.20:11-15). {And I saw a great white throne and Him sat upon it, from whose presence earth and heaven fled away, and no place was found for them. And I saw the dead, the great and the small, standing before the throne, and books were opened; and another book was opened, which is the book of life; and the dead were judged from the things which were written in the books, according to their deeds. And the sea gave up the dead which were in it, and death and Hades gave up the dead which were in them; and they were judged, every one of them according to their deeds. And death and Hades were thrown into the lake of fire. This is the second death, the lake of fire. And if anyone's name was not found written in the book of life, he was thrown into the lake of fire.}

The great white throne judgment will follow the thousand year reign of Christ. This is the final judgment, and only the wicked dead are to be judged. According to: (Page 1224-Rev-20:4). {The rest of the dead did not come to life until the thousand years were completed. This is the first resurrection.}

The believers were resurrected a thousand years before this judgment, and their works were judged at the "judgment seat of Christ": (Page 1116-2Cor. 5:10). {For we must all appear before the judgment seat of Christ, that each one may be recompensed for his deeds in the body, according to what he has done, whether good or bad.}

    (1) At this judgment, the wicked dead will seek a hiding place from the face of the Lord Jesus Christ, the judge. But there is no hiding place.

    (2) At this judgment, the "dead, the great and the small" will stand before God. But the greatness of the great will be of no value. "There is none who does good, There is not even one": (Page 1083-Rom.3:12). {All have turned aside, together they have become useless; there is none who does good, there is not even one.}

    (3) At this judgment, the "book of life" will be opened. Why the "book of life" if there are no saved at this judgment? the wicked will be shown that God in His mercy provided space for them in the "book of life." So that they are without excuse: (Page1082-Rom.

1:18-20). {For the wrath of God is revealed from heaven against all ungodliness and unrighteousness of men, who suppress the truth in unrighteousness, because that which is known about God is evident within them: for God made it evident to them. For since the creation of the world His invisible attributes, His eternal power and divine nature, have been clearly seen, being understood through what has been made, so that they are without excuse.}

(4) At this judgment, the dead will be judged "according to their deeds" God is a just God; and since there are degrees of punishment in hell, some will be punished more than others: (Page 993- Luke 12: 42:48). {And the Lord said, "Who then is the faithful and sensible steward, whom his master will put in charge of his servants, to give them their rations at the proper time? Blessed is that slave whom his master finds so doing when he comes. Truly I say to you, that he will put him in charge of all his possessions. But if that slave says in his heart, 'My master will be a long time in coming,' and begins to beat the slaves, both men and women, and to eat and drink and get drunk; the master of that slave will come on a day when he does not expect him, and at an hour he does not know, and will cut him in pieces, and assign him a place with the unbelievers. And that slave who knew his master's will and did not get ready or act in accord with his will, shall receive many lashes, but the one who did not know it, and committed deeds worthy of a flogging, will receive but few. And from everyone who has been given much shall much be required; to whom they entrusted much, of him they will ask all the more.}

(5) At this judgment, there will be no acquittal, no higher court to which the lost may appeal. It is lost, and lost forever; it is damned to all eternity, and that without hope.

There is a Hades: (Page 998-Luke 16:19-31). {"Now there was a certain rich man, and he habitually dressed in purple and fine linen, gaily living in splendor every day. And a certain poor man named Lazarus was laid at his gate, covered with sores, and longing to be fed with the crumbs which were falling from the rich mans table; besides, even the dogs were coming to lick is sores. Now it came about that the poor man died and he was carried away by the angels to Abraham's bosom; and the rich man also died and was buried. And in Hades he lifted up his eyes, being in torment, and saw Abraham far away, and Lazarus in his bosom. And he cried out and said, "Father Abraham, have mercy on me, and send Lazarus, that he may dip the tip of his finger in water and cool off my tongue; for I am in agony in this flame." But Abraham said, "Child, remember that during your life you received your good things, and likewise Lazarus bad things; but now he is being comforted here, and you are in agony. And besides all this, between us and you there is a great chasm fixed, in order that those who wish to come over from here to you may not be able, and that none may cross over from there to us." And he said, "Then I beg you, Father, that you send him to my father's house- for I have five brothers- that he may warn them, lest they also come to this place of torment.' But Abraham said, 'They have Moses and the Prophets; let them hear them.' But he said, 'No, Father Abraham, but if someone goes to them from the dead, they will repent!' But he said to him, 'If they do not listen to Moses and the Prophets, neither will they be persuaded if someone rises from the dead.'"}

And in Hades, there is no hope, no sympathy, no love; even the love of God does not extend beyond the portals of Hades.

MASTER OUTLINE NUMBER SEVEN
REWARDS

There is a vast difference in the doctrine of salvation for the lost, and the doctrine of rewards for the saved. Salvation is "the gift of God; not as a result of works": (Page 1131-Eph. 2:8.9.). {For by grace you have been saved through faith; and that not of yourselves, it is the gift of God; not as a result of works, that no one should boast.}

Salvation is received by faith in the finished work of the Lord Jesus Christ: (Page 1016-John 3:36). {"He who believes in the Son has eternal life; but he who does not obey the Son shall not see life, but the wrath of God abides on him."}

Rewards are according to the works of the believer: (Page 932-Matt. 16:27). {"For the Son of Man is going to come in the glory of His Father with His angels; and will then recompense every man according to his deeds.} A most revealing Scripture on rewards is found in: (Page 1100-1Cor. 3:8-18). {Now he who plants and he who waters are one; but each will receive his own reward according to his own labor. For we are God's fellow workers; you are God's field, God's building. According to the grace of God which was given to Me, as a wise master builder I laid a foundation, and another is building upon it. But let each man be careful how he builds upon it. For no man can lay a foundation other than the one is laid, which is Jesus Christ. Now if any man builds upon the foundation with gold, silver, precious stones, wood, hay, straw, each man's work will become evident; for the day will show it, because it is to be revealed with fire; and the fire itself will test the quality of each man's work. If any man's work which he has built upon it remains, he shall receive a reward. If any man's work is burned up, he shall suffer loss; but he himself shall be saved, yet so as through fire. Do you not know that you are a temple of God, and that the Spirit of God dwells in you? If any man destroys the temple of God, God will destroy him. For the temple of God is holy, and that is what you are. Let no man deceive himself. If any man among you thinks that he is wise in this age, let him become foolish that he may become wise.}

First, every believer will be rewarded "according to his own labor" (verse 8). We do not labor for salvation.

Second, "We are God's fellow workers" (verse 9)-not for salvation, but for rewards.

Third, the believer is not to build "a foundation other than the one which is laid, which is Jesus Christ" (verse 11).

Fourth, the believer has a "choice of two kinds of building materials: "gold, silver, precious stones"-this is building with eternal materials; or "wood, hay, straw,"-this is building with temporal materials. (verse 12) (Page 1115-2cor 4:18). {while we look not at the things which are seen, but at the things which are seen; for the things that are seen are temporal, but the things which are not seen are eternal.}

The believer who builds on Christ with eternal materials. "gold, silver, precious stones: shall receive a reward. Those who build on Christ with temporal materials, "wood, hay, straw" will receive no reward. The works of "wood, hay, straw" will be destroyed at the judgment seat of Christ," and the believer will suffer loss- not the loss of salvation, but the: loss of reward.

Some believers will be ashamed at the "judgment seat of Christ": (Page 1200-1 John 2:28). {And now, little children, abide in Him, so that when He appears, we may have confidence and not shrink away from Him in shame at His coming.} - ashamed of their works of "wood, hay, straw."

In the first year of my ministry, I sat at the bed side of a dying friend. As we talked of his home going, tears filled his eyes. Being Young in the Lord, I thought he was afraid to die, and attempted to speak words of encouragement to him. He said," I am not afraid to die: I am ashamed to die," He went on to say that Christ was his savior, but he had lived for self, and now had to meet the Lord Jesus Christ empty handed, His life loomed up before him as "wood, hay, straw." He was "saved, yet as through fire."

"Rewards are called "crowns or wreaths" in the New Testament.

THE CROWN OF LIFE

(Page 1184 James 1:12). {Blessed is the man who perseveres under trial; for once he has been approved, he will receive the crown of life, which the Lord has promised to those who love Him.}

This reward could be called the lover's crown. Upon examination of the above verse, we discover that the believer finds strength to overcome temptation and endure trials, through the love of God Paul said, "We also exult in our tribulations." The question is: Do we today exult in tribulations?

We can, only if the "love of God has been poured out within our hearts through the Holy Spirit": (Page 1085-Rom. 5:3-5). {And not only this, but we also exult in our tribulations, knowing that tribulations brings about perseverance.} Without the love of God in the heart of the believer, trials can cause him to become bitter and critical and lose the "crown of life." All believers have eternal life: (Page 1015-John 3:15.16). {that who ever believes may in Him have eternal life. For God so loved the world, that He gave His only begotten Son, that whoever believes in Him should not perish, but have eternal life.}

But not all believers will be rewarded with the "crown of life." This crown will be given to those who are "faithful until death": (Page 1211-Rev.2:10). {Do not fear what you are about to suffer. Behold, the devil is about to cast some of you in prison, that you may be tested, and you will have tribulation ten days. Be faithful until death, and I will give you the crown of life.}

To receive the "crown of life" the believer must love the Lord more than his own life. "For whoever wishes to save his own life (live for self) shall lose it; but whoever loses his life for My sake and the gospel's (live for Christ at all cost) shall save it": (Page 961-Mark 8:35). {"For whoever wishes to save his life shall lose it; but whoever losses his life for My sake and the gospel's shall save it.}

This reward will be given to those who live for Christ, and endure temptations, in the power of the love of God: (Page 1105-1Cor. 10:13). {No temptation has overtaken you but such as is common to man; and God is faithful, who will not allow you to be tempted beyond what you are able, but with the temptation will provide the way of escape also, that you may be able to endure it.}

THE WREATH IMPERISHABLE

(Page 1104-1Cor. 9:24-27). {Do you not know that those who run in a race all run, but only one receives the prize? Run in such a way that you may win. And everyone who competes in the games exercises self-control in all things. They then do it to receive a perishable wreath, but we an imperishable. Therefore I run in such a way, as not without aim; I box in such a way, as not beating the air: but I buffet (bruise) my body and make it my slave, lest possibly, after I have preached to others, I myself should be disqualified.}

Paul makes use of the Greek games to illustrate the spiritual race of the believer. They ran to win a 'perishable wreath; but we an imperishable" wreath. No young man could contend in the games unless he was a Greek citizen, born of Greek parents. No unsaved person can participate in the services of the Lord for rewards; only the born of God are eligible: (Page 1014-John 3:3). {Jesus answered and said to him. "Truly, truly, I say to you, unless one is born again, he cannot see the kingdom of God."}

Just as the athlete must deny himself many gratifications of the body so the believer must say, "I buffet my body and make it my slave" or he will become "disqualified." He will not lose salvation, but he will lose the "imperishable wreath."

The Greek games had hard and fast rules for all participants. The New Testament contains the rules for believers who would enter the spiritual race to win the "imperishable wreath."

(1) The believer must deny self of anything that would weigh him down and hold him back: (Page 1181-Heb. 12:1}. {Therefore, since we have so great a cloud of witnesses surrounding us. Let us also lay aside every encumbrance, and the sin which so easily entangles us, and let us run with endurance the race that is set before us,}
(2) The believer must keep his eyes on Jesus, and not look to the right or the left: (Page 1181-Heb. 12:2). {fixing our eyes on Jesus, the author and perfecter of faith, who for the joy set before Him endured the cross, despises the shame, and has sat down at the right hand of the throne of God.}
(3) The believer must find his strength in the Lord: (Page 1135-Eph. 6:10-18). {Finally, be strong in the Lord, and in the strength if His might. Put on the full armor of God, that you may be able to stand firm against the schemes of the devil. For our struggle is not against flesh and blood, but against the rulers, against the powers, against the world forces of this darkness, against the spiritual forces of wickedness in the heavenly places. Therefore, take up the full armor of God, that you may be able to resist in the evil day, and having done everything, to stand firm. Stand firm therefore, having girded your loins with truth, and having put on the breastplate of righteousness, and having shod your feet with the preparation of the gospel of peace; in addition to all, taking up the shield with which you will be able to extinguish all flaming missiles of the evil one. And take the helmet of salvation, and the sword of the Spirit, which is the word of God. With all prayer and petition pray at all times in the Spirit, and with this in view, be on the alert with all perseverance and petition for all the saints.}
(4) The believer must place his all at the alter of the Lord: (Page 1092-Rom. 12:1.2) {I urge you therefore,

brethren, by the mercies of God, to present your bodies a living sacrifice, acceptable to God, which is you spiritual service of worship. And do not be conformed to this world, but be transformed by the renewing of your mind, that you may prove what the will of God is that which is good and acceptable and perfect.}

(5) The believer must, by faith, refuse anything that would impede spiritual progress: (Page 1180-Heb. 11:24-29). {By faith Moses, when he had grown up, refused to be called the son of Pharaoh's daughter; choosing rather to endure ill-treatment with the people of God, than to enjoy the passing of pleasures of sin; considering the reproach of Christ greater riches than the treasures of Egypt; for he was looking to reward. By faith he left Egypt, not fearing the wrath of the king; for he endured, as seeing Him who is unseen. By faith he kept the Passover and the sprinkling of the blood, so that he who destroyed the first-born might not touch them. By faith they passed through the Red Sea as though they were passing through dry land; and the Egyptians, when they attempted it, were drowned.}

Do not be s spiritual spectator. Enter the race and run to win the "imperishable wreath."

THE CROWN OF EXALTATION

(Page 1149-1Thes. 2:19.20). {For who is our hope or joy or crown of exaltation? Is it not even you, in the presence of our Lord Jesus Christ at His coming? For you are our glory and joy.}

The "crown of exaltation" is the souls winners crown. The greatest work you are privileged to do for the Lord is to bring others to the knowledge of Christ as personal Savior. The degree of your joy in heaven will be determined by the souls you have had a part in bringing to Christ.

Paul tells the Thessalonian believers that they are his "...hope or joy or crown of exaltation" now and when Jesus comes.
   (1) It is wise to win souls to Christ: (Prov.11:30 OT). {If the righteous will be rewarded in the earth, How much more the wicked and the sinner!}
   (2) It is a work against sin to win souls for Christ: (Page 1187-James 5:20). {let him know that he who turns a sinner from error of his way will save his soul from death, and will cover a multitude of sins.}
   (3) It is a cause for joy in heaven to win souls to Christ: (Page 996-Luke 15:10). {"In the same way, I tell you, there is joy in the presence of the angels of god over one sinner who repents."}
   (4) Every soul winner will shine as the stars forever: (Dan.12:3 OT). {"And those who have insight will shine brightly like the brightness of the expanse of heaven, and those who lead the many to righteous, like the stars forever and ever.}

Witness with your life that others may see Christ in you: (Page 1114-2Cor. 3:2). {You are our letter, written in our hearts, known and read by all men.} Also: (Page 1125-Gal 2:20). {"I have been crucified with Christ; and it is no longer I who live, but Christ lives in me; and the life which I now live in the flesh I live by faith in the Son of God, who loved me, and delivered Himself up for me.}

Witness with your mouth, trusting the Holy Spirit to give power to the spoken word: (Page 1041-Acts 1:8). {but you shall receive power when the Holy Spirit has come upon you; and you shall be my witnesses both in Jerusalem, and in all Judea and Samaria, and even to the remotest part of the earth."}

Witness by tithes and offerings that others may preach Christ, and you will have "profit which increases to your account." (Page 1140-Phil.4:15-17). {And you yourselves also know, Philippians, that at first preaching of the gospel, after I departed from Macedonia, no church shared with me in the matter of giving and receiving but you alone; for even in Thessalonica you sent a gift more than once for my needs. Not that I seek the gift itself, but I seek for the profit which increases to your account.} Also: (Page 1119-2Cor. 9:6). {Now this I say, he who sows sparingly shall reap sparingly; and he who sows bountifully shall also reap bountifully.}

God has promised that your toil will not be in vain in the Lord: (Page 1111-1Cor. 15:58). {Therefore, my beloved brethren, be steadfast, immovable, always abounding in the work of the Lord, knowing that your toil is not in vain in the Lord.}

The soul winner will not rejoice alone- all of heaven will rejoice with him when he receives the "crown of exultation": (Page 1017- John 4:36). { "Already he who reaps is receiving wages, and is gathering fruit for life eternal; that he who sows and he who reaps may rejoice together.}

THE CROWN OF RIGHTEOUSNESS

(Page 1162-2Tim. 4:5-8). {But you, be sober in all things, endure hardship, do the work of an evangelist, fulfill your ministry. For I am already being poured out as a drink offering, and the time of my departure has come. I have fought the good fight, I have finished the course, I have kept the faith; in the future there is laid up for me the crown of righteousness, which the Lord, the righteous judge, will award to me on that day; and not only me, but also to all who have loved His appearing.}

The "crown of righteousness" is a reward, but is not to be confused with "righteousness of God" which the believer receives when he becomes a Christian; for at that time, the believer is to"…..become the righteousness of God in Him": (Page 1116-2Cor. 5:21). {He made Him who knew no sin to be sin on our behalf, that we might become the righteousness of God in Him.}

This saving righteousness is a gift to be accepted by the lost. The "crown of righteousness" is a reward earned by the saved. If the believer looks for, and loves the doctrine of the second coming of Christ, it will affect his whole life. Look at the dynamic impact this truth had on the life of the Apostle Paul. He could say:

(1) "I have fought the good fight": (verse 7) Also: (Page 1110-1Cor. 15:32). {If from human motives I fought with wild beasts at Ephesus, what does it profit me? If the dead are not raised, let us eat and drink, for tomorrow we die.} He fought a spiritual battle throughout his Christian life, and won. He never surrendered to the enemies of righteousness: (Page 1135-Eph. 6:12). {For our struggle is not against flesh and blood, but against the rulers, against the power, against the world forces of darkness, against the spiritual forces of wickedness in the heavenly places.}

(2) "I have finished the course." He had a course to travel, and did not detour the hard places; neither did he look back: (Page 989- Luke 9:61.62). {And another also said, "I will follow you, Lord; but first permit me to say goodbye to those at home." But Jesus said to him, "No one, after putting his hand to the plow and looking back is fit for the kingdom of God."} He finished his course with fixed on Christ: (Page 1137- Phil. 1:6). {For I am confident of this very thing, that He who began a good work in you will perfect it until the day of Jesus Christ.}

(3) "I have kept the faith" He preached "…whole purpose of God"—never betraying any of the great doctrines: (Page 1068-Acts 20:24-31). {"But I do not consider my life of any account as dear to myself, in order that I may finish my course, and the ministry which I received from the Lord Jesus, to testify solemnly of the gospel of the grace of God. And now, behold, I know that all of you, among whom I went about preaching the kingdom, will see my face no more. Therefore I testify to you this day, that I am innocent of the blood of all men. For I did not shrink from declaring to you

the whole purpose of God. Be on guard for yourselves and for all the flock, among which the Holy Spirit has made you overseers, to shepherd the church of God which He purchased with His own blood. I know that after my departure savage wolves will come in among you, not sparing the flock; and from among your own selves men will arise, speaking perverse things to draw away the disciples after them. Therefore be on the alert, remembering that night and day for a period of three years I did not cease to admonish each one with tears.}

The Apostle looked ahead to the "judgment seat of Christ" where the "crown of righteousness" will be given to those who "loved His appearing." How important it is for the believer to look with a heart of love for the second coming of our Lord and Savior Jesus Christ, that he may receive the "crown of righteousness": (above verse 8).

THE CROWN OF GLORY

(Page 1192-1Pet. 5:2-4). {Shepherd the flock of God among you, exercising oversight not under compulsion, but voluntarily, according to the will of God; and not be sordid gain, but with eagerness; nor yet as lording it over those allotted to your charge, but proving to be examples to the flock. And when the Chief Shepherd appears, you will receive the unfading crown of glory.}

"The crown of glory" is a special reward for the faithful, obedient God-called pastor. He will receive this reward when the "Chief Shepherd appears." It is eternal; It is "unfading." Every believer may share in the pastors "crown of glory." (Page 923- Matt.10:41). {"He who receives a prophet in the name of a prophet shall receive a prophet's reward; and he who receives a righteous man in the name of a righteous man shall receive a righteous man's reward.}

Support you faithful, God-called pastor by praying for him and encouraging him in the work of the Lord. Under grid his ministry with God's tithes and your offerings: (Mal.3:10 OT). {"Bring the who tithe into the storehouse, so that there may be food in My house, and test Me now in this," says the Lord of hosts, "If I will not open for you the windows of heaven, and pour out for you a blessing until it overflows.}

Giving freely of your time to the service of the Lord. And God will reward you for supporting His chosen servant by allowing you to share in your pastor's reward. The pastor will earn this "crown of glory" by:

(1) Feeding the church. He is to proclaim the Word of God without fear or favor; and, when necessary, he will "reprove, rebuke, exhort, with great patience and instruction": (Page 1162-2Tim. 4:2-5). {preach the word; be ready in season and out of season; reprove, rebuke, exhort, with great patience and instruction. For the time will come when they will not endure sound doctrine; but wanting to have theirs tickled, they will accumulate for themselves teachers in accordance to their own desires; and will turn away their ears from the truth, and will turn aside to myths. But you, be sober in all things, endure hardship, do the work of an evangelist, fulfill your ministry.}

(2) Taking the spiritual oversight of the church, the pastor is responsible to God for the message preached to his people. No pastor should preach to please the people; he is to please his Lord: (Page 1124-Gal. 1:10). {For I am now seeking the favor of men, or of God? Or am I striving to please men? If I were trying to please men, I would not be a bond servant of Christ.}

(3) Being an example to the church. He is not to serve for the reward of money. Yet, the church is responsible to care for his every need: (Page 1157-1Tim 5:18). {For the Scripture says, "You shall not muzzle the ox while he is threshing," and The laborer is worthy of his wages."}

He is to be a spiritual leader, not a dictator. He is to walk with God by faith. "and when the Chief Shepherd appears, you will receive the unfading crown of glory" (above verse 4).

MASTER OUTLINE NUMBER EIGHT

THE CHURCH

Jesus said, "I will build My church" (ecclesia): (Page 931-Matt. 16:18). {"And I also say to you that you are Peter, and upon this rock I will build My church; and the gates of Hades shall not overpower it.} The word "ecclesia" in the New Testament is used to designate any assembly whether it be political: (Page 1067-Acts 19:39). {"But if you want anything beyond this, it shall be settled in the lawful assembly.}

Christian: (Page 1131-Eph. 1:22.23). {And He put all things in subjection under His feet, and gave Him as head over all things to the church. Which is His body, the fullness of Him who fills all in all.}

Or national: (Page 1051-Acts 7:38). {"This is the one who was in the congregation in the wilderness together with the angel who was speaking to him on Mount Sinai, and who was with the fathers; and he received living oracles to pass on to you.}

It means a called-out assembly or congregation. God called Israel out of Egypt; they congregated in the wilderness; they were, "the church in the wilderness." Today, God calls the saved out of the world to congregate in worship. This is the church in the world, in it but not of it.

Unlike the church in the wilderness, the church that Jesus is building will never cease. He said "The gates of Hades shall not overpower it." His church is not synonymous with Christendom in the same way in which it is in the world, in it but not of it. Christendom is made up of those who profess to be Christians, but they know not Christ as a personal; Savior: (Page 919-Matt. 7:21-23). {"Not everyone who says to Me, 'Lord, Lord,' will enter the kingdom of heaved; bur he who does the will of My Father who is in heaven. Many will say to Me on that day, 'Lord, Lord, did we not prophesy in Your name, and in Your name cast out demons, and in Your name perform many miracles?' And I will declare to them, 'I never knew you; Depart from Me, you practice lawlessness.'"}

Also: (Page 1161-2Tim 3:5{holding a form of godliness, although they have denied its power; and avoid such men as these.} And: (Page 1165-Titus 1:16). {They profess to know God, but by their deeds they deny Him, being detestable and disobedient, and worthless for any good deed.}

Only blood-washed, born again, Spirit-baptizes believers constitute the church that Jesus is building. It is called a:

    (1) Mystery: (Page 1132-Eph.3:3-10). {that by revelation there was made known to me the mystery, as I wrote before in brief. And by referring to this, when you read you can understand my insight into the Mystery of Christ, which in other generations was not made known to the sons of men, as it has now been revealed to His holy apostles and prophets in the Spirit; to be specific, that the Gentiles are fellow heirs and fellow members of the body, and fellow partakers of the promise in Christ Jesus through the gospel, of which I was made a minister, according to the gift of God's grace which was given to me according to the working of His power. To me, the very least of all saints, this grace was given, to preach to the Gentiles the unfathomable riches of Christ, and bring to light what is the administration of the mystery which for ages has been hidden in God, who created all things; in order that the manifold wisdom of God might now be made through the church to the rulers and the authorities in the heavenly places.}

    (2) Body: (Page 1107-1Cor. 12:12-31). {For even as the body is one and yet has many members, and all the members of the body, though they are many, are one body, so also in Christ. For by one Spirit we were all baptized into one body, whether Jews or Greeks, whether slaves or free, and we were all made to drink of one Spirit. For the body is not one member, but

many. If the foot should say, "Because I am not a hand, I am not a part of the body," it is not for this reason any the less a part of the body? And if the ear should say, "Because I am not an eye, I am not a part of the body," it is not for this reason any less a part of the body. If the whole body were an eye, where would the hearing be? If the whole were hearing, where would the sense of smell be? But now God has placed the members, each one of them, in the body, just as He desired. And if they were all one member, where would the body be? But now there are many members, but one body. And the eye cannot say to the hand, "I have no need of you"; or again the head to the feet, "I have no need of you." On the contrary, it is much truer that the members of the body which seem to be weaker are necessary; and those members of the body, which we deem less honorable, on these we bestow less honorable, on these we bestow more abundant honor, and our unseemly members come to have more abundant unseemliness, whereas our seemly members have no need of it. But God has so composed the body, giving more abundant honor to that member which lacked, that there should be no division (schism) in the body, but that the members should have the same care for one another. And if one member suffers, all the members suffer with it; if one member is honored, all members rejoice with it. Now you are Christ's body, and individually members of it. And God has appointed in the church, first apostles, second prophets, third teachers, then miracles, then healings, helps, administrations, various kinds of tongues. All are not apostles, are they? All are not prophets, are they? All are not workers of miracles, are they? All do not have gifts of healings, do they? All do not speak in tongues, do they? All do not interpret, do they? But earnestly desire the greater gifts. And I show you a still more excellent way.}

(3) Building: (Page 1131-Eph. 2: 10-22). For we are His workmanship, created in Christ Jesus for good works, which God prepared beforehand, that we should walk I them. Therefore, remember, that formerly you, the Gentiles in the flesh, who are called "Un-circumcision" by the so-called "Circumcision," which is performed in the flesh by human hands- remember that you were at that time separate from Christ, excluded (alienated) from commonwealth of Israel, and strangers to the covenants of promise, having no hope and without God in the world. But now in Christ Jesus you who formerly were far off have been brought near by the blood of Christ. For He Himself is our peace, who made both groups into one, and broke down the barrier of the dividing wall, by abolishing in His flesh the enmity, which is the law of commandants contained in ordinances, that in Himself He might make (create) the two into one new man, thus establishing peace, and might reconcile them both in one body to God through the cross, by is having put to death the enmity. And He came and preached peace to you who were far away, and peace to those who were near; for through Him we both having bur access in one Spirit to the Father. So then you are no longer strangers and aliens, but you are fellow citizens with the saints, and are of God's household, having been built upon the foundation of the apostles and prophets, Christ Jesus Himself being the corner stone, in whom the whole building, being fitted together is growing into a holy (sanctuary) temple in the Lord; in whom you also are being built together into a dwelling of God in the Spirit.}

(4) Bride: (Page 1120-2Cor. 11:2). {For I am jealous for you with a godly jealousy; for I betrothed you to one

husband, that to Christ I might present you as a pure virgin.}

THE CHURCH: IT'S FOUDATION

(Page 931- Matt. 16:13-18). {Now when Jesus came into the district of Caesarea Philippi, He began asking His disciples, saying, "Who do people say that the Son of Man is?" And they said, "Some say John the Baptist; others, Elijah; but still others, Jeremiah, or one of the prophets." He said to them, "But who do you say that I am?" And Simon Peter answered and said, "Thou art the Christ, (the Messiah) the Son of the living God." And Jesus answered and said to him, "Blessed are you, Simon Peter, because flesh and blood did not reveal this to you, but My Father who is in heaven. And I also say to you that you are Peter, and upon this rock I will build My church; and the gates of Hades shall not overpower it."}

"Upon this rock I will build My church." Leading up to this declaration He asked His disciples, "Who do you people say that the son of Man is?" They answered naming some of the prophets. Then He said to them, "But who do you say that I am?" Peter answered, "Thou art the Christ, the Son of the living God"

(Page 931-Matt. 6:16). In verse thirteen Jesus spoke of Himself as the "Son of God." Now Peter speaks of Him as the "Son of the living God." Jesus blessed Peter and said that this great truth came from God the Father. Again He said to Peter, "You are Peter (Petros, a little rock) and upon this rock (Petra, a big rock) I will build My church." Jesus did not say that He would build His church upon Peter, but upon Himself, the Rock of Ages.

Simon Peter called Jesus the "living stone," the precious "corner stone" (corn-er s-tone) a "stone of stumbling," and a "rock of offense." He spoke of all believers, including Himself as "living stones." Christ is the foundation and the believers are the building stones: (Page 1190-1Pet. 2:1-10). {Therefore, putting aside all malice, (wickedness) and all guile and hypocrisy and envy and all slander, like new born babes, long for the pure milk of the word, that by it you may grow in respect to salvation, if you have tasted the kindness (that the Lord is kind) of the Lord. And coming to Him as a living s-tone, rejected by men, but choice and precious in the sight of God, you also as living s-tones, are being built up as a spiritual house for a holy priesthood , to offer up spiritual sacrifices acceptable to God through Jesus Christ. For this is contained in Scripture: "Behold I lay in Zion a choice stone, a precious cornerstone, and he who believes in Him shall not be disappointed." This precious value, then, is for you who believe. But for those who disbelieve, "This s-tone which the builders rejected, This became the very cornerstone," and a stone of stumbling and a rock of offense"; for they stumble because they are disobedient to the word, and to this doom they were also appointed. But you are a chosen race, a royal priesthood, a holy nation, a people for God's own possession, that you may proclaim the excellencies of Him who has called you out of darkness into the marvelous light: for you once were not a people, but now you are the people of God; you had not received mercy, but now you have received mercy.}

Paul speaks of Christ as the foundation of the Apostles and the Prophets: (Page 1132- Eph. 2:19-22). {So then you are no longer strangers and aliens, but you are fellow citizens with the saints, and are of God's household. Having been built upon the foundation of the apostles and prophets, Christ Jesus Himself being the corner stone. In whom the whole building, being fitted together is growing into a holy temple in the Lord; in whom you also are being built together into a dwelling of God in the Spirit.} He also said, "For no man can lay a foundation other than the one which is laid, which is Jesus Christ." (Page 1100-1Cor. 3:11). {For no man can lay a foundation other than the one which is laid, which is Jesus Christ.}

Although the church was a mystery in the Old Testament, yet Isaiah said (Isaiah- 28:16 OT). {Therefore thus says the Lord God, "Behold, I am laying in Zion, a stone, a tested stone, a costly stone for the foundation, firmly placed. He who believes in it will not be disturbed.}

Christ is the sure foundation of His church and all believers are little building stones built into a holy temple in the Lord.

THE CHURCH: ITS HEAD

(Page 1142-Col. 1:18). {He is also the head of the body, the church; and He is beginning, the first-born from the dead; so that He himself might come to have first place in everything.}

"He is also head of the body, the church." Christ is the foundation, cornerstone, and head of His church. He is head of the local church, and He is head of the church in all- inclusive sense, including all born again, bloodwashed Spirit-baptized believers in heaven and earth.

The church is more than a religious organization; it is an organism, with Christ as the living head. It is alive with the life of Christ living in each member: (Page 1107-1Cor.12:1-31). {Now concerning spiritual gifts, brethren, I do not want you to be unaware. You know that when you were pagans, you were led astray to the dumb fool idols, however you were led. Therefore I make known to you; that no one speaking by the Holy Spirit of God says, "Jesus is accursed", and no one can say, "Jesus is Lord," except by the Holy Spirit. Now there are varieties of gifts, but the same Spirit. And there are varieties of ministries, and the same Lord. And there are varieties of effects, but the same God who works all things in all persons. But to each one is given the manifestation of the Spirit for the common good. For to one is given the word of wisdom through the Spirit, and to another the word of knowledge, according to the same Spirit; to another faith by the same Spirit, and to another gifts of healing by the one Spirit, and to another the effecting of miracles, and to another prophecy, and to another the distinguishing of spirits, and to another various kinds of tongues, and to another the interpretation of tongues. But one and the same Spirit works all these things, distributing to each one individually just as He wills. For even as the body is one and yet has many members, and all the members of the body, though they are many, are one body, so also is Christ. For by one Spirit we were all baptized into one body, whether Jews or Greeks, whether slaves or free, and we were all made to drink of one Spirit. For the body is not one member, but many. If the foot should say, "Because I am not a hand, I am not part of the body," it is not for this reason any the less a part of the body. And if the ear should say, "Because I am not an eye, I am not a part of the body," it is not for this reason any the less a part of the body. If the who body were an eye, where would the hearing be? If the whole were hearing, where would the sense of smell be? But now God has placed the members, each one of them, in the body, just as He desired. And if they were all one member, where would the body be? But now there are many members, but one body. And the eye cannot say to the hand, "I have no need of you"; or again the head to the feet, "I have no need of you." On the contrary, it is much truer that the members of the body which seem to be weaker are necessary: and those members of the body, which we deem less honorable, on these we bestow abundant honor, and our unseemly members come to have more abundant seemliness, whereas our seemly members have no need of it. But God has so composed the body, giving more abundant honor to that member which lacked. that there should be no division in the body, but that the members should have the same care for one another. And if one member suffers, all the members suffer with it; if one member is honored, all members rejoice with it. And God has appointed in the church, first apostles, second prophets, third teachers, then miracles, then gifts of healings, helps, administrations, various kinds of tongues. All are not apostles, are they All are not prophets, are they? All are not teachers, are they? All are not workers of miracles, are they? All do not have gifts of healings, do they? All do not speak with tongues, do they? All do not interpret, do they? But earnestly desire the greater gifts. And I show you a still more excellent way.}

Let us examine briefly the church and observe its role as the body of Christ.
- (1) The members of the body are given spiritual gifts according to the will of the Holy Spirit (verse1-11).
- (2) The unity of the body is seen in its many members with different operations all related and coordinated under one head (verse 12).
- (3) All are baptized by one Spirit into one body (verse 13)
- (a)There is one Holy Spirit.
- (b)There is one Holy Spirit baptism.
- (c)There is one body (the church).

This is the church in the broadest sense. You cannot join the church. The only way to become a member of His body is to be spiritually born: (Page 1014-John 3:1-7).{Now there was a man of the Pharisees, named Nicodemus, a ruler of the Jews; this man came to Him by night, and said to Him, "Rabbi" we know that you have come from God as a teacher; for no one can do these signs that you do unless God is with him." Jesus answered and said to him, "Truly, truly, I say to you, unless one is born again, he cannot see the kingdom of God." Nicodemus said to Him, "How can a man be born when he is old? He cannot enter a second time into his mother's womb, can he?" Jesus answered, "Truly, truly, I say to you, unless one is born of water and the Spirit, he cannot enter into the kingdom of God. That which is born of flesh is flesh, and that which is born of Spirit is spirit. Do not marvel that I said to you, 'You must be born again.'"}

And baptized into it by the Holy Spirit:
- (4) The members differ, yet they function as one in the will of God (verses 14-18).
- (5) The least or the weakest member is necessary for the proper function of the whole body (verses 22.23).
- (6) If one member suffers, the whole body suffers; if one is honored, all are honored (verse 26).
- (7) The members are to desire the greater spiritual gifts and minister in love (verse31). The Lord Jesus Christ

has never delegated His authority to anyone, whether he be pope, pastor, deacon, or the majority of the congregation. He is "head over all things to the church": (Page 1131-Eph. 1:22). {And He put all things in subjection under His feet, and gave Him as head over all things to the church,}

Jesus Christ is the only absolute and final authority.

THE CHURCH: ITS ORGANIZATION

(Page 1164-Titus 1:4.5). {to Titus, my true child in a common faith; Grace and peace from the Father God and Christ Jesus our Savior. For this reason I left you in Crete, that you might set in order what remains, and appoint elders in every city as I directed you,}

There is Scriptural evidence of some organization in the local church from its inception. It was a definite and permanent organized congregation, but not as we know it today.

Paul left Titus in Crete to organize the believers into local church bodies and to "set in order what remains, and appoint elders in every city" (above verse 5). The local New Testament church is a microcosm of the complete body of Christ in heaven and earth. The word "church" is used over one hundred times in the New Testament, and the greater majority of the references refer to the local congregation.

Organization in the local church is seen in:

(1) Its officers: He gave to the church "apostles" (this refers to the twelve; there are no apostles in the church today). "prophets" (we have no prophets and have not had since the last book of the New Testament was written), "evangelists" (the evangelists will serve the church until Jesus comes), and "pastors and teachers": (Page 1132-Eph. 4:11.12). And He gave some as apostles, and some as prophets, and some as evangelists, and some as pastors and teachers, for the equipping of the saints for the work of service, to the building up of the body of Christ.} Pastors and

teachers are local ministers; the apostles, and evangelists are ministers at large.

Another officer is the deacon. His qualifications are set forth in 1Timothy: (Page 1156-1Tim. 3:8-13). {Deacons likewise must be men of dignity, not double-tongued or addicted to much wine or fond of sordid gain, but holding to the mystery of the faith with a clear conscious. And let these first also be tested; then let them serve as deacons if they are beyond reproach. Women must likewise be dignified, not malicious gossips, but temperate, faithful in all things. Let deacons be husbands of only one wife, and good managers of their children and their own households. For those who have served well as deacons obtain for themselves a high standing and great confidence in the faith that is in Christ Jesus.}

Deacons are never called a board in the Scriptures. They are not to run the church; they are ordained to assist the pastor by ministering to the saints: (Page 1049-Acts6:1-7). {Now at this time while the disciples were increasing in number, a complaint arose on the part of the Hellenistic Jews against the native Hebrews, because their widows were being overlooked in the daily serving of food. And the twelve summoned the congregation of the disciples and said, "It is not desirable for us to neglect the word of God in order to serve tables. But select among you, brethren, seven men of good reputation, full of the Spirit and of wisdom, whom we may put in charge of this task. But we will devote ourselves to prayer, and to the ministry of the word." And the statement found approval with the whole congregation; and they chose Stephen, a man full of faith and of the Holy Spirit, and Philip, Prochorus, Nicanor, Timon, Parmenas and Nicholas, a proselyte from Antioch. And these they brought before the apostles; and after praying, they laid their hands on them. And the word of God kept on spreading; and the number of the disciples continued to increase greatly in Jerusalem, and a great many of the priests were becoming obedient to the faith.}

(2) Membership records: The church must have kept records of its members. The book of Acts tells us that there were about 120 in the upper room: (Page 1042- Acts 1:15-26) {And at this time Peter stood up in the midst of the brethren (a gathering of about one hundred and twenty persons was there together), and said "Brethren, the Scripture had to be fulfilled, which the Holy Spirit foretold by the word of mouth of David concerning Judas, who became a guide to those who arrested Jesus. For he was counted among us, and received his portion in this ministry." (Now this man acquired a field with the price of wickedness; and falling headlong, he burst open in the middle and all his bowels fell out. And it became known to all who were living in Jerusalem; so that in their own language that field called Hakeldalma, that is field of blood .) For it is written in the book of Psalms, 'Let his homestead be made desolate, and let no man dwell in it'; and, 'his office let another man take.' It is therefore necessary that the men who have accompanied us all the time that the Lord Jesus went in and out among us- beginning with the baptism of John, until the day that He was taken up from us-one of these should become a witness with us of His resurrection." And they put forward two men, Joseph called Barsabbas (who was called Justus), and Matthias. And they prayed, and said, "Thou Lord, who knowest the hearts of all men, show which one of these Thou hast chosen to occupy this ministry and apostleship from which Judas turned aside to go to his own place." And they drew lots for them, and the lot fell to Matthisa; and he was numbered with the seven apostles.}

The account reads like the average local church business meeting. Simon Peter is the Pastor; he takes the lead and gives direction in choosing one to take the place of Judas. "And they drew lots," and Matthias was chosen to be an apostle. On the day of Pentecost about 3,000 were added to the body of Christ by Holy Spirit baptism: (Page 1107-1Cor.12:13). {For by one Spirit we are all baptized into one body, whether Jews or Greeks; whether slaves or free, and we were all made to drink of one Spirit.}

And to the local church in Jerusalem by water baptism: (Page 1044-Acts 2:41). {So then, those who had received his word were baptized; and there were added that day about three thousand souls.}

Again the records show another 5,000 added: (Page 1045-Acts 4:4). {But many of those who had heard the message believed; and the number of the men came to about five thousand.}

The Scriptures tells us that "the Lord was adding to their number day by day those who were being saved": (Page 1044-Acts 2:47). {Praising God, and having favor with all the people. And the Lord was adding to their number day by day those who were being saved.}

   (3) Its ordinances:
     (a) Baptism (baptize means to immerse). The Lord commands the believer to be baptized. This is the believer's first opportunity to obey his Lord and Savior Jesus Christ. In the early church no one ever questioned water baptism; they obeyed: (Page 948-Matt.28:18-20). {And when they saw Him, they worshiped Him; but some were doubtful. And Jesus came up and spoke to them, saying, "All authority has been given to Me in heaven and on earth. Go therefore and make disciples of all the nations, baptizing them in the name of the Father and the Son and the Holy Spirit, teaching them to observe all that I commanded you; and lo, I am with you always,

even to the end of the age."}
Also:
(Page 1086-Rom. 6:1-4). {What shall we say then? Are we to continue in sin that grace might increase? May it never be! How shall we who died to sin still live in it? Or do you not know that all of us who have been baptized into Christ Jesus have been baptized into His death? Therefore we have been buried with Him through baptism into death, in order that as Christ was raised from the dead through the glory of the Father, so we too might walk in newness of life.} Baptism does not save. It is a picture of your faith in His death, burial, and resurrection. It is faith in Christ that saves: (Page 1016-John 3:36). {"He who believes in the Son has eternal life; but he who does not obey the Son shall not see life, but the wrath of God abides on him."} The ordinance of baptism that identifies the believer with the risen Savior.

(b) The Lords supper: There is no saving power in the Lords Supper. It is memorial. The bread is symbolical of His broken body and the wine of His shed blood for the remission of our sins. Baptism identifies the believer with Christ in His death, burial, and resurrection: and the Lords Supper is a memorial to be observed by the believer to "proclaim the Lord's death until He comes": (Page 1106-1Cor. 11:23-34). {For I received from the Lord that which I also delivered to you, that the Lord Jesus in the night in which He was betrayed took bread; and when He had given thanks, He broke it, and said, "This is my body, which is for you; do this in remembrance of Me." In the same way He took the cup also, after supper, saying. "This cup is the new covenant in My blood; do this, as often as you drink it, in remembrance of Me." For as often as you eat this bread and drink the cup, you proclaim the Lord's death until He comes. Therefore whoever eats the bread or drinks the cup of the Lord in an unworthy manner, shall be guilty of the body and the blood of the Lord. But let a man examine himself, and so let him eat of the bread and drink of the cup. For He who eats and drinks, eats and drinks judgment to himself, if he does not judge the body rightly. For this reason many among you are weak and sick, and a number sleep. But if we judge ourselves rightly, we should not be judged. But when we are judged, we are disciplined by the Lord in order that we may not be condemned along with the world. So then my brethren, when you come together to eat, wait for one another. If anyone is hungry, let him eat at home, so that you may not come together for judgment. And the remaining matters I shall arrange when I come.}

THE CHURCH: ITS DISCIPLINE

(Page 933-Matt.18:15-17). {And if your brother sins, go and reprove him in private; if he listens to you, you have won your brother. But if he does not listen to you, take one or two more with you, so that by the mouth of two or three witnesses every fact may be confirmed. And if he refuses to listen to them, tell it to the church; and if he refuses to listen to the church, let him be to you as a Gentile and a tax-gatherer.}

This is the most difficult and necessary function of the local assembly, and its importance cannot be exaggerated. "Do you not know that a little leaven leavens the whole lump of dough? Clean out the old leaven": (Page 1101- 1Cor. 5:6.7). {Your boasting is not good. Do you not know that a little leaven leavens the whole lump of dough? Clean out the old leaven, that you may be a new lump, just as you are in fact unleavened. For Christ our Passover also has been sacrificed.}

Leaven in the Scripture is always a type of evil. The church is to clean out any evil in its membership. The motive for disciplining a brother is love: (Page 1202-1John4:7-11). {Beloved, let us love one another, for love is from God; and everyone who loves is born of God and knows God. The one who does not love does not know God, for God is love. By this the love of God was manifested In us, that God has sent His only begotten Son into the world so that we might live through Him. In this is love, not that we loved God, but that He loved us and sent His Son to be propitiation for our sins. Beloved, if God so loved us, we also ought to love one another.}

The goal is to restore him to fellowship with his Lord and the church. "If your brother sins…"

(1) The first step is to be taken by the one sinned against. He is to go to his brother alone, not seeking revenge or self-justification, "If he listens to you, you have one your brother."

(2) If he does not repent, the second step is to take one or two believers and go to him again.

(3) If he will not hear the one or two, the third step is to take it to the church. A good example of church discipline is reported in Paul's letter to the church at Corinth. He used strong words calling upon the church to discipline a member for fornication. He wrote, "Remove the wicked man from among your selves." (Page 1101-1Cor.5:1-13).{It is actually reported that there is immorality among you, and immorality of such a kind as does not exist even among the Gentiles, that someone has his father's wife. And you have become arrogant, and have not mourned instead, in order that the one who had done this deed might be removed from your midst. For I on my part, though absent in body but present in spirit, have already judged him who has so committed this, as though I were present. In the name of our Lord Jesus, when you were assembled, and I with you in spirit, with the power of our Lord Jesus, I have decided to deliver such a one to Satan for the destruction of the flesh, that his spirit

may be saved in the day of the Lord Jesus. Your boasting is not good. Do you not know that a little leaven leavens the whole lump of dough? Clean out the ole leaven, that you may be a new lump, just as you are in fact unleavened. For Christ our Passover also has been sacrificed. Let us therefore celebrate the feast, not with old leaven, nor with the leaven of malice and wickedness, but with unleavened bread of sincerity and truth. I wrote you my letter not to associate with immoral people; I did not at all mean with the immoral people of this world, or with the covetous and swindlers, or with idolaters; for then you would have to go out of this world. But actually, I wrote to you not to associate with any so called brother if he should be an immoral person, covetous, or an idolater, or a reviler, or a drunkard, or a swindler-not even to eat with such a one. For what have I to do with judging outsiders? Do not judge those who are within the church? But those who are outside, God judges. Remove the wicked man from among yourselves.}
In his second letter to the Corinthian church we learn that the man repented and was restored to the fellowship of God's people. Now Paul writes, "forgive and comfort him....reaffirm your love for him": (Page 1114-2Cor. 2:3-11) {And this is the very thing I wrote you, lest, when I came, I should have sorrow from those who ought to make me rejoice; having confidence in you all, that my joy would be the joy of all. For out of much affliction and anguish of heart I wrote to you with many tears; not that you should be made sorrowful, but that you might know the love which I have especially for you. But if any has caused sorrow, he has caused sorrow not unto me but in some degree-in order not to say much-to all of you. Sufficient for such a one is this punishment which was inflicted by the majority. So that on the contrary you

should rather forgive and comfort him, lest somehow such a one be overwhelmed by excessive sorrow. Wherefore I urge you to reaffirm your love for him. For to this end also I wrote that I might put you to test, whether you are obedient in all things. But whom you forgive anything, I forgive also; for indeed what I have forgiven, if I have forgiven anything, I did it for your sakes in the presence of Christ. In order that no advantage be taken of us by Satan; for we are ignorant of his schemes.}

The attitude of the church toward a repenting brother should always be that of forgiveness in love.

THE CHURCH: ITS WORSHIP AND WORK

(Page 948-Matt. 28:16-20). {But the eleven disciples proceeded to Galilee, to the mountain which Jesus had designated. And when they saw Him, they worshiped Him; some were doubtful. And Jesus came up and spoke to them, saying, "All authority has been given to Me in heaven and on earth. Go therefore and make disciples of all the nations, baptizing them in the name of the Father and the Son and the Holy Spirit. And teaching them to observe all that I commanded you; and lo, I am with you always, even to the end of the age."}

First, the church: its worship. "When they saw Him, they worshiped Him" (above verse 17). To worship is to bow down in awe; to pay divine honors to God in humble, reverent homage. There are three essentials in worship, they are:

- (1) Faith: "the people believed....then they bowed low and worshiped": (Page 54-Ex.4:31 OT). {So the people, believed; and when they heard that the Lord was concerned about the sons of Israel and that He had seen their affliction, then they bowed low and worshiped.}
- (2) Spirit: "those who worship Him must worship in spirit…." (Page 1016-John4:23.24). {"But an hour is coming, and now is, when true worshipers shall worship the Father in spirit and truth; for such people

the Father seeks to be His worshipers. "God is spirit, and those who worship Him must worship in spirit and truth."}

   (3) Truth: "those who worship Him must worship in spirit and truth" (Page 1016-John 4:24). {"God is spirit, and those who worship Him must worship in spirit and truth."}

Jesus Christ is truth, "I am the way, and the truth, and the life": (Page 1031-John 14:6). {Jesus said to him, "I am the way, and the truth, and the life; no one comes to the Father, but through Me.}

Therefore, there can be no pretense or hypocrisy in true worship. The parable of the Pharisee and the publican illustrates true worship: (Page 1000-Luke 18:9-14). {And He also told this parable to certain ones who trusted in themselves that they were religious, and viewed others with contempt: "Two men went up into the temple to pray, one a Pharisee, and the other a tax gatherer. The Pharisee stood and was praying thus to himself, 'I thank Thee that I am not like the other people: swindlers, unjust, adulterers, or even like this tax-gatherer. I fast twice a week, I pay tithes of all that I get.' But the tax-gatherer, standing some distance away, was even unwilling to lift up his eyes to heaven, but was beating his breast, saying, 'God, be merciful to me, the sinner!' I tell you, this man went down to his house justified rather than the other; for everyone who exalts himself shall be humbled, but he who humbles himself shall be exalted."}

The publican worshiped in truth and he went home justified. The Pharisee worshiped in religious pride and he went home rejected. Second, The church: its work. "For the word has sounded forth from you" (Page 1148- 1Thes. 1:8). {For the word of the Lord has sounded forth from you, not only in Macedonia and Achaia, but also in every place your faith toward God has gone forth, so that we have no need to say anything.}

The church in Thessalonica did the work of the Lord so well that the apostles did not have to evangelize Macedonia and Achaia. The church shared its faith with the lost, and after all that is the main work of the church.

This is how that, "this took place for two years....all who lived in Asia heard the word of the Lord, both Jews and Greeks: (Page 1066- Acts 19:8-10). {And he entered the synagogue and continued speaking boldly for three months, reasoning and persuading them about the kingdom of God. But when some were becoming hardened and disobedient, speaking evil of the way before the multitude, he withdrew from them and took the disciples, reasoning daily in the school of Tyrannus. And this took place for two years, so that all who lived in Asia heard the word of the Lord, both Jews and Greeks.}

All of Asia did not journey to Ephesus to hear Paul. It is evident that the believers went everywhere sharing the gospel. The work of the church is to go with the gospel, because:

    (1) The church is commissioned to work (above verse018-20).

    (2) The church is to work with Christ: (Page 1117-2Cor 6:1). {And working together with Him, we also urge you not to receive the grace of God in vain.} And the Holy Spirit: (Page 1049-Acts 5;32). {"And we are witnesses of these things; and so is the Holy Spirit, whom God has given to those who obey Him."}

    (3) The church is to work with Christ in His field (the world): (Page 927-Matt. 13:36-43). {Then He left the multitudes, and went into the house. And His disciples came to him saying, "Explain to us the parable of the tares of the field." And He answered and said, "The one who sows the good seed is the Son of Man, and the field is the world; and as for the good seed, these are the sons of the kingdom; and the tares are the sons of the evil one; and the enemy who sowed them is the devil, and the harvest is the end of the age; and the reapers are angels. Therefore just as the tares are gathered up and burned with fire, so shall it be at the end of the age. The Son of Man will send forth His angels, and they will gather out of His kingdom all

stumbling blocks, and those who commit lawlessness. And will cast them into the furnace of fire; in that place there shall be weeping and gnashing of teeth. Then the righteous will shine forth as the sun in the kingdom of their Father, He who has ears, let him hear."} Also: (Page 972- Mark 16:15). {And He said to them, "Go into all the world and preach the gospel to all creation.}

(4) The need for the church to work is great: (Page 1017- John 4:35). {"Do you not say, 'There are yet four months, and then comes the harvest'? Behold, I say to you, lift up your eyes, and look on the fields, that they are white for harvest.}

(5) The time for the church to work is now: (Page 1117- 2Cor. 6:2). {for He says, At the acceptable time I listened to you, And on the day of salvation I helped you"; behold, now is the acceptable time, "behold, now is the day of salvation."}

(6) The church is to work until Jesus comes to judge the works of the saints: (Page 1116-2Cor. 5:10). {For we must all appear before the judgment seat of Christ, that each one may be recompensed for his deeds in the body, according to what he has done, whether good or bad.}

(7) The church will be rewarded for its work: (Page 1100- 1Cor.3:9-15). {For we are God's fellow workers; you are Foe's field, God's building. According to the grace of God which was given to me, as a wise master builder I laid a foundation, and another is building upon it. But let each man be careful how he builds upon it. For no man can lay a foundation other than the one which is laid, which is Jesus Christ. Now if any man builds upon the foundation with gold, silver, precious stones, wood hay, straw, each man's work will become evident; for the day will show it, because it is to be revealed with fire; and the fire itself will test

the quality of each man's work. If any man's work which he has built upon it remains, he shall receive a reward. If any man's work is burned up, he shall suffer loss; but he himself shall be saved, yet so as through fire.}

God's program for the local church is come and worship, go and work (witness): (Page 1052- Acts 8:1-4). {And Saul was in hearty agreement with putting him to death. And on that day a great persecution arose against the church in Jerusalem; and they were scattered throughout the regions of Judea and Samaria, except the apostles. And some devout men buried Stephen, and made loud lamentation over him. But Saul began ravaging the church, entering house after house; and dragging off men and women, he would put them in prison. Therefore, those who had been scattered went about preaching the word.}

THE CHURCH; ITS POWER

(Page 1041- Acts 1:8) {But you shall receive power when the Holy Spirit has come upon you; and you shall be My witnesses both in Jerusalem, and in all Judea and Samaria, and even to the remotest part of the earth."}

On the day of Pentecost the church received power to evangelize the world. When the hundred and twenty came down from the upper room, they came in the dynamic of the Holy Spirit. It was a spiritual phenomenon issuing forth in joyful ecstasy and miracle-working power, resulting in conviction of sin, "repentance toward God and faith in our Lord Jesus Christ": (Page 1068-Acts 20:21). {solemnly testifying to both Jews and Greeks of repentance toward God and faith in our Lord Jesus Christ.} Some were empowered for special service, but all received power to witness.

The real power of the church is not found in:
    (1) Modern buildings or unique methods of preaching and teaching.
    (2) Its great wealth or how that wealth is used.
    (3) The church's prominence or popularity.

The Laodicean church was the first "bragging congregation" but not the last: (Page 1212-Rev.3:14-22). {"And to the angel of the church in Laodicea write: The Amen, the faithful and true Witness, the Beginning of the creation of God says this: I know your deeds, that you are neither cold nor hot, I would that you were cold or hot. So because you are lukewarm, and neither hot nor cold, I will spit you out of My mouth. Because you say, I am rich, and have become wealthy, and have need of nothing. And you do not know that you are wretched and miserable and poor and blind and naked, I advise you to buy from Me gold refined by fire, that you may become rich, and white garments, that you may clothe yourself, and that the shame of your nakedness may not be revealed; and eye salve to anoint your eyes, that you may see. Those whom I love, I reprove and discipline; be zealous therefore, and repent. Behold, I stand at the door and knock; if anyone hears My voice and opens the door, I will come in to him, and will dine with him, and he with Me. He who overcomes, I will grant to him to sit down with Me on My throne, as I also overcame and sat down with My Father on His throne. He who has an ear, let him hear what the Spirit says to the churches."}

They said, "We are rich." God said they are poor.

They said, "We are wealthy." God said they were wretched.

They said, "We do not need anything." God said they need everything.

They said, "We are busy in the church." God said they were miserable.

They said, "We have a vision." God said they were blind.

They said, "We are clothed in fine garments." God said they were naked.

They said, "We are satisfied." God said they made Him sick.

You can always recognize a Holy Spirit-powered church. The evidence is obvious, they have power to:

    (1) Evangelize: They share their faith with the lost and souls are saved. Evangelism is the only way to make full proof of your ministry: (Page 1162- 2 Tim. 4:5).

{But you, be sober in all things, endure hardship, do the work of an evangelist, fulfill your ministry.} When a church is not involved in winning souls, it grieves the Holy Spirit and is void of power.

(2) Reproduce: Souls are born into the family of God by the "imperishable" seed which is the word of God: (Page 1190-1 Pet.1:23). {And He did so in order that He might make known the riches of his glory upon vessels of mercy, which He prepared before hand for glory.} The Spirit-filled believer sows the seed; this is evangelism. The Holy Spirit hovers over the seed, convicting and leading the lost to repentance. This is the spiritual birth.

(3) Change:

People: (Page 1044-Acts 2:37-41). {Now when they heard this, they were pierced to the heart, and said to Peter and the rest of the apostles, "Brethren, what shall we do?" And Peter said to them, "Repent, and let each of you be baptized in the name of Jesus Christ for the forgiveness of sins; and you shall receive the gift of the Holy Spirit. For the promise is for you, and your children, and for all who are far off, as many as the Lord our God shall call to Himself." And with many other words he solemnly testified and kept on exhorting them, saying, "Be saved from this perverse generation!" So then, those who had received his word were baptized; and there were added that day about three thousand souls.}

Places: (Page 1048- Acts.5:28). {saying, "We gave you strict orders not to continue teaching in His name, and behold, you have filled Jerusalem with your teaching, and intend to bring this man's blood upon us."}

And things: (Page 932-Matt. 17:20.21).{And He said to them, "Because of the littleness of your faith; for truly I say to you, it you have faith as a mustard seed, you shall say to this mountain, 'Move from here to there,' and it shall; move; and nothing shall be impossible to you. [But this kind does not go out except by prayer and fasting."]}

(4) Turn the world upside down: (Page 1063-Acts 17:6). {And when they did not find them, they began dragging Jason and some brethren before the city authorities, shouting. "These men who have upset the world have come here also."}

This is the power that filled the upper room congregation on the day of Pentecost. That power is with the believer today in the person of the Holy Spirit. He is the power of the church.

THE CHURCH: ITS FUTURE

(Page 1150-Thess.4:16.17). {For the Lord Himself will descend from heaven with a shout, with the voice of the Archangel , and with the trumpet of God; and the dead in Christ will rise first. Then we who are alive and remain shall be caught up together with them in the clouds to meet the Lord in the air, and thus we shall always be with the Lord.}

The true Church of Jesus Christ has a glorious, victorious future in the world, in the air, and the kingdom and in eternity; it cannot fail. The gates of Hades shall not overpower it": (Page 931-Matt. 16:18). {"And I also say to you Peter, and upon this rock I will build My church; and the gates of Hades shall not overpower it.}

(1) The future of the church in the world. At Pentecost the Holy Spirit set the course for the church as it journeys from the upper room to the Rapture. It is to:

(a) Wage war: (Page 1135- Eph. 6:10-18). {Finally, be strong in the Lord, and in the strength of His might. Put on the full armor of God, that you may be able to stand firm against the schemes of the devil. For struggle is not against flesh and blood, but against the rulers, against the powers, against the world forces of this darkness, against the spiritual forces of wickedness in the heavenly places. Therefore, take up the full armor of God, that you may be able to resist in the evil day, and having done everything, to stand firm. Stand firm therefore, having girded your loins with truth, and having put on the breastplate of righteousness, and having shod your feet with the preparation of the gospel of peace; in addition to all, taking up the shield of faith with which you will be able to extinguish all the flaming missiles of the evil one. And take the helmet of salvation, and the sword of the Spirit, which is the word of God. With all prayer and petition pray at all times in the Spirit, and with this in view, be on the alert with all perseverance and petition for all the saints,}

(b) Run a race: (Page 1181- Heb. 12:1.2). {Therefore, since we have so great a cloud of witnesses surrounding us, let us also lay aside every encumbrance, and the sin so easily entangles us, and let us run with endurance the race that is set before us. Fixing our eyes of Jesus, the author and the perfecter of faith, who for the joy set before Him endured the cross, despising the shame, and has sat down at the right hand of the throne of God.}

(c) Work in love: (Page 1100-1Cor. 3:9). {For we are God's fellow workers; you are God's field, God's building.}

The church of Jesus Christ will emerge triumphant for, "we overwhelmingly conquer through Him who loved us." (Page 1089- Rom. 8:35-39). {Who shall separate us from the love of Christ? Shall tribulation, or distress, or persecution, or famine, or nakedness, or peril, or sword? Just as it is written, "for Thy sake we are being put to death all day long; We were considered as sheep to be slaughtered." But in all these things we overwhelmingly conquer through Him who loved us. For I am convinced that neither death, nor life, nor angels, nor principalities, northing present, nor things to come, nor powers, nor height, nor depth, nor any other created thing, shall be able to separate us from the love of God, which is in Christ Jesus our Lord.}

The church cannot fail because Christ is its head, the Holy Spirit is its power, and the word of God is its guide.

   (2) The future of the church in the air: We shall be caught up (above verse). Caught up:

    (a) In our imperishable, glorified bodies: (Page 1110-1Cor.15:42-44). {So also is the resurrection of the dead. It is sown a perishable body, it is raised an imperishable body; it is sown in dishonor, it is raised in glory, it is sown in weakness, it is raised in power; it is sown a natural body, it is raised a spiritual body. If there is a natural body, there is a spiritual body.}

    (b) To meet the Lord in the heavens and for the great majority of the church we will see him in His resurrected body for the first time: (Page 1200-1John 3:2) {Beloved, now we are children of God, and it has not appeared as yet what we shall be. We know that, when He appears, we shall be just like Him, because we shall see Him just as He is.}

    (c) That our deeds may be judged at the judgment seat of Christ: (Page 1116-2Cor. 5:10) {For we must all appear before the judgment seat of Christ, that each one may be recompensed for his deeds in the body, according to what he has done, whether good or bad.}

    (d) That we may be rewarded or suffer loss of reward: (Page 1100- 1Cor.3:11-15) {For no man can lay a foundation other than the one which is laid, which is Jesus Christ. Now if any man builds upon the foundation with gold, silver, precious stones, wood, hay, straw, each man's work will become evident; for the day will show it, because it is to be revealed with fire; and the fire itself will test the quality of each mans work. If any man's work which has built upon it remains, he shall receive a reward. If any man's work is burned up, he shall suffer loss; but he himself shall be saved, yet so as through fire.}

(3) The future of the church in the kingdom.
  (a) The twelve apostles will sit on the thrones and judge the twelve tribes of Israel: (Page 935-Matt. 19:28). {And Jesus said to them, "Truly I say to you, that you who have followed Me, in the regeneration when the Son of Man will sit on His glorious throne, you also shall sit upon twelve thrones, judging the twelve tribes of Israel."}
  (b) All who overcomes the evils of Christendom (Laodicea) will sit with Christ on His Kingdom Throne: (Page 1213-Rev. 3:21). {He who overcomes, I will grant to him to sit down with Me on My throne, as I also overcame and sat down with My father on His throne.}
  (c) We shall reign with Him for a thousand years: (Page 1224—Rev.20:4-6). {And I saw thrones, and they sat upon them, and judgment was given to them. And I saw the souls of those who had been beheaded because of the testimony of Jesus and because of the word of God, and those who had not worshiped the beast or his image, and had not received the mark upon their forehead and upon their hand; and they came to life and reigned with Christ for a thousand years. The rest of the dead did not come to life until the thousand years were completed. This is the first resurrection, Blessed and holy is the one who has a part in the first resurrection; over these the second death has no power, but they will be priests of God and of Christ and will reign with Him for a thousand years.}

(4) The future of the church in eternity: After the kingdom reign of one thousand years there will be a new heaven and a new earth. (Page 1225-Rev. 21:1). {And I saw a

new heaven and a new earth; for the first heaven and the first earth passed away, and there is no longer any sea.}

The earth will be restored to its original, created state: (Page 1-Gen. 1:1 OT). {In the beginning God created the heavens and the earth.} God's earthly people Israel will inherit the new earth.

(Page 82-Ex.32:13 OT). {"Remember Abraham, Isaac, and Israel, Thy servants to whom Thou didst swear by Thyself, and didst say to them, 'I will multiply your descendants as the stars of the heavens, and all this land of which I have spoken I will give your descendants, and they shall inherit it forever.'"} The church, His bride will remain in His presence forever. If in His human form He is in the new heaven or the new earth, we will be with Him, to serve Him, and to worship Him. He will continue to bestow upon His bride the riches of His eternal grace: (Page 1131-Eph. 2:6.7). {and raised us up with Him, and seated us with Him in the heavenly places, in Christ Jesus, in order that in the ages to come He might show the surpassing riches of His grace in kindness toward us in Christ Jesus.}

Even in our perfect glorified bodies it will take eternity (time without end) to begin to comprehend the greatness of His grace.

MASTER OUTLINE NUMBER NINE

PRAYER

Prayer is as old as man, as universal as religion, and as instinctive as breathing. (Page 5-Gen.4:26). {And to Seth, to him also a son was born; and he called his name Enosh. Then men began to call upon the name of the Lord.} It is practiced in some form by all men of all faiths. Prayer springs from the heart with a need-a need greater than man's ability to encounter.

Prayer is man's acknowledgment of a higher being than self. Most men try to pray, yet so few know how. There are two kinds of prayers: the prayer that does not reach God and the prayer that does reach God. This is illustrated by our Lord in the parable of the Pharisee and the publican: (Page 1000- Luke 18:9-14). {And He also told this parable to certain ones who trusted in themselves that they were righteous, and viewed others with contempt: "Two men went into the temple to pray, one a Pharisee, and the other a tax-gatherer. The Pharisee stood and was praying thus to himself, 'God, I thank Thee that I am not like other people: swindlers, unjust, adulterers, or even like this tax-gatherer. I fast twice a week; I pay tithes of all that I get.' But the tax-gatherer, standing some distance away, was even unwilling to life his eyes to heaven, but was beating his breast, saying, 'God, be merciful to me, the sinner!' I tell you, this man went down to his house justified rather than the other; for everyone that exalts himself shall be humbled, but he who humbles himself shall be exalted."}

Both men went to the same place, at the same time, for the same purpose-to pray.

The Pharisee prayed in his righteous pride, expecting God to answer because he thought himself worthy. He informed God of his own goodness, that he was better than others. He boasted of his good works. He said, "I fast, I pay." This is the kind of prayer that does not reach God. It is self-righteous prayer.

Now look at the publican and his prayer. He came to God in great humility, conscious of his unworthiness, confessing himself a sinner, and begging for mercy This is kind of prayer that reaches God. This is righteous prayer. It is a rare privilege to pray; because it brings you into close relationship with God, admitting your need for Him and your utter dependence upon Him.

WHAT IS PRAYER

(Page 919-Matt 7:7-11). "Ask, (keep asking) and it shall be given to you; seek (keep seeking) and you shall find; knock and it shall be opened to you. For everyone who asks receives, and he who seeks finds, and to him who knocks it shall be opened. Or what man is there among you, when his son shall ask him a loaf, will give him a stone? Or if he shall ask for a fish, he will not give him a snake? If you then, being evil, know how to give good gifts to your children, how much more shall your Father who is in heaven give what is good to those who ask Him!"

Prayer is asking and receiving; it is talking with God. It is making your request known to Him in faith. The above Scripture is so simple on the surface, that we are in danger of failing to recognize its immensity. Our Lord instructs the believer to ask, and knock; because these three words cover the whole spectrum of prayer.

(1) Prayer is asking and receiving. When you know the will of God regarding a need, whether it is material or spiritual, you can ask and receive. This is prayer according to the revealed will of God. (Page 1203-1John 5:14.15). {And this is the confidence which we have toward Him, that, if we ask anything according to His will, He hears us. And if we know that He hears us in whatever we ask, we know that we have the request which we have asked from Him.}

(2) Prayer is seeking and finding. When you do not know the will of God regarding a need, whether it is, material or spiritual, then you are to seek His will in prayer

concerning this need until you find it. This is prayer for knowledge of the unrevealed will of God in a specific need: (Page 1145-Col. 3:1). {If then you have been raised up with Christ, keep seeking the things above, where Christ is, seated at the right hand of God.} Also: (Page 717-Jer. 29:12.13). {Then you will call upon Me and come and pray with Me, and I will listen to you. And you will seek Me when you search for Me with all your heart.}

(3) Prayer is knocking and opening. When you know the will of God, and yet you find a closed door, you are to knock, and keep knocking until God opens the door. This is tenacious prayer-prayer for mountain-moving faith. Knocking prayer perseveres until the impossible becomes the possible.

This is miracle-working prayer: (Page 932-Matt. 17:14-21).And when they came to the multitude, a man came up to Him, falling on His knees before Him, and saying, "Lord, have mercy on my son, he is a lunatic, and is very ill; for he often falls into the fire, and often into the water. And I brought him to your disciples, and they could not cure him." And Jesus answered and said, "O unbelieving and perverted generation, how long shall I be with you? How long shall I Put up with you? Bring him here to me." And Jesus rebuked him, and the demon came out of him, and the boy was cured (from that hour) at once. Then the disciples came to Jesus privately and said, "Why could we not cast it out?" And He said to them, "Because of the littleness of your faith; for truly I say to you, if you have faith as a mustard seed, you shall say to this mountain, 'Move from here to there,' and it shall move; and nothing shall be impossible to you. But this kind does not go out except by prayer and fasting." And while they were gathering together in Galilee, Jesus said to them, "The Son of Man is going to be delivered into the hands of men; and they will kill Him, and He will be raised on the third day." And they were deeply grieved. And when they had come to Capernaum, those who collected the two drachma tax came to Peter, and said, "Does your teacher not pay the two-drachma tax?"}

All things are possible when you ask, seek, and knock.

WHY PRAY

(Page 999-Luke 18:1). {Now He has telling them a parable to show that all times they ought to pray and not to lose heart.}

Pray:
- (1) Because Jesus said, "at all times they ought to pray" (Page 999-Luke 18:1). Prayer is imperative. You are commanded to pray. (Page 944-Matt. 26:41). {"Keep watching and praying, that you may not enter into temptation; the spirit is willing, but the flesh is weak."}
- (2) Because prayer is the only way to get things from God. "You do not have because you do not ask": (Page 1186- James 4:2). {You lust and do not have; so you commit murder. And you are envious and cannot obtain; so you fight and quarrel. You do not have because you do not ask.}
- (3) Because there is joy in prayer: (Page 1034- John 16:24). {"Until now, you have asked for nothing in My name' ask, and you will receive, that your joy may be made full.}
- (4) Because prayer will save you out of all your troubles: (Page 519-Ps. 34:6). {This poor (afflicted) man cried and the Lord heard him, And saved him out of all his troubles.}
- (5) Because prayer can unlock the treasure chest of God's wisdom: (Page 1184-James 1:5). {But if any of you lacks wisdom, let him ask God, who gives to all men generously and without reproach, and it will be given to him.}
- (6) Because prayer is a channel of power: (Page 723-Jer.33:3OT). {'Call to Me, and I will answer you, and I will tell you great and mighty things, which you do not know.'}

(7) Because it is sin not to pray: (Page 266-1Sam. 12:23 OT). {"Moreover, as for me that I should sin against the Lord be ceasing to pray for you; but I will instruct you in the good and right way.}

(8) Because sinners can be saved when they pray in faith: (Page 1090-Rom 10:13.14). {for "Whoever will call upon the name of the Lord will be saved." How then shall they call upon Him in whom they have not believed? And how shall they believe in Him whom they have not heard? And how shall they hear without a preacher?}

(9) Because Jesus, while here in the flesh, prayed often to the Father. Now if Jesus, the Son of God, needed to pray, then we should "pray without ceasing": (Page 1150-1Thess.5:17). {pray without ceasing.}

HOW TO PRAY

(Page 918-Matt.6:9-13). {"Pray, then in this way: 'Our Father who art in heaven, Hollowed be thy name. Thy kingdom come. Thy will be done, on earth as it is in heaven. Give us this day our daily bread. And forgive us our debts, as we also have forgiven our debtors. And do not lead us into temptation, but deliver us from evil. (The evil one) [For Thine is the kingdom, and the power, and the glory, forever. Amen.]"}

"Pray, then in this way," Our Lord gave this as a model prayer after one of His disciples said to Him, "Lord, teach us to pray just as John also taught his disciples." (Page 991-Luke 11:1). {And it came about that while He was praying in a certain place, after He had finished one of His disciples said to Him, "Lord, teach us to pray just as John also taught his disciples."}

(1) We are to pray to "Our Father who art in heaven," because He is all-wise, all-loving, and all-powerful. We are also instructed to pray in the name of Jesus: (Page 1301- John 14:13.14). {"And whoever asks in My name, that will I do, that the Father may be glorified in the Son. If you ask Me anything in My

name, I will do it."} Depending on the mediating influence of the Holy Spirit: (Page 1088-Rom. 8:26.27). {And in the same way the Spirit also helps our weakness; for we do not know how to pray as we should, but the Spirit Himself intercedes for us with groaning too deep for words; and He who searches the hearts knows the mind of the Spirit is, because He intercedes for the saints (holy ones) according to the will of God.}

(2) We are to pray for His will to be done in everything: (Page 1187-James 4:15). {Instead, you ought to say, "If the Lord wills, we shall live and also do this or that."}

(3) We are to pray for the coming of the kingdom: (Page 942-Matt. 25:31-46). {But when the son of Man comes in His glory, and all His angels with Him, then He will sit on His glorious throne. And all the nations will be gathered before Him: and He will separate them from one another, as the shepherd separates the sheep from the goats; and He will put His sheep on His right, and the goats on the left. Then the King will say to those on His right, "Come, you who are blessed of My Father, inherit the kingdom prepared for you from the foundation. For I was hungry, and you gave Me something to eat; I was thirsty, and you gave Me to drink; I was a stranger, and you invited Me in; naked, and you clothed Me; I was sick, and you visited Me; I was in prison, and you came to Me." Then the righteous will answer him, saying, "Lord, when did we see you hungry, and feed you, or thirsty, and give You drink? And when did we see You a stranger, and invite You in, naked, and clothe You? And when did we see You sick, or in prison, and come to You?" And the King will answer and say to them, "Truly I say to you, to the extent that you did to one of these brothers of mine, even the least of them, you did to Me." Then

He will say to those on His left. "Depart from Me, accursed ones, into the lake of fire which has been prepared for the devil and his angels; for I was hungry, and you gave Me nothing to eat; I was thirsty, and you gave Me nothing to drink; I was a stranger, and you did not invite Me in; and you did not cloth Me; sick, and in prison, and you did not visit Me." Then they themselves will answer, saying, "Lord, when did we see You hungry, or thirsty, or a stranger, or naked, or sick, or in prison, and did not take care of You?" Then He will answer them, saying, "Truly, I say to you, to the extent that you did not do it to one of the least of these, you did not do it to Me." And these will go away into eternal punishment, but the righteousness into eternal life.}

(4) We are to pray for our daily necessities: (Page 991-Luke 11:3). {"And forgive us our daily sins, For we ourselves also forgive everyone who is indebted to us. And lead us not into temptation."}

(5) We are to pray forgiveness, and practice forgiving others: (Page 934-Matt.18:21.22). {Then Peter came and said to Him, "Lord, how often shall my brother sin against me and I forgive him? Up to seven times?" Jesus said to him, "I do not say to you, up to seven times, but up to seventy times seven."}

(6) We are to pray for the leading of the Lord, and deliverance from evil: (Page1006-Luke 22:42). {saying "Father, if Thou art willing, remove this cup from Me; yet not My will, but Thine be done."}

(7) We are to pray in faith, for "without faith it is impossible to please Him": (Page 1180- Heb. 11:6). {And without faith it is impossible to please Him, for he who comes to God must believe that He is, and that He is a rewarder of those who seek Him.}

The model prayer is brief, to the point, and not repetitious. It is the perfect prayer.

WHERE TO PRAY

(Page 1057-Acts 12:5). {So Peter was kept in the prison, but prayer for him was being made fervently by the church to God.}

There was a remarkable change in the prayer life of the disciples after the resurrection of Jesus, and it is noted again after Pentecost. Before the death of Jesus, the disciples slept while Jesus prayed in the Garden: (Page944-Matt.26:36-46). {Then Jesus came with them to a place called Gethsemane, and said to his disciples, "Sit here while I go over there and pray." And He took with Him Peter and the two sons of Zebedee, and began to be grieved and distressed. Then He said to them, "My soul is deeply grieved, to the point of death; remain here and keep watch with Me." and He went a little beyond them, and fell on His face and prayed, "My Father, if it is possible, let this cup pass from Me; yet not as I will, but as Thou wilt." And He came to the disciples and found them sleeping, and said to Peter, "So you men could not keep watch with Me for one hour? Keep watching and praying, that you may not enter into temptation; the spirit is willing, but the flesh is weak." He went away again a second time and prayed, saying, "My Father, if this cannot pass away unless I drink it, Thy will be done." And again He came and found them sleeping, for their eyes were heavy. And He left them again, and went away and prayed a third time, saying the same thing once more. Then He came to the disciples, and said to them, "Are you still sleeping and taking your rest? Behold the hour is at hand and the Son of Man is being betrayed into the hands of sinners. Arise, let us be going; behold, the one who betrays Me is at Hand!"}

But after His death and resurrection:
- (1) They assembled in the upper room, waiting for the coming of the Holy Spirit; and they prayed. We should always pray when assembled with believers: (Page 1042-Acts 1:13.14). {And when they had entered, they went up to the upper room, where they were staying; that is, Peter and John and James and Andrew, Philip and Thomas, Bartholomew and Matthew, James the

son of Alphaeus, and Simon the zealot, and Judas, the son of James. These all with one mind were continually devoting themselves to prayer, along with the women, and Mary the mother of Jesus, and with His brothers.}

(2) They prayed as they went from house to house: (Page 1044-Acts 2:42-47). {And they were continually devoting themselves to the apostles teaching and to fellowship, to the breaking of bread and to prayer. And everybody kept feeling a sense of awe; and many wonders and signs were taking place through the apostles. And all those who had believed were together, and had all things in common; and they began selling their property and possessions, and were sharing them with all, as anyone might have need. And day by day continuing with one mind in the temple, and breaking bread from house to house, they were taking their meals together with gladness and sincerity of heart, praising God, and having favor with all the people. And the Lord was adding to their number day by day those who were being saved.}

(3) They prayed in the church when Peter was in prison (above verse 5-19). (4)Paul and Silas prayed in prison: (Page 1062-Acts. 16:25). {But about midnight Paul and Silas were praying and singing hymns of praise to God, and the prisoners were listening to them.} Here we see Christians praying in the presence of unbelievers, but not to be heard of them. Never pray to please others present; pray only to please God.

(5) The most important place to pray is in any place you can be alone with God: (Page 917- Matt.6:6). {"But you, when you pray, go into your inner room, and when you have shut your door, pray to your Father who is in secret, and your Father who sees in secret will repay you.}

(6) We are instructed to pray in all places at all times: (Page 1155- 1Tim. 2:8). {Therefore I want the men in every place to pray, lifting holy hands, without wrath and dissension.}

It is a great joy to be able to talk to God, any time, any place, under any condition, and to know that He will hear and answer.

HINDRANCES TO PRAYER

(Page 1191-1Pet.3:7). {You husbands likewise, live with your wives in an understanding way, as with a weaker vessel, since she is a woman; and grant her honor as a fellow heir of the grace of life, so that your prayers may not be hindered.}

When prayers are not answered and you should examine yourself in the light of God's Word. If you find anything not pleasing to God, confess it believing God for forgiveness that your prayers may be answered: (Page 1199-1 John 1:9). {If we confess our sins, He is faithful and righteous to forgive us our sins and to cleanse us from unrighteousness.}

(1) An unharmonious relationship between husband and wife will hinder prayer (Above verse 1-7).

(2) Selfishness will hinder prayer: (Page 1186-James 4:3). {You ask and do not receive, because you ask with wrong motives, so that you may spend it on your pleasures.}

(3) An unforgiving spirit will hinder prayer: (Page 916- Matt. 5:22-24). {"But I say to you that everyone who is angry with his brother shall be guilty before the court; and whoever shall say to his brother, Raca (good for nothing) shall be guilty before the supreme court; and whoever shall say, you fool, shall be guilty enough to go into the fiery hell. If therefore you are presenting your offering at the alter, and there remember that your brother has something against you, leave your offering there before the alter, and go your way; first be reconciled to your brother, and then come and present your offering.} Many Christians go without answers to

prayer because they have wronged others, or have failed to humble themselves and seek reconciliation.

(4) Unbelief will hinder prayer: (Page 1184- James 1:6.7). {But let him ask in faith without any doubting, for the one who doubts is like the surf of the sea driven and tossed by the wind. For let not that man expect that he will receive anything from the Lord.} Also: (Page 1180- Heb. 11:6). {And without faith it is impossible to please Him, for he who comes to God must believe that He is, and that He is a rewarder of those who seek Him.}

(5) Known sin in the heart will hinder prayer: (Page 678 Is. 59:1.2OT). {Behold, the Lord's hand is not so short That it cannot save; Neither is His ear so dull That if cannot hear. But your iniquities have made a separation between you and your God, And your sins have hidden His face from you, so that He does not hear.} Also: (Page 535-Ps. 66:18OT). {If I regard wickedness in my heart, The Lord will not hear.}

When you pray, go to God in all humility. Ask Him to reveal anything in your life that is not pleasing to Him. Then judge it; confess it, calling it by name and forsake it. Pray in all simplicity and earnestness, believing, and God will hear and answer.

DOES GOD ANSWER ALL PRAYERS

(Page 1032-John 15:7). {"If you abide in Me and My words abide in you, ask whatever you wish, and it shall be done for you.} The Bible is filled with answered prayer from Genesis to Revelation.

You are commanded to pray, and God has promised to answer: (Page 724-Jer. 33:3 OT). {Call to Me and I will answer you, and I will tell you great and mighty things, which you do not know.'}

In the above Scripture, there are two requirements for answers to prayer. First, you are to abide in Him; that is to continue in Him. It means to remain in His perfect will at all cost: (Page 1092-Rom. 12:1.2). {I urge you therefore, brethren, by the mercies of God, to present your bodies a living and holy sacrifice, acceptable to God, which is your spiritual service of worship. And do not be conformed to this world, but be transformed by the renewing of your mind, that you may prove what the will of God is, that which is good and acceptable and perfect.}

Second, His words are to abide in you; they are to become a vital part of your life. You are to be filled up with His words: (Page 1145-Col. 3:16.17). {Let the word of Christ richly dwell within you, with all wisdom teaching and admonishing one another with psalms and hymns and spiritual songs, singing with thankfulness in your hearts to God. And whatever you do in word or deed, do all in the name of the Lord Jesus, giving thanks through Him to God the Father.}

Meet these two requirements, and your prayers will be answered.

> (1) The answer is sometimes immediate. Peter walked on the water to go to Jesus, and as he began to sink, he prayed, "Lord, save me!" The answer was immediate: (Page 929-Matt. 14:22-31). {And immediately He made the disciples get into the boat, and go ahead of Him to the other side, while He sent the multitudes away. And after He had sent the multitudes away, He went up to the mountain by Himself to pray; and when it was evening, He was there alone. But the boat was already many stadia away from the land, battered by the waves; for the wind was contrary. And in the fourth watch of the night He came to them, walking on the sea. And when the disciples saw Him walking on the sea, they were frightened, saying, "It is a ghost!" And they cried out for fear. But immediately Jesus spoke to them, saying, "Take courage, it is I; do not be afraid." And Peter answered Him and said, "Lord, if it is you, command me to come to You on the water."

And He said , "Come!" And Peter got out of the boat, and walked on the water and came to Jesus. But seeing the wind, he became afraid, and beginning to sink, he cried out, saying, "Lord, save me!" And immediately Jesus stretched out His hand and took hold of him, and said to him, "O you of little faith, why did you doubt?"}

(2) The answer is sometimes delayed. The delay is according to His will: (Page 1088-Rom. 8:28). {And we know that God causes all things to work together for good to those who love God, to those who are called according to His purpose.} The resurrection of Lazarus is a good example of delayed answer to prayer. Lazarus was sick. Mary and Martha sent for Jesus to come and heal him. But Jesus delayed coming until Lazarus was dead and in the tomb for four days. Then He came and raised Lazarus from the dead. The answered but not denied: (Page 1026-John 11:1-44.) {Now a certain man was sick, Lazarus of Bethany, the village of Mary, and her sister Martha. And it was the Mary who anointed the Lord with ointment, and wiped His feet with her hair, whose brother Lazarus was sick. The sisters therefore sent to Him saying, "Lord, behold, he whom you love is sick." But when Jesus heard it, He said, "This sickness is not unto death, but for the glory of God, that the Son of God may be glorified by it." Now Jesus loved Martha, and her sister, and Lazarus. When therefore He heard that he was sick, He stayed two days longer in the place where He was. Then after this He said to the disciples, "Let us go to Judea again." The disciples said to Him, "Rabbi, the Jews were just now seeking to stone you, and you are going there again?" Jesus answered, "Are there not twelve hours in a day? If anyone walks in a day, he does not stumble, because he sees the light of the world. But if anyone walks in the night, he

stumbles, because the light is not in him." This He said, and after that He said to them, "Our friend Lazarus has fallen asleep; but I go, that I may awaken him out of sleep." The disciples therefore said to Him, "Lord, if he has fallen asleep, he will recover." Now Jesus had spoken of his death, but they thought that He was speaking of literal sleep. Then Jesus therefore said to them plainly, "Lazarus is dead, and I am glad for your sakes that I was not there, so that you may believe; but let us go to him." Thomas therefore, who is called Didymus, said to his fellow disciples, "Let us also go, that we may die with him." So when Jesus came, He found that he had already been in the tomb four days. Now Bethany was near Jerusalem, about two miles off: and many of the Jews had come to Martha and Mary to console them concerning their brother. Martha therefore, when she heard that Jesus was coming, went to meet Him; but Mary still sat in the house. Martha therefore said to Jesus, "Lord, if You had been here, my brother would not have died. Even now I know that whatever You ask of God, God will give You." Jesus said to her, "Your brother shall rise again." Martha said to Him, "I know that he will rise again in the resurrection on the last day." Jesus said to her, "I am the resurrection and the life; he who believes in Me shall live even if he dies, and everyone who lives and believes in Me shall never die. Do you believe this?" She said to Him, "Yes, Lord; I have believed that You are the Christ, the Son of God, even He comes into the world." And when she had said this, she went away, and called Mary her sister, saying secretly, "The teacher is here and is calling for you." And when she heard it, she arose quickly, and was coming to Him. Now Jesus had not yet come into the village, but was still in the place where Martha had met Him. The Jews then who were with her in the house, and consoling her, when they saw that Mary rose up quickly and went out, followed her, supposing that she was going to the tomb to weep there. Therefore when Mary came where Jesus was, she saw Him, and fell at His feet, my brother would not have died." When Jesus therefore saw her weeping and the Jews who came with her, also weeping, He was deeply moved in spirit, and was troubled, and said, "Where have you laid him?" They said to Him, "Lord, come and see." Jesus Wept. And so the Jews were saying, "Behold how He loved him!" But some of them said, "Could not this man, who opened the eyes of him who was blind, have kept this man also from dying?" Jesus therefore again being deeply moved within, came to the tomb. Now it was a cave, and a stone was lying against it. Jesus said, "Remove the stone," Martha, the sister of the deceased, said to Him, "Lord, by this time there will be a stench, for he has been dead four days." Jesus said to her, "Did I not say to you, if you believe, you will see the glory of God?" And so they removed the stone, and Jesus raised His eyes and said, "Father, I thank Thee that Thou hearest Me. And I knew that Thou hearest Me always; but because of the people standing around I said it, that they may believe that Thou didst send Me." And when He had said these things, He cried out loud with a loud voice, "Lazarus, come forth." He who had died came forth, bound hand and foot with wrappings; and his face was wrapped around with a cloth. Jesus said to them, "Unbind him and let him go."}

(3) The answer is sometimes "no" When God answers with a "no" He always accompanies the answer with peace: (Page 1139-Phil 4:6.7). {Be anxious for nothing, but in everything by prayer and supplication with thanksgiving let your requests be made known to God. And the peace of God, which surpasses all comprehension shall guard your hearts and your minds

in Christ Jesus.} And grace: (Page 1121-2Cor. 12:7-10). {And because of the surpassing greatness of the revelations, for this reason, to keep me from exalting myself, there was given me a thorn in the flesh, a messenger of Satan to buffet me-to keep me exalting myself! Concerning this I entreated the Lord three times that it might depart from me. And He has said to me, "My grace is sufficient for you, for power is perfected in weakness." Most gladly, therefore, I will rather boast about my weakness, that the power of Christ may dwell in me. Therefore I am well content with weakness, with insults, with distresses, with persecutions, with difficulties, for Christ's sake; for when I am weak, then I am strong.}

The answer is sometimes different from what you expect. You pray for perseverance and God sends tribulation- because "tribulation brings about perseverance": (Page 1085-Rom. 5:3). {And not only this, but we also exult in our tribulations, knowing that tribulations brings about perseverance.}

God answers all prayers-not according to your wishes, but according to His perfect will.

MASTER STUDY OUTLINE NUMBER TEN

FAITH

The righteous shall live by faith. This declaration of the Christians principle of life is found four times in the Bible: (Hab.2:1-5 OT). {I will stand on my guard post And station myself on the rampart; And I will keep watch to see what He will speak to me, And how I may reply when I am reproved. Then the Lord answered me and said, Record the vision And inscribe it on tablets, That the one who reads it may run. For the vision is yet for the appointed time; It hastens toward the goal, and it will not fail. Though it tarries, wait for it; For it will certainly come, it will not delay. Behold, as for the proud one. His soul is not right within him; But the righteous will live by faith. Furthermore, wine betrays the haughty man, so that he does not stay at home. He enlarges his appetite like Sheol, And he is like death, never satisfied. He also gathers to himself all nations And collects to himself all peoples.}

(Page 1081-Rom. 1:17). {For in it the righteousness of God is revealed from faith to faith; as it is written, "But the righteous shall live by faith."}

(Page 1125-Gal. 3:10.11). {For as many as are of the works of the law are under a curse; for it is written, "Cursed is everyone who does not abide by all things written in the book of the law, to perform them." Now that no one is justified by the law before God is evident; for, "the righteous man shall live by faith,"}

(Page 1179-Heb. 10:38). {"But the righteous one shall live by faith; And if he shrinks back, My soul has no pleasure in him."} In Habakkuk we see the difference between the lives of the unrighteous and the righteous. The unrighteous are puffed up and live by their own self sufficiency. But the righteous live by faith- their confidence is in God. To them, faith is more than a philosophy of life; It is the very principle of life (Hab.2:4). The righteous shall live his whole life by faith.

He is saved by faith: (Page 1063-Acts 16:31). {And they said, "Believe in the Lord Jesus, and you shall be saved, you and your household."}

He is kept by faith: (Page 1189- 1Pet. 1:5). {For we are protected by the power of God through faith for a salvation ready to be revealed in the last time.}

And he lives by faith: (Page 1125-Gal. 2:20). {"I have been crucified with Christ; and it is no longer I who live, but Christ lives in me; and the life which I now live in the flesh I live by faith in the Son of God, who loved me, and delivered Himself up for me.}

His faith shall be tried many times and in many ways: (Page 1189-1Pet. 1:7) .{that the proof of your faith, being more precious than gold which is perishable, even though tested by fire, may be found to result in praise and glory and honor at the revelation of Jesus Christ.}

But faith will always be vindicated, because it is more than equal to any occasion. Faith knows how to wait on the Lord: (Page 660-Is. 40:31 OT). {Yet those who wait (hope in) for the Lord will gain new strength; They will mount up with wings like eagles. They will run and not get tired, They will walk and not become weary.}

And it is always victorious: (Page 1203- I John5:4). {For whatever is born (begotten) of God overcomes the world; and this is the victory that has overcome the world-our faith.}

Faith defies reason; it moves mountains: (Page 932- Matt. 17:14-21). {And when they came to the multitude, a man came up to Him, falling on his knees before Him, and saying, "Lord, have mercy on my son for he is a lunatic, and is very ill; for he often falls into the fire, and often into the water. And I brought him to your disciples, and they could not cure him." And Jesus answered and said, "O unbelieving and perverted generation, how long shall I be with you? How long shall I put up with you? Bring him here to Me." And Jesus rebuked him, and the demon came out of him, and the boy was cured at once. Then the disciples came to Jesus privately and said, "Why could we not cast it out?" And He said, "If you have faith as a mustard seed, you shall say to this mountain, 'Move from here to there,' and it shall move; and nothing shall be impossible to you. But this kind does not go out except by prayer and fasting."}

Faith does not always face facts; it never gives up: (Page 1180-Heb.11:32-39). {And what more shall I say? For time will fail me if I tell of Gideon, Barak, Samson, Jephthah, of David and Samuel and the prophets, who by faith conquered kingdoms, performed acts of righteousness, obtained promises, shut the mouths of lions, quenched the power of fire, escaped the edge of sword, from weakness were made strong, became mighty in war, put foreign armies to flight. Women received back their dead by resurrection; and others were tortured, not accepting their release, in order that they might obtain a better resurrection: and others experienced mockings and scourgings, yes, also chains and imprisonment. They were stoned, they were sawn in two, they were tempted, they were put to death with the sword; they went about in sheepskins, in goatskins, being destitute, afflicted, ill-treated (men of whom the world was not worthy), wandering in deserts and mountains and caves and holes in the ground. And all these things, having gained approval through their faith, did not receive what was promised.}

Faith says, "God is working out His perfect will in my life, and I can wait, endure, and suffer." Faith does not make anything easy, but it does make all things possible.

WHAT IS FAITH

(Page 1179-Heb. 11:1-3). {Now faith is the assurance of things hoped for, the conviction of things not seen, For by it the men of old gained approval. By faith we understand that the worlds (ages) were prepared by the word of God, so that what is seen was not made out of the things which were visible.}

"Now faith is the assurance (title deed) of things hoped for….." Your faith is your title deed to eternal life. Just as a title deed is evidence of real estate, so your faith is evidence of your eternal estate in God. (Page 1115-2Cor. 4:18). {While we look not at the things which are seen, but at the things which are not seen; for the things which are seen are temporal, but the things which are not seen are eternal.}

(1) Faith is taking God at His word and not asking questions: (Page 1180-Heb. 11:6). {And without faith it is impossible to please Him, for He who comes to God must believe that He is, and that He is a rewarder of those who seek Him.}

(2) Faith is knowing that: "God causes all things to work together for good to those who love God": (Page 1088-Rom. 8:28). {And we know that God causes all things to work together for good to those who love God, to those who are called according to His purpose.}

(3) Faith does not believe that all things are good, or that all things work well. It does believe that all things (good or bad) work together for good for those that love God.

(4) Faith has two sides. One side has to do with the intellect. It is an intellectual conviction that Jesus Christ is God. The other side has to do with the will. It is volitional surrender of the will to Jesus Christ as Master. This is seen when Thomas believed and confessed, "My Lord and My God": (Page 1038-John 20:29). {Jesus said to them, "Because you have seen Me, have you believed? Blessed are they who did not see me, and yet believed."} "My Lord"-this was volitional surrender; "My God"-This was intellectual conviction. Together you have saving faith: (Page 1039-John 20:31) {but these have been written that you may believe that Jesus is the Christ, the Son of God; and that believing you may have life in His name.} Saving faith is an intellectual conviction that Jesus is God, and volitional surrender to Him as Lord (Master) of your life. By faith, the mind trusts God; the

heart responds to the love of God; the will submits to the commands of God; and the life obeys in the service of God.

(5) Faith is paradoxical, it goes beyond reason. It believes without understanding "why."

It sings in prison: (Page 1062-Acts 16:25). {But about midnight Paul and Silas were praying and singing hymns of praise to God, and the prisoners were listening to them.}

It exults in tribulations: (Page 1085-Rom 5:3). {And not only this, but we exult in our tribulations, knowing that tribulation brings about perseverance.}

It chooses to endure ill treatment: (Page1180-Heb. 11:25). {choosing rather to endure ill-treatment with the people of God, than to enjoy the passing pleasures of sin.}

It accepts all things as a part of God's will: (Page 1137-Phil 1:12). {Now I want you to know, brethren, that my circumstances have turned out for the greater progress of the gospel,}

You are not born with this faith. It comes by hearing the Word of God: (Page 1091-Rom. 10:17). {So faith comes by hearing, and hearing by the word of Christ.} This is why we are commanded to preach the gospel to every creature, that they may hear and believe: (Page 1090-Rom. 10:13.14). {for "Whoever will call upon the name of the Lord will be saved." How then shall they call upon Him in whom they have not believed? And how shall they believe in Him whom they have not heard? And how shall they hear without a preacher?}

THE IMPORTANCE OF FAITH

(Page 1135-Eph. 6:16). {In addition to all, taking up the shield of faith with which you will be able to extinguish all the flaming missiles of the evil one.}

The shield of faith is a vital part of the Christian armor. You are to put on the "...full armor of God", because the Christian life is a warfare, a spiritual conflict. As Paul names the different parts of the Christian armor, he comes to the shield and emphasizes its importance by saying, "In addition to all, taking up the shield of faith…" For with my shield of faith, nothing can hurt you: (Page 1089-Rom. 8:37). {In all these things we overwhelmingly conquer through Him who loved us.}

The importance of faith:
- (1) You cannot be saved without faith: (Page 1016- John 3:36). {"He who believes in the son has eternal life; but he who does not obey the Son shall not see life, but the wrath of God abides on him."}
- (2) You cannot live victoriously over the world without faith: (Page 1203- 1John 5:4). {For whatever is born of God overcomes the world; and this is the victory that has overcome the world-our faith.}
- (3) You cannot please God without faith: (Page 1180-Heb. 11:6). {And without faith it is impossible to please Him for he who comes to God must believe that He is and that he is a rewarded of those who seek Him.}
- (4) You cannot pray without faith: (Page 1184- James 1:6). {But let him ask in faith without any doubting, for the one who doubts is like the surf of the sea driven and tossed by the wind.}
- (5) You cannot have peace without God and faith: (Page 1085- Rom 5:1). {Therefore having been justified by faith, we have peace with God through our Lord Jesus Christ.}
- (6) You cannot have joy without faith: (Page 1189-1Pet. 1:8); {and though you have not seen Him, you love Him, and though you do not see Him now, but believe in Him, you greatly rejoice with joy inexpressible and full of glory.}
- (7) You are justified by faith and not by works: (Page 1125-Gal. 2:16). {nevertheless knowing that a man is not justified by the works of the law but through faith in Christ Jesus, even we have believed in Christ Jesus,

that we may be justified by faith in Christ, and not by the works of the law; since by the works of the law shall no flesh be justified.}

(8) You are to live by faith: (Page 1125-Gal. 2:20). {"I have been crucified with Christ; and it is no longer I who live, but Christ lives in me; and the life I now live the flesh I live by faith in the Son of God, who loved me, and delivered Himself up for me.}

(9) You are righteous by faith: (Page 1090-Rom. 10:1-4). {Brethren, my hearts desire and my prayer to God for them is for their salvation. For I bear them witness that they have a zeal for God, but not in accordance with knowledge. For not knowing about God's righteousness, and seeking to establish their own, they did not subject themselves to the righteousness of God. For Christ is the end of the law for righteousness to everyone who believes.}

(10) Christ dwells in your heart by faith: (Page 1132-Eph. 3:17). {so that Christ may dwell in your hearts through faith; and that you, being rooted and grounded in love.}

(11) The Holy Spirit is received by faith: (Page 1124- Gal. 3:2). {This is the only thing I want to find out from you; did you receive the Spirit by the works of the law, or by hearing with faith?}

(12) "Whatever is not faith is sin": (Page 1094- Rom. 14:23). {But he who doubts is condemned if he eats, because his eating is not from faith; and whatever is not from faith is sin.}

LITTLE FAITH

(Page 929- Matt.14:28-33). {And Peter answered Him and said, "Lord, if it is You, command me to come to You on the water." And He said, "Come!" And Peter got out of the boat, and walked on the water and came toward Jesus. But seeing the wind, he became afraid, and beginning to sink, he cried out, saying, "Lord, save me!" And immediately Jesus stretched out His hand and took hold of him, and said to him, "O you of little faith, why do you doubt?" And when they got into the boat, the wind stopped. And those who were in the boat worshiped Him, saying, "You are certainly God's Son!"}

At this stage in the spiritual growth of Peter, he was a man of "little faith." However, after Pentecost, he became a spiritual giant. Let us take a good look at his "little faith" and profit from it. Jesus came to His distressed disciples, walking on the water in the midst of the storm. Peter asked to come to Jesus on the water. He must have thrilled at the thought of doing the impossible. Jesus said, "Come."

> (1) Peter did the impossible thing: He walked on the water by faith.
> (2) Next, Peter did the conceivable thing: He saw the storm, and had a second thought-he doubted. For a moment, he lost sight of Jesus. He may have turned and started back to the boat: (Page 989- Luke 9:62). {But Jesus said to him, "No one, after putting his hand to the plow and looking back, is fit for the kingdom of God."}
> (3) Now Peter did the natural thing: He feared destruction. Doubt always breeds fear.
> (4) Then Peter did the expected thing: He began to sink-he failed.
> (5) Now Peter did the right thing: He prayed, "Lord, save me." Immediately Jesus stretched forth His hand and caught him. Once more Peter made contact with Jesus by faith.
> (6) Again Peter did the impossible thing: He walked on the water with Jesus, to the boat. In this lesson, we see the success and failure of "little faith."

Now let us recap the steps that led to failure. Peter started by faith, and walked on the water. Then he saw the storm, and had a second thought that led to doubt, that produced fear, that caused him to turn back, that brought about failure.

You need a faith that is bigger than the elements that would drag you down to defeat. You can have big faith by "prayer and fasting" (Page 1091- Rom.10:17). {So faith comes from hearing, and hearing by the word of Christ.}

You can have mountain-moving faith.

THREE KINDS OF FAITH

(Page1027-John 11:21-44). {Martha therefore said to Jesus, "Lord, if You had been here, My brother would not have died. Even now I know that whatever You ask of God, God will give you." Jesus said to her, "Your brother shall rise again." Martha said to Him, "I know that he will rise again in the resurrection on the last day." Jesus said to her, "I am the resurrection and the life; he who believes in Me shall life even though he dies, and everyone who lives and believes in Me shall never die. Do you believe this?" She said to Him, "Yes, Lord: I have believed that you are the Christ, the Son of God, even He comes into the world." And when she had said this, she went away, and called Mary her sister, saying secretly, "The teacher is here, and is calling for you." And when she heard it, she arose quickly, and was coming to Him. Now Jesus had not yet come into the village, but was still in the place where Martha met Him. The Jews then who were with her in the house, and consoling her, when they saw that Mary rose quickly and went out, followed her, supposing that she was going to the tomb to weep there. Therefore, when Mary came to where Jesus was, she saw Him, and fell at His feet, saying to Him, "Lord, if you had been here, my brother would not have died." When Jesus therefore saw her weeping, and the Jews came with her, also weeping, He was deeply moved in spirit, and was troubled, and said, "Where have you laid Him?" They said to Him. "Lord, come and see." Jesus Wept. And so the Jews were saying, "Behold how He loved him!" But some of them said, "Could not this man, who opened the eyes of the blind, have kept this man also from dying?" Jesus therefore again being deeply moved within, came to the tomb. Now it was a cave, and a stone was lying against it. Jesus said, "Remove the stone." Martha, the sister of the deceased, said to Him, "Lord, by this time there will be a stench, for he has been dead four days." Jesus said to her, "Did I not say to you, if you believe, you will see the glory of God?" And so they removed the stone, And Jesus raised His eyes and said, "Father, I thank Thee that thou heardest Me. And I knew that Thou hearest Me always; but because of the people standing around I said it, that they may believe that Thou didst send Me." And when He had said these things, He cried with a loud voice, "Lazarus, come forth." He who had died came forth, bound hand and foot with wrappings; and his face was wrapped around with a cloth. Jesus said to them, "Unbind him, and let him go."}

   In this chapter, we see the faith of Martha in connection with the resurrection of her brother Lazarus. Now Lazarus fell ill, and Martha and her sister Mary sent for Jesus to come and heal him. Jesus delayed His coming until Lazarus was dead and in the tomb for four days. Then He came to raise him from the dead, and found the limited, fundamental faith of Martha His only obstacle.

> (1) Martha's faith was limited. She said, "Lord, if You had been here, my brother would not have died" (verse 21). The death of Lazarus meant the end of Martha's faith. She believed that Jesus had the power her brother up from the sick bed, but not from the dead. Her limited faith restricted the power of Christ: (Page 928-Matt13:58). {And He did not do many miracles there because of their unbelief.} Limited faith is controlled by circumstances, motivated by fear of failure.
>
> (2) Martha's faith was fundamental. Jesus said, "Your brother shall rise again" (verse 23). These words were spoken to kindle hope and faith in Martha; but she said, "I know that he will rise again in the resurrection on the last day" (verse 24). Martha declared her fundamental faith in a great truth, but that is not enough. Jesus stated, "I am the resurrection and the life" (verse 25). Jesus was saying that He had all the

power over life and death. Then He asked, "Do you believe this? (verse 21). Martha evaded the question by stating her fundamental faith in her creed (verse 27). It is not enough to believe in creed only; faith must go beyond your creed, to the living, all powerful Christ. Her faith limited the power of Christ: (Page 964-Mark 10:27). {Looking upon them, Jesus said, "With men it is impossible, but not with God; for all things are possible with God."} And "Jesus wept" (verse35). Jesus wept when He came to raise Lazarus from the dead and found limited, fundamental belief faith only.

(3) At last, unlimited faith came from Martha when she consented to have the stone moved from the grave (verse 41). When Jesus first ordered the stone taken from the grave, Martha objected in unbelief (verse 39). Then Jesus challenging her belief, said, "Did I not say to you, if you believe, you will see the glory of God?" (verse 40). Martha believed and waited to see the glory of God, and she was not disappointed. We often hear that "seeing is believing," but this is not so. You believe, and then see. Faith comes before sight. Now Martha's faith no longer limited the power of Christ. She consented to have the stone moved from the tomb and Jesus "cried out with a loud voice, 'Lazarus, come forth'" (verse 43), and Lazarus was raised up.

Don't be satisfied with limited, fundamental faith only, when you can have unlimited faith that pleased God and reveals His glory.

THE HALL OF FAITH

(Page 1180-Heb.11:32-39). {And what more shall I say? For time will fail me if I tell Gideon, Barak, Samson, Jephthah, of David and Samuel and the prophets, who by faith conquered kingdoms, performed acts of righteousness, obtained promises, shut the mouths of lions, quenched the power of fire, escaped the edge of the sword, from weakness were made strong, became mighty in war, put foreign armies to flight. Women received back their dead by resurrection; and others were tortured, not accepting their release, in order that they might obtain a better resurrection; and other experienced mockings and scourgings, yes, also chains and imprisonment, They were stoned, they were sawn in two, they were tempted, they were put to death with the sword; they went about in sheepskins, and goatskins, being destitute, afflicted, ill-treated (men of whom the world was not worthy), Wandering in deserts and mountains and caves and holes in the ground. And all these, having gained approval through their faith, did not receive what was promised,}

    This chapter is often called the "Hall of Faith." You need to come here often and linger long, that your faith may be come strong in the Lord; for in this Scripture we get a view of the history of Israel and the church, as it is written by faith, in the blood of the saints. They worshiped by faith as Abel. They walked by faith as Enoch. They worked by faith as Noah. They lived by faith as Abraham. They governed by faith as Israel. They fought by faith as Joshua. They conquered by faith as Gideon, They subdued kingdoms by faith as David. They closed the mouth of lions by faith as Daniel. They walked through fire by faith as the three Hebrew children. They suffered by faith as Paul. They died as Stephen, the first Christian martyr:

    (Page 1051)-Acts 7:54-60). {Now when they heard this, they were cut to the quick, and they began gnashing their teeth at him. But being full of the Holy Spirit, he gazed intently into heaven and saw the glory of God, and Jesus standing at the right hand of God. And He said, "Behold, I see the heavens opened up and the Son of Man standing at the right hand of God." But they cried out with a loud voice, and covered their ears, and they rushed upon him with one impulse. And when they had driven him out of the city, they began stoning him and the witnesses laid aside their robes at the feet of a young man Saul. And they went on stoning Stephen as he called upon then Lord and said, "Lord Jesus, receive my spirit!" And falling on his knees, he cried out with a loud voice. "Lord do not hold this sin against them!" And having said this, he fell asleep.}

By faith they were patient in suffering, courageous in battle, made strong out of weakness, and were victorious in defeat. They were more than conquerors by faith. It is only by faith in the all-powerful Christ that you can be superior to circumstances and victorious over all the evil forces that would destroy you. (Page 1181-Heb. 12:2). {Fixing our eyes on Jesus, the author and perfecter of faith, who for the joy set before Him endured the cross, despising the shame, and has sat down at the right hand of the throne of God.}

The faith of the saints inspires us, but we look to Jesus as our example of faith.

MASTER OUTLINE NUMBER ELEVEN

THE ABUNDANT LIFE

"…I came that they might have life, and might have it abundantly." (Page 1025-John 10:10). {"The thief comes only to steal, and kill, and destroy; I came that they might have life, and might have it abundantly.}

The only way into eternal life is through faith in Christ as personal savior: (Page 1015- John 3:15). {that whoever believes in Him have eternal life.}

But do not stop here; to have eternal life is great- but there is more. Christ came that you might have life more abundantly. All believers have life, but not all have abundant life. You are living beneath your privilege if you are a believer and not enjoying the abundant life.

For life to be abundant, it must have abundant resources, and the only unlimited source of life is in the person of Jesus Christ the Son of God: (Page 1031- John 14:6). {Jesus said to him, "I am the way, and the truth, and the life; no one comes the Father, but through Me.}

To possess this fuller, the believer must abide in Him: (Page 1032-John 15:1-5). {"I am the true vine, and My Father is the vinedresser. Every branch in Me that does not bear fruit, He takes away; and every branch that bears fruit, He prunes it, that it may bear more fruit. You are already clean because of the word which I have spoken to you. "Abide in Me, and I in you. As the branch cannot bear fruit itself, unless it abides in the vine, so neither can you, unless you abide in Me. I am the vine, you are the branches; he who abides in Me, and I in him, he bears much fruit, for apart from Me you can do nothing."}

Dynamic, abundant living is not for just a few- it is God's norm for all believers. It is spiritual life in depth, and without it, the Christian life becomes inane and meaningless.

If you do not have abundant life within you, you will soon yield to the fleshly life around you: (Page 1100-1Cor 3:1-4).

{And I brethren, could not speak to you as to spiritual men, but as to men of flesh, as to babes in Christ. I gave you milk to drink, not solid food; for you were not yet able to receive it. Indeed, even now you are not yet able, for you are still fleshly. For since there is jealousy and strife among you, are you not fleshly, and are you not walking like mere men? For when one says, "I am of Paul," and another, "I am of Apollos," are you not mere men?}

The fleshly life is circumstance- controlled; the abundant life is Holy Spirit-controlled. The fleshy Christian life leads to defeat; the abundant life leads to victory in Christ. Man seems to know everything about life except how to live it abundantly. From this moment on, determined not to be satisfied with anything less that God's best: Living life abundantly.

THE ABUNDANT LIFE IS A YIELDED LIFE

(Page 1086-Rom. 6:10-13). {For the death that He died, He died to sin, once and for all; but the life that He lives, He lives to God. Even so consider yourselves to be dead to sin, but alive to God in Christ Jesus. Therefore do not let sin reign in your mortal body that you should obey its lusts, and do not go on presenting the members of your body to sin as instruments of unrighteousness; but present yourselves to God as those alive from the dead, and your members as instruments of righteous to God.}

How to live the abundant life is no secret; it is revealed in out Lord and Savior Jesus Christ. "For the death that He died, He died to sin, once for all; but the life that He lives, He lives to God" (above verse 10). Faith that saves identifies you with Christ in His death-this is eternal life. Faith that yields identifies you with Christ in His resurrection- this is abundant life: (Page 1145-Col. 3:1-4). {If then you have been raised up with Christ, keep seeking the things above, where Christ is, seated at the right hand of God. Set your mind on the things above, not on the things that are on earth. For you have died and your life is hidden with Christ in God. When Christ, who is your life, is

revealed, then you also will be revealed with Him in glory.}
  (1) It is one thing to have eternal life by faith. It is quite another thing to have abundant life by faith.
  (2) It is one thing for you to "...become the righteousness of God in Him": (Page 1116- 2Cor. 5:21). {He made Him who knew no sin to be sin on our behalf, that we might become the righteousness of God in Him.} It is another thing for you to realize His righteous life is in you: (Page 1201-1John 3:7). {Little children, let no one deceive you; the one who practices righteousness is righteous, just as He is righteous.}
  (3) It is one thing for you to live in Christ: (Page 1116-2Cor. 5:17). Therefore if any man is in Christ, he is a new creature; the old things passed away; behold, new things have come.} It is another thing for Christ to live His life through you: (Page 1143-Col. 1:27). {To whom God willed to make His known what is the riches of the glory of this mystery among the Gentiles, which is Christ in you, the hope of glory.}

In the above (verse 13), the believer has a choice. He may yield to God by faith and enjoy abundant life, or he may yield to sin and endure a defeated life: (Page 1212-Rev. 3:1). {And to the angel of the church in Sardis write: He who has the seven Spirits of God, and the seven stars, says this: "I know your deeds, that you have a name that you are alive, but you are dead."}

God would have you know the power of a yielded life; it will lift you above circumstances that circumvent abundant living. The abundant life begins when you yield to Him as Master, allowing Him to live His life through you by faith.

THE ABUNDANT LIFE IS A SERVICE LIFE

(Page 1092-Rom. 12:1.2). {I urge you therefore, brethren, by the mercies of God to present your bodies a living and holy sacrifice, acceptable to God, which is your spiritual service of worship. And do not be conformed to this world, be transformed by the renewing of your mind, that you may prove what the will of God is, that which is good and acceptable and perfect.}

To live abundantly, you must serve the Lord Jesus Christ, who Himself became our example. He served all the way to Calvary, and there was the obedient servant, "…obedient to the point of death, even death on a cross": (Page 1137-Phil. 2:7.8). {but emptied Himself, taking the form of a bond-servant, and being made in the likeness of men. And being found in appearance as a man, He humbled Himself by becoming obedient to the point of death, even death on a cross.}

In the above (verses 1.2), the believer is urged to take the necessary steps for abundant living:

(1) You are to "present." This volitional surrender to the perfect will of God, even though you may not know God's perfect will for your life; it is, on your part, an act of faith: (Page 1021- John 7:17). {"If any man is willing to do His will, he shall know of the teaching, whether it is of God, or whether I speak from Myself.}

(2) You are to "present your bodies." God must control and use the whole man. "And may your spirit and soul and body be preserved complete, without blame at the coming of the Lord Jesus Christ." Your whole man was redeemed on the cross and sanctified (set apart for service): (Page 1151-1Thess. 5:23). {Now may the God of peace Himself sanctify you entirely; and may your spirit and soul and body be preserved complete, without blame at the coming of our Lord Jesus Christ.}

(3) You are to "…present your bodies a living a holy sacrifice." This is exemplified in the life of the Apostle Paul; he was a living sacrifice. In life, he was "a bond servant of Christ Jesus": (Page 1081- Rom. 1:1). {Paul, a bond servant of Christ Jesus, called as an apostle, set apart for the gospel of God.} In the battle, he was a warrior: (Page 1135- Eph. 6:10-18). {Finally, be strong in the Lord, and in the strength of His might. Put on the full armor of God, that you may be able to

stand firm against the schemes of the devil. For our struggle is not against flesh and blood, but against the rulers, against the powers, against the world forces of this darkness, against the spiritual forces of wickedness in the heavenly places. Therefore, take up the full armor of God, that you may be able to resist in the evil day, and having done everything, to stand firm. Stand firm therefore, having girded your loins with truth, and having put on the breastplate of righteousness, and having shod your feet with the preparation of the gospel of peace; in addition to all, taking up the shield of faith with which you will be able to extinguish all the flaming missiles of the evil one. And take the helmet of salvation, and the sword of the Spirit, which is the word of God. With all prayer and petition pray at all times in the Spirit, and with this in view, be on the alert with all perseverance and petition for all the saints.}

In the will of God, he was a "prisoner of Christ Jesus": (Page1132-Eph.3:1). {For this reason I, Paul the prisoner of Christ Jesus for the sake of the Gentiles.} These words were spoken from a Roman prison: he never referred to himself as a prisoner of Rome. To the Apostle, prison was a part of the perfect will of God. With this conviction, he lived abundantly: (Page 1137-Phil. 1:12). {Now I want you to know, brethren, that my circumstances have turned out for the greater progress of the gospel.} In death, he was victorious: (Page 1162-2Tim. 4:7.8). {I have fought the good fight, I have finished the course, I have kept the faith; in the future there is laid up for me the crown of righteousness, which the Lord, the righteous judge, will award to me on that day; and not only to me, but also to all who have loved His appearing.}

    You have been "transformed"--changed by the power of God, and no longer "conform to this world"; but now you can be conformed to the "good and acceptable and perfect" will of God-and live abundantly!

THE ABUNDANT LIFE IS A SEPERATED LIFE

(Page 1081-Rom. 1:1). {Paul, a bond servant of Christ Jesus, called as an apostle, set apart for the gospel of God.}

Separation is both positive and negative. You are to be "…set apart for the gospel of God"—this is positive (above verse. You are to come out from anything that is contrary to the perfect will of God. This is negative: (Page 1117-2Cor. 6:17). {"Therefore, come out from their midst and be separate," says the Lord. "And do not touch the unclean; And I will welcome you.} To be separated means to be (set apart) for salvation and service.

(1) The Word of God has the power to separate the believer from sin: (Page 1035- John 17:17). {"Sanctify them in the truth; Thy word is truth}. Also: (Page 568-Ps. 119:11OT). {Thy word I have treasured in my heart, That I may not sin against Thee.}

(2) God the Father has the power to separate the believer to the "…coming of the Lord Jesus Christ": (Page 1151-1Thess. 5:23). {Now may the God of peace Himself sanctify you entirely; and may your spirit and soul and body be preserved complete, without blame at the coming of the Lord Jesus Christ.}

(3) God the Son has the power to separate the believer to righteousness, "…having no spot or wrinkle": (Page1134-Eph. 5:24-27). {But as the church is subject to Christ, as also the wives ought to be to their husbands in everything. Husbands, love your wives, just as Christ also loved the church and gave Himself up for her; that He might sanctify her, having cleansed her by the washing of water with the word, that He might present to Himself the church in all her glory, having no spot or wrinkle or any such thing; but that she should be holy and blameless.}

(4) God the Holy Spirit has the power to separate the believer unto salvation and service: (Page 1153-2Thess. 2:13). {But we should always give thanks to God for you, brethren beloved by the Lord, because God has chosen you from beginning for salvation through sanctification by the Spirit and faith in the truth.}

Without being separated, you can have a relationship; but you cannot have fellowship with Him. You may be united to Him in Calvary, but separated from Him in sin: (Page 678-Is.59:1.2 OT). {Behold, the Lord's hand is not so short that it cannot save: Neither is His ear so dull That He cannot hear. But your iniquities have made a separation between you and your God, and your sins have hidden His face from you, so that He does not hear.}

Without separation, you can have influence without power, movement without achievement; you may try, but not trust; serve, but not succeed; war, but not win. Without separation to God from sin, your whole Christian life will be "wood, hay, straw." The abundant life is made possible by the death, burial, and resurrection of our Lord and Savior Jesus Christ, and made a reality by being separated to Him.

THE ABUNDANT LIFE IS A SPIRIT-FILLED LIFE

(Page 1134-Eph.5:18-20). {And do not get drunk with wine, for that is dissipation, but be filled with the Spirit, speaking to one another in psalms and hymns and spiritual songs, singing and making melody with your heart to the Lord; always giving thanks for all things in the name of our Lord Jesus Christ to God, even the Father.}

The Holy Spirit indwells every believer. You may be immature, weak and imperfect; but, if you have been "born again" of the Spirit: (Page 1014-John 3:3-7). {Jesus answered and said to him, "Truly, truly, I say to you, unless one is born again, he cannot see the kingdom of God." Nicodemus said to Him, "How can a man be born when he is old? He cannot enter a second time into his mother's womb, can he?" Jesus answered, "Truly, truly, I say to you, unless one is born of water and the Spirit, he cannot enter the kingdom of God. That which is born of flesh is flesh, and that which is born of Spirit is spirit. Do not marvel that I said to you, 'You must be born again.'"}

He indwells in you: (Page 1102-1Cor. 6:19). {Or do you not know that your body is a temple of the Holy Spirit who is in you, whom you have from God, and that you are not your own?} Also: (Page 1088-Rom.8:9). {and those who are in the flesh cannot please God.}

It is one thing for you to have the Holy Spirit dwelling in you, but does the Holy Spirit have you, that He may fill you with abundant life? The abundant life is not found in environment or circumstances, or in the things you may possess. It is found in the infilling of the Holy Spirit. "Be filled with the Spirit" (above verse 18) is a command. You may be filled many, many times: (Page 1043-Acts2:4). {And they were all filled with the Holy Spirit, and began to speak with other tongues, as the Spirit was giving them utterance.} Also: (Page 1047-Acts 4:31). {And when they had prayed, the place where they had gathered together was shaken, and they were filled with the Holy Spirit, and began to speak the word of God with boldness.}

The apostles were filled in Acts chapter 2, were filled again in Acts chapter 4. To be filled with the Holy Spirit is to be Spirit-possessed, Spiritempowered, and Spirit-controlled: (Page 1052-Acts 8:26-40). {But an angel of the Lord spoke to Philip saying, "Arise and go south to the road that descends from Jerusalem to Gaza." (This is a desert road.) And he arose and went; and behold, there was an Ethiopian eunuch, a court official of Candace, queen of Ethiopians, who was in charge of all her treasure; and he had come to Jerusalem to worship. And he was returning and sitting in his chariot, and was reading the prophet Isaiah, and the Spirit said to Philip, "Go up and join this chariot." And when Philip had run up, he heard him reading Isaiah the prophet, and said, "Do you understanding what you are reading?" And he said, "Well, how could I, unless someone guides me?" And he invited Philip to come up and sit with him. Now the passage of Scripture which he was reading was this: "He was led as sheep to the slaughter; And as lamb before its shearer is silent, So He does not open His mouth, In humiliation His judgment was taken away; Who shall relate His generation? For His life is removed from the earth." And the eunuch answered Philip and said, "Please tell me, of whom does the prophet say this? Of himself, or of someone else?" And Philip opened his mouth, and beginning from Scripture he preached Jesus to him. As they went along the road they came to some water; and the eunuch said, "Look! Water! What prevents me from being baptized?" And Philip said, "If you believe with all your heart, you may." And he answered and said, "I believe that Jesus Christ is the Son of God." And he ordered the chariot to stop; and they both went down into the water, Philip as well as the eunuch; and he baptized him. And when they came out of the water, the Spirit of the Lord snatched Philip away; and the eunuch saw him no more, but went on his way rejoicing. But Philip found himself at Azotus; and as he passed through he kept preaching the gospel to all the cities, until he came to Caesarea.}

(1) You are filled with the Spirit that you might have joy (above verse 19 and 20).
(2) You are filled with the Spirit for service: (Page 1049-Acts 6:3). {"But select from among you, brethren, seven men of good reputation, full of the Spirit and wisdom, whom we may put in charge of this task.} Also: (Page 1043-Acts 2:4-7). {I say this in order that no one may delude you with persuasive argument. For even though I am absent in body, nevertheless I am with you in spirit, rejoicing to see your good discipline and stability of your faith in Christ. As you therefore have received Christ Jesus the Lord, so walk in Him, having been firmly rooted and now being built up in Him and established in your faith, just as you were instructed, and overflowing with gratitude.}

(3) You are filled with the Spirit for power to be a witness: (Page 1041-Acts 1:8). {But you shall receive power when the Holy Spirit has come upon you; and you shall be my witnesses both in Jerusalem, and in all Judea and Samaria, and even to the remotest part of the earth.} Also: (Page 1056-Acts 11:22-24). {And the news about them reached the ears of the church of Jerusalem, and they sent Barnabas off to Antioch. Then when he had come and witnessed the grace of God, he rejoiced and began to encourage them all with resolute heart to remain true to the Lord; for he was a good man, and full of the Holy Spirit and of faith. And considerable numbers were brought to the Lord.}

(4) You are filled with the Spirit for the hour of persecution: (Page 1051-Acts 7:54-60). {Now when they heard this, they were cut to the quick, and they began gnashing their teeth at him. But being full of the Holy Spirit, he gazed intently into heaven and saw the glory of God, and Jesus standing at the right hand of God; And he said, "Behold, I see the heavens opened up and the Son of Man standing at the right hand of God." But they cried out with a loud voice, and covered their ears, and they rushed upon him with one impulse. And when they had driven him out of the city, they began stoning him, and the witnesses laid aside their robes at the feet of a young man named Saul. And they went stoning Stephen as he called upon the Lord and said, "Lord Jesus, receive my spirit!" And falling on his knees, he cried out with a loud voice, "Lord, do not hold this sin against them!" And having said this, he fell asleep.}

(5) You are filled with the Spirit that you may :walk by the Spirit" (Page 1127-Gal. 5:16-26). {But I say to you, walk by the Spirit, and you will not carry out the desires of the flesh. For the flesh sets its desire against the Spirit, and the Spirit against the flesh; for these are

in opposition to one another, so that you may not do the things that you please. But if you are led by the Spirit, you are not under the law. Now the deeds of the flesh are evident, which are: immorality, impurity, sensuality, idolatry, sorcery, enmities, strife, jealousy, outbursts of anger, disputes, dissentions, factions, envying, drunkenness, carousing, and things like these, of which I forewarn you just as I have forewarned you that those who practice such things shall not inherit the kingdom of God.}

(6) You are filled with the Spirit that you may lead with the Spirit: (Page 1088-Rom. 8:14). {For all who are being led by the Spirit, these are the sons of God.} How can you be filled with the Holy Spirit? First, you must desire Him to fill you. Second, you must ask Him to fill you. Third, you must believe that He does fill you: (Page 1016-John4:14). {but whoever drinks of the water that I shall give him shall never thirst; but the water that I shall give him shall become in him a well of water springing up to eternal life.} Also: (Page1022-John 7:37:38). {Now on the last day, the great day of the feast, Jesus stood and cried out, saying, "If any man is thirsty, let him come to Me and drink. He who believes in Me, as the Scriptures said, 'From his innermost being shall flow rivers of living water.'"}

THE ABUNDANT LIFE IS A MUTURE LIFE

(Page 1197-2Pet. 3:18). {But grow in the grace and knowledge of our Lord and Savior Jesus Christ. To Him be the glory, both now and to the day of eternity. Amen.}

The Scriptures reveal four stages of spiritual growth in the Christian life:

(1) The baby stage: (Page 1100-1Cor. 3:1-4). {And I, brethren, could not speak to you as to as spiritual men, but as to men of flesh, as to babes in Christ. I gave you

milk to drink, not solid food; for you were not yet able to receive it. In deed, even now you are not yet able, for you are still fleshy. For since there is jealousy and strife among you, are you not fleshy, and are you not walking like mere men? For when one says, "I am of Paul," and another, "I am of Apollos." Are you not mere men?} A baby thinks only of it self; and, if denied the things desired, it will raise a rumpus. It seeks its own; its feelings are easily hurt and it is often jealous. A baby lives to be served-it never serves. It drinks milk, and cannot eat strong meat. It cries, but never sings. It tries to talk, but never makes sense. These infant characteristics are so prominent in the lives of many church members. They have been born into the family of God, but have failed to develop spiritually. They are spiritual babies-carnal Christians.

(2) The little child stage: (Page 1200-1John 2:12). {I am writing to you, little children, because your sins are forgiven you for His names sake.} Some Christians grow to be little children spiritually. But stop there. Here are some of the characteristics of children: they are often untruthful, envious, and cruel. If rebuked, they become martyrs; if crossed, they are resentful and make a scene. They are talebearers, repeating everything they hear (in adults it is called gossip). They are given to emotional outbursts, and are easily puffed up. They love praise, and will accept it from any source. They seek only the things that appeal to self. Are you a spiritual child?

(3) The young man stage: (Page 1200-1 John 2:13). {I am writing to you, fathers, because you know Him who has been from the beginning. I am writing to you, young men, because you have overcome the evil one. I have written to you, children because you know the Father.} Spiritual growth to that of a young man is not reached by many, He is strong and virile and is well

able to overcome his enemy. He has a vision for the future and the faith and courage to tackle it. He is preparing for his productive years. You too can become a young man spiritually by doing away with childish things" and grow: (Page 1108-1Cor.13:11). {When I was a child, I used to speak as a child, think as a child, reason as a child; when I became a man, I did away with childish things.}

(4) The father stage: (Page 1200-1 John 2:13). {I am writing to you, fathers, because you know Him who has been from the beginning. I am writing to you, young men, because you have overcome the evil one. I have written to you, children, because you know the Father.} This stage of spiritual development can be reached by all, but so few ever attain it.

The spiritual father has peace with God: (Page 1085-Rom. 5:1). {Therefore having been justified by faith, we have peace with God through our Lord Jesus Christ.}

He knows the peace of God: (Page 1139-Phil 4:7). {And the peace of God, which surpasses all comprehension, shall guard your hearts and your minds in Christ Jesus.}

He rejoices in His spiritual children: (Page 1149-1Thess. 2:19). {For who is our hope or joy or crown of exultation? Is it not even you, in the presence of our Lord Jesus at His coming?} Also: (Page 1154- 1Tim. 1:2). {to Timothy, my true child in the faith; grace and mercy and peace from God the Father and Christ Jesus our Lord.}

He has learned contentment under all circumstances: (Page 1139-Phil. 4:11). {Not that I speak from want; for I have learned to be content in whatever circumstances I am.}

He knows the only source of strength: (Page 1139-Phil. 4:13.14). {I can do all things through Him who strengthens me.}

He does not brood over the past, but looks to the future: (Page 1139-Phil.3:13.14). {Brethren, I do not regard myself as having laid hold of it yet; but one thing I do: forgetting what lies behind and reaching forward to what lies ahead. I press on toward the goal for the prize of the upward call of God in Christ Jesus.}

He knows that all things work together in his life for his eternal good: (Page 1088-Rom. 8:28). {And we know that God causes all things to work together for good to those who love God, to those who are called according to His purpose.}

He enjoys the abundant life now and will enjoy it in the life to come: (Page 1131- Eph. 2:7). {in order that the ages to come He might show the surpassing riches of His grace in kindness toward us in Christ Jesus.}

MASTER OUTLINE NUMBER TWELVE

REPENTANCE

(Prov.28:13 OT). {"He who conceals his transgressions will not prosper, But he who confesses and forsakes them will find compassion"}

God desires; "truth in the inner most being" (Page 529 Ps.51:6 OT). {Behold, thou dost desire truth in the innermost being, And in the hidden part of Thou wilt make me know wisdom.}

And commands all men everywhere to repent: (Page 1064-Acts 17:30) {"Therefore having over looked the times of ignorance, God is now declaring to men that everywhere should repent,}

The sinner must repent before he can become the recipient of salvation by grace through faith: (Page 1131-Eph. 2:8.9). {For by grace you have been saved through faith; and that not of your selves, it is the gift of God; not as a result of works, that no man should boast.}

The saved must practice repentance if he is to enjoy unbroken fellowship with God: (Page 500 Job-42:1-6). {Then Job answered the Lord, and said, "I know that Thou canst do all things, And that no purpose of Thine can be thwarted. Who is this that hides counsel without knowledge? Therefore I have declared that which I did not understand, Things too wonderful for me, which I did not know. Hear now and I will speak; I will ask Thee, and do Thou instruct me. I have heard of Thee by the hearing of the ear; But now my eyes sees Thee. Therefore I retract, And I repent in dust and ashes."}

Some one said, "I repented before I understood the meaning of the word, but since then as a Christian I have repented many times."

Repentance is granted by God: (Page 1049-Acts 5:31). {"He is the One whom God exalted to His right hand as a Prince and a Savior, to grant repentance to Israel, and forgiveness of sins.}

"The kindness of God leads to repentance": (Page 1082-Rom. 2:4). {Or do you think lightly of the riches of His kindness and forbearance and patience, not knowing that the kindness leads to repentance?} The kindness of God is not merited; therefore, the results of His kindness which is repentance is a gift. This gift of repentance is an inward change produced by the convicting power of the Holy Spirit as the Word of
God is proclaimed: (Page 1044-Acts 2:37.38). {Now when they heard this, they were pierced to the heart, and said to Peter and the rest of the apostles, "Brethren, what shall we do?" And Peter said to them, "Repent, and let each of you be baptized in the name of Jesus Christ for the forgiveness of your sins; and you shall receive the gift of the Holy Spirit."} Also: (Page 1033-John 16:7-11). {But I tell you the truth, it is to your advantage that I go away; for if I do not go away, the Helper shall not come to you; but if I go, I will send Him to you. And He, when He comes, will convict the world concerning sin, and righteousness, and judgment; concerning sin, because they do not believe in Me; and concerning righteousness, because I go to the Father, and you no longer behold Me; and concerning judgment, because the ruler of this world has been judged.}

The results, "repentance toward God and faith in our Lord Jesus Christ": (Page 1068-Acts 20:21). {Solemnly testifying to both Jews and Greeks of repentance toward and faith in our Lord Jesus Christ.}

Faith that Christ died for our sins; and that He was buried and that He rose from the dead: (Page 1109-1Cor.15:1-4). {Now I make known to you, brethren, the gospel which I preached to you, which also you received, in which also you stand, by which also you are saved, if you hold fast the word which I preached to you, unless you believed in vain. For I delivered to you as of first importance what I also received, that Christ died for our sins according to the Scriptures, and that He was buried, and that He was raised on the third day according to the Scriptures,}

Repentance qualifies a man for salvation, but it takes faith in Christ to acquire it. True repentance is always coupled with faith. It is impossible to have saving faith and not repent. "Repentance toward God and faith in our Lord Jesus Christ: are essential and inseparable in salvation.

REPENTANCE DEFINED

Faith with out repentance is the ultimate hypocrisy, and repentance without faith in the death, burial, and resurrection of Christ is sheer folly. (Page 1196-2Pet. 3:9). {The Lord is not slow about His promise, as some count slowness, but is patient toward you, not wishing for any to perish but for all to come to repentance.}

First, let us see that repentance is not:

(1) Sorrow. "Sorrow that is according to the will of God produces a repentance without regret, leading to salvation": (Page 1117-2Cor.7:9.10). {I now rejoice, not that you were made sorrowful, but that you were made sorrowful to the point of repentance; for you were made sorrowful according to the will of God, in order that you might not suffer loss in anything through us. For sorrow that is according to the will of God produces a repentance without regret, leading to salvation; but the sorrow of the world produces death.} Godly sorrow is a guilty feeling that leads to repentance but it is not repentance.

(2) Penance. Penance is an act on the part of the guilty to render payment for sin. It is to make an effort, in some way, to atone for wrongs done against God or man. God calls all men to repentance, not to do penance.

(a) Jesus did not say, do penance and believe the gospel. He said, "repent and believe in the gospel": (Page 952-Mark 1:15). {and saying, "The time is fulfilled, and the kingdom of God is at hand; repent and believe in the gospel."}

(b) Peter did not say, do penance and be baptized everyone of you in the name of Jesus Christ. He said, "Repent, and let each of you be baptized in the name of Jesus Christ for the forgiveness of your sins": (Page 1044-Acts 2:38). {And Peter said to them, "Repent and let each of you be baptized in the name of Jesus Christ for the forgiveness of your sins; and you shall receive the gift of the Holy Spirit.}

(c) Paul did not say, God is declaring all men everywhere to do penance. He said, "God is now declaring to men that all everywhere should repent": (Page 1064-Acts 17:30). {Therefore having overlooked the times of ignorance, God is now declaring to men that all everywhere should repent.} If penance is repentance then salvation is not the gift of God, and we are not saved by grace through faith: (Page 1131- Eph. 2:8.9). {For by grace you have been saved through faith; and that not of your selves, it is the gift of God. Not as a result of works, that no one should boast.}

Reformation. Reformation is a change brought about by the efforts of man for self glory: (Page 926-Matt.12:43-45). {Now when the unclean spirit goes out of a man, it passes through waterless places, seeking rest, and it does not find it. Then it says, "I will return to my house from which I came," and when it comes, it finds it unoccupied, swept, and put in order. Then it goes, and takes along with it seven other spirits more wicked than itself, and they go in and live there; and the last state of that man becomes worse that the first. That is the way it will also be with this evil generation."}

It is turning away from sin, or giving up a bad habit, or trying to overhaul the old nature, or turning over a new leaf, or making restitution. Judas reformed but it did not save him and neither can it save you: (Page 945-Matt. 27:3-5). {Then when Judas , who had betrayed Him, saw that He had been condemned, he felt remorse and returned the thirty pieces of silver to the chief and elders, saying, "I have sinned by betraying innocent blood." But they said, "What is that to us? See to that yourself!" And he threw the pieces of silver into the sanctuary and departed; and he went away and hanged himself.}

Second, let us see what repentance is:

(1) A change. The change is always evidenced in three elements.
   (a) The intellectual element, a change of mind.
   (b) The emotional element, a change of heart.
   (c) The volitional element, a change of will.
(2) The parable of the prodigal is a perfect illustration of repentance. He had a change of mind, a change of heart, and a change of will: (Page 997-Luke 15:11-32). {And He said, "A certain man had two sons; and the younger of them said to his father, 'Father, give me the share of the estate that falls to me.' And he divided his wealth between them. And not many days later, the younger son gathered everything together and went on a journey into the distant country, and there he squared his estate with loose living. Now when he had spent everything, a severe famine occurred in that country, and he began to be in need. And he went and attached himself to one of the citizens of that country, and he sent him into his fields to feed swine. And he was longing to fill his stomach with the pods that the swine were eating, and no one was giving anything to him. But when he came to his senses, he said, 'How many of my fathers hired men have more than enough bread, but I am dying here with hunger! I will get up and go to my father, and will say to him, "Father, I have sinned against heaven and in your sight. I am no longer worthy to be called your son; make me as one of your hired men."' And he got up and came to his father. But while he was still a long way off, his father saw him, and felt compassion for him, and ran and embraced him and kissed him. And the son said to him, 'Father, I have sinned against heaven and in your sight; I am no longer worthy to be called your son.' But the father, said to the slaves, 'Quickly bring out the best robe and

put it on him, and put a ring on his hand and sandals on his feet; and bring the fattened calf, kill it, and let us eat and be merry; for this son of mine was dead, and has come to life again; he was lost, and has been found.' And they began to be merry. Now his older son was in the field, and when he came and approached the house, he heard music and dancing, And he summoned one of the servants and began inquiring what these things might be. And he said to him, 'Your brother has come, and your father has killed a calf, because he has received him back safe and sound.' But he became angry, and was not willing to go in; and his father came out and began entreating him. But he answered and said to his father, 'Look! For so many years I have been serving you, and I have never neglected a command of yours; and yet you have never given me a kid, that I might be merry with my friends; but when this son of yours came, who has devoured your wealth with harlots, you killed the fattened calf for him.' And he said to him. 'My child, you have always been with me, and all that is mine is yours. But we had to be merry and rejoice, for this brother of yours was dead and has begun to live, and was lost and has been found.'"}

(a) The intellectual element, "He came to his senses."
(b) The emotional element, "I have sinned."
(c) The volitional element, "I will get up and go to my father."

Repentance is a change. The prodigal had a change had mind; and his change of mind effected a change of heart; and his change of heart effected a change of will. No one is ever saved until he wills to be: (Page 1226-Rev. 22:17). {And the Spirit and the bride say, "Come," And let the one who hears say, "Come." And let the one who is thirsty come; let the one who wishes take the water of life without cost.}

Repentance is a change of mind, of heart, and of will.

REPENTANCE PREACHED

(Page 951-Mark. 1:1-4). {The beginning of the gospel of Jesus Christ, the Son of God. As it is written in Isaiah the prophet, "Behold, I send My messenger before your face, Who will prepare your way; The voice of one crying in the wilderness, 'Make ready the way of the Lord, Make His paths straight.'" John the Baptist appeared in the wilderness preaching a baptism of repentance for the forgiveness of sins.}

Repentance was preached in the Old Testament before the birth of Christ, and during the life and ministry of Christ. It was preached on the day of Pentecost, and in the Book of Acts after Pentecost. It is taught in the Epistles and the Book of Revelation. It is a doctrine to be preached and practiced in all dispensations.

(1) John the Baptist preached repentance:
  (a) He preached the baptism of repentance: (Page 978-Luke 3:3). {And he came into all the district around Jordan, preaching a baptism of repentance of sins;}
  (b) He preached. "Repent, for the kingdom of heaven is at hand": (Page 914-Matt. 3:2). {"Repent, for the kingdom of heaven is at hand."} "The voice of one crying in the wilderness, 'Make ready the way of the Lord'": (Page 914-Matt. 3:3). {For this is the one referred to by Isaiah the prophet, saying, "The voice of one crying in the wilderness, 'Make ready the way of the Lord, Make His paths straight!'"}

John's preaching of repentance exalted Christ, denounced sin, warned of judgment, and it cost him his head: (928-Matt. 14:6-11). {But when Herod's birthday came, the daughter of Herodias danced before them and pleased Herod. Thereupon he promised with an oath to give her whatever she asked. And having been prompted by her mother, she said, "Give me here on a platter the head of John the Baptist." And although he was grieved, the king commanded it to be given because of his oaths, and because of his dinner guests. And he sent and had John beheaded in the prison. And his head was brought on a platter

and given to the girl; and she brought it to her mother.}
  (2) Jesus preached repentance:
    (a) He preached, "Repent and believe in the gospel": (Page 952-Mark 1:14.15). {And after John had been taken into custody, Jesus came to Galilee, preaching the gospel of God. And saying, "The time is fulfilled, and the kingdom if God is at hand; repent and believe in the gospel."} He went about doing mighty works and calling sinners to repent and to have faith in the good news of God.
    (b) His preaching of repentance was an ultimatum, repent of perish (Page 994-Luke 13:1-5). {Now on the same occasion there were some present who reported to Him about the Galileans, whose blood Pilate had mingled with their sacrifices. And He answered and said to them, "Do you suppose that these Galileans were greater sinners than all other Galileans, because they suffered this fate? I will tell you, but unless you repent, you will all likewise perish. Or do you suppose that those eighteen on whom the tower in Siloam fell and killed them, were worse culprits than all the men who liven in Jerusalem? I tell you, no, but unless you repent, you will all likewise perish."} Salvation by grace is for the repentant soul, and judgment without mercy for those who resist.
  (3) Peter preached repentance:
    (a) At Pentecost he preached, "Repent, and let each of you be baptized in the name of Jesus Christ for the forgiveness of your sins": (Page1044-Acts 2:38). {And Peter said to them, "Repent, and let each of you be baptized in the name of Jesus Christ for the forgiveness of sins; and you shall receive the gift of the Holy Spirit.}
    (b) In His second Epistle he preached that, the Lord "is patient toward you, not wishing for any to perish but

for all to come to repentance": (Page 1196-2Pet. 3:9). {The Lord is not slow about His promise, as some count slowness, but is patient toward you, not wishing for any to perish but for all to come to repentance.} Every soul that goes to hell goes against the will of God.

(4) Paul preached repentance:

(a) He preached that God "Is now declaring to men that all everywhere should repent" (Page 1064-Acts 17:30). {"Therefore having overlooked the times of ignorance, God is now declaring to men that all everywhere should repent.} This message was given on Marshill to the intelligentsia of Athens. The results were three-fold. First, some sneered; second, some procrastinate; third, some believed: (Page 1065-Acts 17:32-34). {Now when they heard of the resurrection of the dead, some began to sneer, but others said, "We shall hear you again concerning this." So Paul went out of their midst. But some men joined him and believed, among whom also was Dionysius the Areopagite and a woman named Damaris and others with them.}

REPENT FROM DEAD WORKS

(Page 1174-Heb. 6:1). {Therefore leaving the elementary teaching about Christ, let us press on to maturity, not laying again a foundation of repentance from dead works and of faith toward God.}

What does the writer of Hebrews mean by, "repentance from dead works"? First, we need to see the other two categories of works. They are:

(1) Good works: (Page 916-Matt. 5:16). {"Let your light shine before men in such a way that they may see your good works, and glorify your Father who is in heaven.} Only saved souls can do good works and please God. Of the lost He said, "There is no one who does good,

not even one." (Page 508-Ps.14:1-3). {The fool has said in his heart, "There is no God." They are corrupt, they have committed abominable deeds; There is no one else who does good. The Lord has looked down from heaven upon the sons of men, To see if there are any who understand, Who seek God. They have all turned aside; together they have become corrupt. There is no one who does good, not even one.} The believer is not to hide his good works, but let them be seen to the glory of the heavenly Father. Mary of Bethany anointed the head and feet of Jesus with precious perfume while He sat at the table of Simon the leper. Some of the disciples called her deed an extravagant waste. But Jesus said, "She has done a good deed to Me...She has done what she could": (Page 968-Mark 14:3-9). {And while He was in Bethany at the home of Simon the leper, and reclining at the table, there came a woman with an alabaster vial of very costly perfume of pure nard; and she broke the vial and poured it over His head. But some were indignantly remarking to one another, "Why has this perfume been wasted? For this perfume might have been sold for over three hundred denarii, and the money given to the poor." And they were scolding her. But Jesus said, "Let her alone; why do you bother her? She has done a good deed to Me. For the poor you always have with you, and whenever you wish, you can do them good; but you do not always have Me. She has done what she could; she has anointed my body beforehand for the burial. And truly I say to you, wherever the gospel is preached in the whole world, that also which this woman has done shall be spoken of in memory of her."} Like Mary we are to do all we can to the glory of God, not in order to be saved but because we are saved, having no other motive. This is the way to do good works.

(2) Evil deeds: (Page 1143-Col 1:20.21). {And through Him to reconcile all things to Himself, having made peace through the blood of His cross; through Him, I say, whether things on earth or things in heaven. And although you were formerly alienated and hostile in mind, engaged in evil deeds.} Evil deeds are deeds done by the un-regenerated, natural man: (Page 1099-1Cor.2:14). {But a natural does not except the things of the Spirit of God; for they are foolish to him, and he cannot understand them, because they are spiritually appraised.} He walks according to this world system. He is motivated by the "prince of the power of the air Satan." His talk is filled with lust of the flesh and he lives to gratify the desires of the flesh and the natural mind, He is a child of wrath and his works are wicked because he is dead in sin: (Page 1131-Eph. 2:1-3). {And you were dead in your trespasses and sins, in which you formerly walked according to the course of this world, according to the prince of the power of the air, of the spirit that is now working in the sons of disobedience.}

(3) Dead works (above verse).Dead works could be called religious works. They are done by the religious for the purpose of meriting eternal life. It is a legalistic effort to keep the moral and ceremonial laws of God for the purpose of winning God's favor and be saved by works: (Page 1131-Eph. 2:8.9). {For by the grace you have been saved through faith; and that not of yourselves, it is a gift of God; not as result of works, that no one should boast.} Paul said, "Because by the works of the law no flesh will be justified in His sight": (Page 1083-Rom. 3:20). {Because by the works of the law no flesh will be justified in His sight; for through the law comes the knowledge of sin.}

Dead works are performed by the religious, "For not knowing God's righteousness, and seeking to establish their own, they did not subject themselves to the righteousness of God": (Page 1090-Rom. 10:1-4). {Brethren, my heart's desire and my prayer for them is for their salvation. For I bear them witness that they have a zeal for God, but not in accordance with knowledge. For not knowing about God's righteousness, and seeking to establish their own, they did not subject themselves to the righteousness of God. For Christ is the end of the law for righteousness to everyone who believes.}

Paul is a good illustration of repentance from dead works. He clearly stated that he had "no confidence in the flesh"; then he lists his dead works of which he had to repent: (Page 1138-Phil.3:1-9). {Finally, my brethren, rejoice in the Lord. To write the same things again is no trouble to me, and it is a safeguard for you. Beware of the dogs, beware of the evil workers, beware of the false circumcision; for we are the true circumcision, who worship in the Spirit of God and glory in Christ Jesus and put no confidence in the flesh. although I my self might have confidence even in the flesh. If anyone else has a mind to put confidence in the flesh, I far more: circumcised the eighth day, of the nation of Israel, of the tribe of Benjamin, a Hebrew of Hebrews; as to the law, a Pharisee; as to zeal, a persecutor of the church; as to the righteousness which is in the law, found blameless. But whatever things were gain to me, those things I have counted as loss for the sake of Christ. More than that, I count all things to be loss in view of the surpassing value of knowing Christ Jesus my Lord, for whom I have suffered the loss of all things, and count them but rubbish in order that I may gain Christ, and may be found in Him, not having a righteousness of my own derived from the law, but that which is through faith in Christ, the righteousness which comes from God on the basis of faith.}

When he compared this righteousness which is by dead works of the law, with the righteousness of Christ which is by faith, he counted the former but rubbish. He knew the meaning of "repentance from dead works."

REPENTANCE AND GOD

(Page 1176-Heb. 7:21). {For they indeed became priests without an oath, but He with an oath through the One who said to Him, "The Lord has sworn And will not change His mind, 'Thou art a Priest forever.'"}

(Page 150Numbers 23:19 OT). {"God is not a man, that He should lie, Nor a son of man, that He should repent; Has He said, and will He not do it? Or has He spoken, and will He not make it good?} Yet the Bible tells us that He does repent: (Page 5-Gen. 6:5-7). {Then the Lord saw that the wickedness of man was great on the earth, and that every intent of the thoughts of his heart was evil continually. And the Lord was sorry that He had made man on the earth, and He was grieved in His heart.}

There is no contradiction. It is paradoxical, but not contradictory. God made two covenants with man: The first is unconditional. When He makes an unconditional covenant He never repents ("change His mind.") (Page 564-Ps.110:4 OT). {The Lord has sworn and will not change His mind, Thou art a priest forever according to the order of Melchizedek."}

He made such a covenant with Israel: (Page 1092-Rom.11:25-36). {For I do not want you, brethren, to be uninformed of this mystery, lest you be wise in your own estimation, that a partial hardening has happened to Israel until the fullness of the Gentiles has come in; and thus all Israel will be saved; just as it is written, "The deliverer will come from Zion, He will remove ungodliness from Jacob. And this is My covenant with them, When I take away her sins. From the stand point of the gospel they are enemies for your sake, but from the standpoint of God's choice they are beloved for the sake of the fathers: for the gifts and the calling of God are irrevocable. For just as you once were disobedient to God, but now have been shown mercy because of their disobedience, so these also now have been disobedient, in order that because of the mercy shown to you they also may now be shown mercy. For God has shut up all disobedience that He might show mercy to all. Oh, the depth of the riches both of the wisdom and knowledge of God! How unsearchable are his judgments and unfathomable His ways! For who has known the mind of the Lord, or who became His counselor? Or who has first given to Him that it might be paid back to Him again? For from Him and through Him and to Him all things. To Him be the glory forever. Amen."}

The second conditional. {The Lord said, "My Spirit shall not strive with man forever, because he also is flesh; nevertheless his days shall be one hundred and twenty years"} (Page 6-Gen.6:3).

In the days of Noah, God gave the human race 120 years to repent. Only Noah and his family repented and "found favor in the eyes of the Lord" (Page 6-Gen. 6:8). They met God's condition and were not judged with the rest of the human race who refused to repent. {"The Lord is not slow about His promise as some count slowness, but is patient toward you, not wishing for any to perish but for all to come to repentance."} (Page 1196- 2Pet.3:9). It is clear that God wills to save all lost souls. He is "not wishing for any to perish." To be saved the lost must meet His condition, "repentance toward God and faith in our Lord Jesus Christ." (Page 1068-Acts 20:21): {solemnly testifying to both Jews and Greeks of repentance toward God and faith in our Lord Jesus Christ.}

Now if a man does not repent and believe in the Lord Jesus Christ, God will repent. He will change and judge that man. In love He bestows grace; but, if salvation by grace is rejected, in justice He terminates it. In this way God repents.

REPENTANCE, IMPOSSIBLE TO RENEW

(Page 1174-Heb.6:4-6). {For in the case of those who have once been enlightened and have tasted of the heavenly gift and have been made partakers of the Holy Spirit, and have tasted the good word of God and the powers of the age to come, and then have fallen away, it is impossible to renew them to repentance, since they again crucify to themselves the Son of God, and put Him to open shame.}

The key that unlocks the mystery to this difficult portion of Scripture is the word, "impossible" in verse 6. The writer is saying, that the person who so sins will find it impossible to repent again.

First, let us see what the writer does not mean. He does not mean a backslidden Christian. Simon Peter backslid: (Page 945-Matt. 26:69-75). {Now Peter was sitting outside in the courtyard, and a certain servant-girl came to him and said, "You too were with Jesus the Galilean." But he denied it before them all, saying, "I do not know what you are talking about." And when he had gone out to the gateway, another servant-girl saw him and said to those who were there, "This man was with Jesus of Nazareth." And again he denied it with an oath, "I do not know the man." And a little later the bystanders came up and said to Peter, "Surely you too are one of them; for the way you talk gives you away." Then he began to curse and swear, "I do not know the man!" And immediately a cock crowed. And Peter remembered the word Jesus and said, "Before a cock crows, you will deny Me three times." And he went out and wept bitterly.}

Repented: (Page 1039-John21:3-17). {Simon Peter said to them, "I am going fishing," They said to him, "We will also come with you." They went out, and got into the boat; and that night they caught nothing. But when the day was breaking, Jesus stood on the beach; yet the disciples did not know that it was Jesus. Jesus therefore said to them, "Children, you do not have any fish, do you?" They answered Him, "No" And He said to them, "Cast the net on the right side of the boat, and you will find a catch." They cast therefore, and then they were not able to haul it in because of the great number of fish. That disciple therefore whom Jesus loved said to Peter, "It is the Lord." And so when Simon Peter heard that is was the Lord, he put his outer garment on (for he was stripped for work), and threw himself into the sea. But the other disciples came in the little boat, for they were not for from the land, but about one hundred yards away, dragging the net full of fish. And so when they got out upon the land, they saw a charcoal fire already laid, and fish placed on it, and bread. Jesus came to them, "Bring some of the fish which you have caught." Simon Peter went up and drew the net to land, full of large fish, a hundred and fifty three; and although there were so many, the net was not torn. Jesus said to them, "Come and have breakfast." None of the disciples ventured to question Him, "Who are You?" knowing that is was the Lord. Jesus came and took the bread, and gave them, and the likewise. This is the third time that Jesus was manifested to the disciples, after He was raised from the dead. So when they had finished breakfast, Jesus said to Simon Peter, "Simon, son of John, do you love Me more than these?" He said to Him, "Yes Lord; You know that I love you." He said to him, "Tend my lambs." He said to him a second time. "Simon, son of John, do you love Me?" He said to Him, "Yes Lord; You know that I love You." He said to him, "Shepherd My sheep." He said to him a third time, "Simon, son of John, do you love Me?" Peter was grieved because he said to him the third time, "Do you love Me?' And he said to Him, "Lord, You know all things; You know that I love you," Jesus said to him, "Tend My sheep.}

And was restored to fellowship with the Lord. King David sinned: (Page 296-2Sam. 11:1-27). {Then it happened in the spring, at the time when dings go out in battle, that David sent Joab and his servants with him and all Israel, and they destroyed the sons of Ammon and besieged Rabbah. But David stayed in Jerusalem. Now when evening came David arose from his bed and walked around on the roof of the king's house, and from the roof he saw a woman bathing; and the woman was very beautiful in appearance. So when David sent and inquired about the woman. And one said, "Is this not Bathsheba, the daughter of Elam, the wife of Uriah the Hittite?" And Davis sent messengers and took her, and when she came to him he lay with her; and when she had purified herself from her uncleanness, she returned to her house. And the woman conceived; and she sent and told David, and said, "I am pregnant." Then David sent to Joab. "Send me Uriah the Hittite." So Joab sent Uriah to David. When Uriah came to him, David asked concerning the welfare of Joab and the people and the state of the war. Then David said to Uriah, "Go down to your house, and wash your feet." And Uriah went to the king's house, and a present from the king was sent out after him. But Uriah slept at the door of the king's house with all the servants of his lord, and did not go down to the house. Now when they told David, saying, "Uriah did not go down to the house." David said to Uriah, "Have you not come from a long journey? Why did you not go down to your house?" And Uriah said to David, "The art and Israel and Judah are staying in temporary shelters, and my lord Joab and the servants of my lord are camping in the open field. Shall I then go to my house to eat and to drink and to lie with my wife? By your life and the life of your soul, I will not do this thing." Then David said to Uriah, "Stay here today also, and tomorrow I will let you go." So Uriah remained in Jerusalem that day and the next. Now David called him, and he ate and drank before him, and he made him drunk: and in the evening he went out to lie on his bed with his lord's servants, but he did not go down to his house. Now it came about in the morning that David wrote a letter to Joab, and sent it by the hand of Uriah. And he had written in the letter, saying, "Place Uriah in the front line of the fiercest battle and withdraw from him, so that he may be struck down and die." So it was as Joab kept on watch on the city, that he put Uriah at the place where he knew there were valiant men. And the men of the city went out and fought against Joab, and some of the people among David's servants fell; and Uriah the Hittite fell also died. Then Joab sent and reported to David all the events of the war. And he charged the messenger, saying, "When you have finished telling all the events of the war to the king, and it happens that the king's wrath rises and he says to you, "Why did you go so near the city to fight? Did you not know that they would shoot from the wall? Who struck down Abimelech, the son of Jerubbesheth? Did not a woman throw an upper millstone on him from the wall so that he died at Thebez? Why did you go so near the wall?' Then you shall say, 'Your servant Uriah the Hittite is dead also.'" So the messenger departed and came and reported to David all that Joab had sent him to tell. And the messenger said to David, "The men prevailed against us and came out against us in the field, but we pressed them as far as the entrance of the gate. Moreover the archers shot at your servants from the wall; so some of the king's servants are dead, and your servant Uriah the Hittite is also dead." Then David said to the messenger, "Thus you shall say to Joab, 'Do not let this thing displease you, for the sword devours one as well as another; make your battle against the city stronger and overthrow it; and so encourage him." Now when the wife of Uriah heard that Uriah her husband was dead, she mourned for her husband. When the time for mourning was over, David sent and brought her to his house and she became his wife; then she bore him a son. But the thing that David had done was evil in the sight of the Lord.}

Repented: (Page 529-Ps.51:1-19 OT). {Be gracious to me O God, according to Thy loving kindness; According to the greatness of Thy compassion blot out my transgressions. Wash me thoroughly from my iniquity, And cleanse me from my sin. For I know my transgressions, And my sin is ever before me. Against Thee, Thee only, I have sinned, And done what is evil in Thy sight, So that Thou art justified when Thou dost speak, And blameless when Thou dost judge. Behold, I was brought forth in iniquity, and in my sin my mother conceived me. Behold, Thou dost desire truth in the innermost being, And in the hidden part Thou wilt make me know wisdom. Purify me with hyssop, and I shall be clean; Wash me, and I shall be whiter than snow. Make me hear joy and gladness, Let the bones which Thou hast broken rejoice. Hide Thy face from my sins And blot out all my iniquities. Create in me a clean heart, O God, And renew a steadfast spirit within me. Do not cast me away from Thy presence, And do not take Thy Holy Spirit from me. Restore to me the joy of Thy salvation, And sustain me with a willing spirit. Then I will teach transgressors Thy ways, And sinners will be converted to Thee. Deliver me from blood guiltiness. O God, Thou God of my salvation; Then my tongue will joyfully sing of Thy righteousness. O Lord, open my lips, That my mouth may declare Thy praise. For thou dost not delight in sacrifice, otherwise I would give it: Thou art not pleased with burnt offering. The sacrifices of God are a broken spirit; A broken and a contrite heart, O God, Thou wilt not despise. By Thy favor do good to Zion; Build the walls of Jerusalem. Thou wilt delight in righteous sacrifices, In burnt offering and whole burnt offering; Then the young bulls will be offered on Thine alter.}

And was restored to fellowship with the Lord: (Page297-2Sam.12:13OT). {Then David said to Nathan, "I have sinned against the Lord.' And Nathan said to David. "The Lord also has taken away your sin; you shall not die.}

Any backslidden Christian can repent and be restored to fellowship with God.

Second, let us see what the writer does mean. Hebrews 6:4-6 is proof that being religious is not enough to save you. They professed, but did not possess eternal life. In outward appearance they would be called Christians.

But Jesus said, "Not everyone who says to Me, 'Lord, Lord,' will enter the kingdom of heaven": (Page 919-Matt. 7:21-23). {"Not everyone who says to Me, 'Lord, Lord,' will enter the kingdom of heaven; but he who does the will of My Father who is in heaven. Many will say to Me on that day. 'Lord, Lord, did we not prophesy in Your name, and in Your name cast out demons, and in Your name perform many miracles?' And then I will declare to them, 'I never knew you, depart from Me, you who practice lawlessness.'}

Esau so sinned against the Lord when He sold his birthright to Jacob for a bowl of stew. (Page Gen.25:27-34). {When the boys grew up, Esau became a skilled hunter, a man of the field; but Jacob was a peaceful man, living in tents. Now Isaac loved Esau, because he had a taste for game, but Rebekah loved Jacob. And when Jacob had cooked stew, Esau came in from the field and he was famished; and Esau said to Jacob, "Please let me have a swallow of that red stuff there, for I am famished."

Therefore his name was called Edom. But Jacob said, "irst sell me your birthright." And Esau said, "Behold, I am about to die; so of what use is the birthright to me?" And Jacob said, "First swear to me"; so he swore to him, and sold his birthright to Jacob. Then Jacob gave Esau bread and lentil stew; and he ate and drank, and rose and went on his way. Thus Esau despised his birthright.}

Later he tried to repent, but found it impossible to do so. The Scripture says, "he found no place for repentance, though he sought for it with tears": (Page 1181-Heb. 12:16.17). {That there be no immoral or godless person like Esau, who sold his own birthright for a single meal. For you know that even after words, when he desired to inherit the blessing, he was rejected, for he found no place for repentance, though he sought it with tears.}

At the great white throne judgment where only the wicked dead are judged: (Page 1224-Rev. 20:11-15). {And I saw a great white throne and Him who sat upon it, from whose presence earth and heaven fled away, and no place was found for them. And I saw the dead, the great and the small, standing before the throne, and books were opened; and another book was opened, which is the book of life; and the dead were judged from the things which were written in the books, according to their deeds. And the sea gave up the dead which were in it, and death and Hades gave up the dead which were in them; and they were judged, every one of them according to their deeds. And death and Hades were thrown into the lake of fire. This is the second death, the lake of fire. And if anyone's name was not found written in the book of life, he was thrown into the lake of fire.}

They too will try to repent but will find it impossible.

REPENTANCE THE IMPORTANTCE OF

(Page 1064-Acts 17:30). {"Therefore having over looked the times of ignorance, God is now declaring to men that all everywhere should repent.}

Repentance is so important that God commands that "all everywhere should repent" (above verse).

(1) The lost are to repent. Jesus said, "I did not come to call the righteous, but sinners." (Page 921-Matt. 9:13). {"But go and learn, what this means, 'I desire compassion, and not sacrifice,' for I did not come to call the righteous, but sinners."} Again He says, "Unless you repent, you will all likewise perish": (Page 994- Like 13:3-5). {"I tell you, now, but, unless you repent, you will all likewise perish. Or do you suppose that those eighteen on whom the tower in Siloam fell and killed them, were worse culprits than all the men who lived in Jerusalem? I tell you, no, but unless you repent, you will all likewise perish."}

(2) Backsliders are to repent. Paul said, "I now rejoice, not that you were made sorrowful, but that you were made sorrowful to the point of repentance": (Page 1117-2Cor.7:9). {I now rejoice, not that you were made sorrowful, but that you were made sorrowful to the point of repentance; for you were made sorrowful according to the will of God, in order that you might not suffer loss in anything through us.} There were fleshly Christians in the church at Corinth. In Paul's first letter to them he called upon the church to discipline the guilty. In his second letter he rejoices because the guilty repented.

(3) Local churches are to repent. In the book of Revelation (Page 1211, 1212-Rev. 2:3), {Our Lord sent seven letters to seven churches. He called upon five of the seven to repent.

The church at Ephesus was to repent because she had left her first love.

The church at Pergamos was to repent because she permitted the doctrine of Balaam to be taught, and to eat things sacrificed to idols, and to commit acts of immorality.

> The church at Thyatira was to repent because she tolerated Jezebel to teach and lead God's servants to commit acts of immorality.
> The church at Sardis was to repent because she was a dying congregation.
> The church at Laodicea was to repent because she thought she was rich and did not need anything. In her opinion, she had arrived. She did not know that she was neither hot or cold, but lukewarm and God was ready to spit her out of his mouth.
> The Lord called upon these five local churches to repent or else He would remove their candlestick and they would cease to be a light in darkness.

The lost are to repent. The backslider is to repent or be disciplined. The local church is to repent or lose its effectiveness in a world lost in sin.

REPENTANCE, EVIDENCE OF

(Page 1074-Acts 26:19.20). {"Consequently, King Agrippa, I did not prove disobedient to the heavenly vision, but kept declaring both to those of Damascus first, and also at Jerusalem and then throughout all the region of Judea, and even to the Gentiles, that they should repent and turn to God, performing deeds appropriate to repentance.}

The evidence of repentance toward God and faith toward our Lord Jesus Christ is seen in:

> (1) The repentance of unbelieving Thomas: (Page 1038-John 20:24-29). {But Thomas, one of the twelve, called Didymus, was not with them when Jesus came. The other disciples therefore were saying to him, "We have seen the Lord!" But he said to them, "Unless I shall see in His hands the imprint of the nails, and put my finger into the place of the nails, and put my hand into His side, I will not believe." And after eight days again His disciples were inside, and Thomas with them. Jesus came, the doors having been shut, and

stood in their midst, and said, "Peace be with you." Then He said to Thomas, "Reach here your finger, and see My hands; and reach here your hand, and put it into My side; and be not unbelieving." Thomas answered and said to Him, "My Lord and My God!" Jesus said to him, "Because you have seen Me, have you believed? Blessed are they who did not see Me and yet believed."} Thomas would not believe that Christ had been raised from the dead until he saw the risen Savior and was given the opportunity to touch His nail-pierced hands and put his hand into His wounded side. Thomas repented, believed, and made his great confession of faith, "My Lord and my God!"

(2) Three thousand changed their minds, hearts, and wills on the day of Pentecost and immediately gave evidence of repentance: (Page 1044-Acts2:41-47). {So then, those who had received his word were baptized; and there were added that day about three thousand souls. And they were continually devoting themselves to the apostles' teaching and to fellowship, to the breaking bread and to prayer. And everyone kept feeling a sense of awe; and many wonders and signs were taking place through the apostles And all those who had believed were together, and had all things in common; and they were selling their property and possessions, and were sharing them with all, as anyone might have need. And day by day continuing with one mind in the temple, and breaking bread from house to house, they were taking their meals together with gladness and sincerity of heart, praising God, and having favor with all the people. And the Lord was adding to their number day by day those who were being saved.}

(3) Saul of Tarsus experienced repentance when he met Jesus on the Damascus road and gave evidence of repentance: (Page 1053-Acts 9:1-22). {Now Saul, still breathing threats and murder against the disciples of

the Lord, went to the high priest, and asked for letters from him to the synagogues at Damascus, so that if he found any belonging to the way, both men and women, he might bring them bound to Jerusalem. And it came about that as he journeyed, he was approaching Damascus, and suddenly a light from heaven flashed around him; and he fell to the ground, and heard a voice saying to him, "Saul, Saul, why are you persecuting Me?" And he said, "Who art thou, Lord?" And He said, "I am Jesus whom you are persecuting, but rise, and enter the city, and it shall be told you what you must do." And the men who traveled with him stood speechless, hearing the voice, but seeing no one. And Saul got up from the ground, and though his eyes were open, he could see nothing; and leading him by hand, they brought him into Damascus. And he was three days without sight, and neither ate nor drank. Now there was a certain disciple at Damascus, named Ananias; and the Lord said to him in a vision, "Ananias." And he said, "Behold here am I, Lord." And the Lord said to him, "Arise and go to the street called Straight, and inquire at the house of Judas for a man from Tarsus named Saul, for behold he is praying. And he has seen in a vision of a man named Ananias come in and lay his hands on him, so that he might regain his sight." But Ananias answered, "Lord, I have heard from many about this man, how much harm he did to Thy saints at Jerusalem; and he has authority from the chief priests to bind all who call upon Thy name." But the Lord said to him, "Go, for he is a chosen instrument of Mine, to bear My name before Gentiles and kings and the sons of Israel; for I will show him how much he must suffer for My names sake." And Ananias departed and entered the house, and after laying his hands on him said, "Brother Saul, the Lord Jesus, who appeared to you on the road by which you were coming has sent me so that you may regain your sight, and be filled with the Holy Spirit." And immediately there fell from his eyes something like scales, and he regained his sight, and he arose and was baptized; and he took food and was strengthened. Now for several days he was with the disciples who were at Damascus, and immediately he began to proclaim Jesus in the synagogues, saying, "He is the Son of God." And all those hearing him continued to be amazed, and were saying, "Is this not he who in Jerusalem destroyed those who called on His name, and who had come here for the purpose of bringing them bound before the chief priests?" But Saul kept increasing in strength and confounding the Jews who lived at Damascus by proving that this Jesus is the Christ.}

(4) Cornelius, his family, and friends repented when they heard the gospel preached by Simon Peter, and evidence of repentance followed: (Page 1055-Acts 10:24-48). {And on the following day he entered Caesarea. Now Cornelius was waiting for them, and had called together, his relatives and close friends. And when it came about Peter entered Cornelius met him, and fell at his feet and worshiped him. But Peter raised him up, saying, "Stand up; I too am just a man." And as he talked with him, he entered, and found many people assembled. And he said to them, "You yourselves know how unlawful it is for a man who is a Jew to associate with a foreigner or to visit him; yet God has shown me that I should not call any man unholy or unclean. That is why I came without even raising objection when I was sent for. And so I ask for what reason you have sent for me." And Cornelius said, "Four days ago to this hour, I was praying in my house during the ninth hour; and behold, a man stood before me in shining garments, and he said, 'Cornelius,

your pray has been heard and your alms have been remembered before God. Send therefore to Joppa and invite Simon, who is called Peter, to come to you; he is staying at the house of Simon the tanner by the sea.' And so I went to you immediately, and you have been kind enough to come. Now then, we are all here present before God to hear all that you have been commanded by the Lord." And opening his mouth, Peter said: "I most certainly understand now that God is not one to show partiality, but in every nation the man who fears Him and does what is right, is welcome to Him. The word which He sent to the sons of Israel, preaching peace through Jesus Christ (He is Lord of all) you yourselves know the thing which took place throughout all Judea, starting from Galilee, after the baptism which John proclaimed. You know Jesus of Nazareth, how God anointed Him with the Holy Spirit and with power, and how He went about doing good, and healing all who were oppressed by the devil; for God was with Him. And we are witnesses of all the things He did both in the land of the Jews and in Jerusalem. And they also put Him to death by hanging Him on a cross. God raised Him up on the third day, and granted that He should become visible, not to all the people, but to witnesses who were chosen beforehand by God, that is, to us, who ate and drank with Him after He arose from the dead. And He ordered us to preach to the people, and solemnly to testify that this is the One who has been appointed by God as judge of the living and the dead. Of Him all the prophets bear witnesses that through His name everyone who believes in Him receives forgiveness of sins." While Peter was still speaking these words, the Holy Spirit fell upon all those who were listening to the message. And all the circumcised believers who had come with Peter were amazed, because the gift of the Holy Spirit had been poured out upon the Gentiles also. For they were hearing them speaking in tongues and exalting God. Then Peter answered, "Surely no one can refuse the water for these to be baptized who have received the Holy Spirit just as we did, can He?" And he ordered them to be baptized in the name of Jesus Christ. Then they asked him to stay on for a few days.}

(5) The Philippian jailer and his house repented when witnessed to by Paul and Silas; the evidence of repentance followed: (Page 1062-Acts 16:26:34). {And suddenly there came a great earthquake, so that the foundations of the prison house were shaken; and immediately all the doors were opened, and everyone's chains were unfastened. And when the jailer had been aroused out of sleep and had seen the prison doors were opened, he drew his sword and was about to kill himself, supposing that the prisoners had escaped. But Paul cried out with a loud voice, saying, "Do yourself no harm, for we are all here!" And he called for lights and rushed in and, trembling with fear, he fell down before Paul and Silas, and after he brought them out, he said, "Sirs, what must I do to be saved?" And he said, "Believe in the Lord Jesus, and you shall be saved, I you and your household." And they spoke with the word of the Lord to him together with all who were in the house. And he took them that very hour of the night and washed their wounds, and immediately he was baptized, he and all his household. And he brought them into his house and set food before them, and rejoiced greatly, having believed in God with his whole household. }

Repentance is a change of heart, and the will.
The proof of repentance is:
 (1) Turning from "transgressions": (Page770-Ezek.18:30 OT). {"Therefore I will judge you, O house of Israel,

each according to his conduct," declares the Lord God. "Repent and turn away from all your transgressions, so that iniquity may not become a stumbling block to you.}

(2) Turning to God.
(3) Followed by good deeds (above verse).

MASTER OUTLINE NUMBER THIRTEEN

THE NEW BIRTH

It is of the utmost importance that we have a clear understanding of what Jesus meant when, speaking with Nicodemus, He said, "You must be born again." The new birth is a spiritual birth. It is as much as the natural birth; it is not just a figure of speech. The first birth is of the seed of man.

The second birth is of the seed of God. (Page 1190-1Pet. 1:23). {For you have been born again not of seed which is perishable, but imperishable, that is, through the living and abiding word of God.}

Therefore, you cannot become a child of God by joining the church, any more than a monkey could become a man by joining the human race. He may act like a man, dress like a man and try to live like a man-but he would still be a monkey. Now, if by some miracle, the monkey could be born again of the seed of man then- and only then-could he become a man. The only way to become a child of God is to be "born again": (Page 1014-John 3:3). {Jesus answered and said to him, "Truly, truly, I say to you, unless one is born again, he cannot see the kingdom of God."}

Not of the seed which is perishable but imperishable, that is, through the living and abiding word of God." What is the new birth?

The new birth is a new creation: (Page 1116-2Cor. 5:17). {Therefore if any man is in Christ, he is a new creature; the old things passed away; behold, new things have come.}

The new birth is a spiritual resurrection:(Page 1131-Eph.2:1-9). {And you were dead in your trespasses and sins, in which you formerly walked according to the course of this world, according to the prince of the power of the air, of the spirit that is now working in the sons of disobedience. Among them we too all formerly lived in the lusts of our flesh, indulging the desires of the flesh and of the mind, and were by nature children of wrath, even as the rest. But God, being rich in mercy, because of His Great love with which He loved us, even when we were dead in our transgressions, made us alive together with Christ (by grace you have been saved), and raised up with Him, and seated us with Him in the heavenly places, in Christ Jesus, in order that in the ages to come He might show surpassing riches of His grace in kindness toward us in Christ Jesus. For by grace you have been saved through faith; and that not of your selves, it is the gift of God; not as a result of works, that no one should boast.}

The new birth is regeneration: (Page 1166-Titus 3:5). {He saved us, not on the bases of deeds which we have done in righteousness, but according to His mercy, by the washing of regeneration and renewing by the Holy Spirit.}

The new birth is partaking of the divine nature of God: (Page 1194-2Pet. 1:4). {For by these He has granted to us His precious and magnificent promises, in order that by them you might become partakers of the divine nature, having escaped the corruption that is in the world of lust.}

The new birth is receiving Jesus Christ as Savior and Lord, by faith: (Page 1012-John1:12). {But as many as received Him, to them He gave the right to become children of God, even those who believe in His name.}

The new birth is being made the "righteousness of God": (Page 1116-2Cor. 5:21. {He made Him who knew no sin to be sin on our behalf, that we might become the righteousness of God in Him}.

The new birth is compulsory if you are to become a child of God: You must be born again."

JESUS AND THE TWO BIRTHS

(Page 1014-John 3:1-8). {Now there was a man of the Pharisees, named Nicodemus. A ruler of the Jews; This man came to Him by night, and said to Him, "Rabbi, we know that you have come from God as a teacher; for no one can do these things signs that You do unless God is with him." Jesus answered and said to him, "Truly, truly. I say to you, unless one is born again, he cannot see the kingdom of God." Nicodemus said to Him, "How can a man be born when he is old? He cannot enter a second time into his mother's womb and be born, can he?" Jesus answered, "Truly, truly, I say to you, unless one is born of water and the Spirit, he cannot enter into the kingdom of God. That which is born of the flesh is flesh, and that which is born of the Spirit is spirit. Do not marvel that I said to you, 'You must be born again.' The wind blows where it wishes and you hear the sound of it, but do not know where it comes from and where it is going; so is everyone who is born of the Spirit."}

In the above Scriptures, we see Jesus and Nicodemus face to face- Jesus the Son of God, and Nicodemus the son of natural man. Nicodemus was a very religious man, but he was not a child of God. What a shock it must have been to learn that his religion was not enough! He came to Jesus, addressing Him saying, "You have come from God as a teacher." Jesus knew Nicodemus, as He knows all men: (Page1014-John 1:24.25). {But Jesus on His part, was not entrusting Himself to them, for He knew all men, and because He did not need anyone to bear witness concerning man for He Himself knew what was in man.}

And Jesus knew that he needed more than a teacher - he need a Savior. He needed more than religion - he needed regeneration. He needed more than the law - he needed life. Jesus began by going right to the point when He said, "You must be born again." Nicodemus asked, "How can a man be born when he is old?" Then Jesus pointed out dissimilarity in the two births: "That which is born of the flesh is flesh" (the flesh will never change); and "that which is born of the Spirit is spirit" (the Spirit will never change, above verse).

First, let us take a brief look at the flesh birth.
- (1) It produces an old, sinful nature: (Page 529-Ps. 51:5 OT). {Behold, I was brought forth in iniquity, And in sin my mother conceived me.}

(2) It produces a perishable nature: (Page 1190-1Pet. 1:23). {for you have been born again not of seed which is perishable but imperishable, that is through the living and abiding word of God.}

(3) It produces an old nature under the sentence of death: (Page 1087-Rom 6:23). {For the wages of sin is death, but the free gift of God is eternal life in Christ Jesus our Lord.}

(4) It produces an old nature that makes every person a child of the devil: (Page 1201-1John 3:10). {By this the children of God and the children of the devil are obvious: anyone who does not practice righteousness is not of God, nor the one who does not love his brother.} Also: (Page 1024-John8:44). {"You are of your father the devil, and you want to do the desires of your father. He was a murderer from the beginning, and does not stand in the truth, because there is no truth in him. Whenever he speaks a lie, he speaks his own nature; for he is a liar, and the father of lies.}

Second, let us say a word about the new birth:

(1) It produces a sinless nature: (Page 1201- 1John3:9). {No one who is born of God practices sin, because His seed abides in him; and he cannot sin, because he is born of God}.

(2) It produces a nature that cannot sin: (Page 1201-1John 3:9).

(3) It produces a divine nature: (Page 1116-2Cor.5:21). {He made Him who knew no sin to be sin on our behalf, that we might become the righteousness of God in Him.}

(4) It produces a divine nature: (Page 1194-2Pet. 1:4). {For by these He has granted to us His precious and magnificent promises, in order that by them you might become partakers of the divine nature, having escaped the corruption that is in the world by lust.}

Every born again person has two natures: the old from the old birth, and the new from the new birth. By the old birth, we are children of the flesh; by the new birth, we are the children of God. This is why "You must be born again."

THE NEW BIRTH ISSUES A NEW, SINLESS NATURE

(Page 1201-1John3:9). {No one who is born of God practices sin, because His seed abides in him; and he cannot sin, because he is born of God.}

This is one of the most misunderstood verses of the Bible. Do not try to understand it in the light of personal experience. Keep in mind that the above verse is speaking of the new nature- not the old nature- because the old nature is not born of God. The old nature is born of fallen man and is depraved. The new nature is born of God and is holy.

First let us see what this verse says about the new nature:
(1) The new nature does not commit sin, because it is the product of the seed. (sperm of God.)
(2) The new nature cannot sin, because it is the divine nature of God: (Page 1194-2Pet. 1:4). {For by these He has granted to us His precious and magnificent promises, in order that by them you might become partakers of the divine nature, having escaped the corruption that is in the world by lust.} And since God cannot sin, the new nature that issues from His holy seed cannot sin.

Second, let us see what the Bible says about the old nature:
(1) The old nature does sin any time you let in sin: (Page 1086- Rom. 6:12). {Therefore do not let sin reign in your mortal body that you should obey its lusts.} As a child of God, you will keep under the old nature: (Page 1105-1cor. 9:27). {but I buffet my body and make it my slave, lest possibly, after I have preached to others, I myself should be disqualified.} By not yielding to the desires of the flesh; or the old nature will keep you

under, and you will live a defeated Christian life: (Page 1086-Rom.6:13). {and do not go on presenting the members of your body to sin as instruments of unrighteousness; but present yourselves to God as those alive from dead, and your members as instruments of righteousness to God.}

(2) There is nothing good in the old nature: (Page 1087-Rom. 7:18). {For I know that nothing good dwells in me, that is, in my flesh; for the wishing is present in me, but the doing of the good is not.} The power to live a righteous life cannot be found in the old nature; it can be found only in the new: (Page 1124-Gal. 2:20). {"I have been crucified with Christ; and it is no longer I who live, but Christ lives in me; and the life which I now live in the flesh I live by faith in the Son of God, who loved me, and delivered Himself up for me."}

If you have been "born again" you have two natures- the old and the new-and you are walking according to one of the two. Examine your Christian walk in the light of God's word: (Page 1088-Rom. 8:5.6). {For those who are according to the flesh set their minds on the things of the flesh, but those who are according to the Spirit, the things of the Spirit. For the mind set on the flesh is death, but the mind set on the Spirit is life and peace.}

THE NEW BIRTH IS IMPERISHABLE

(Page 1190- 1Pet. 1:23). {For you have been born again not of seed perishable but imperishable, that is, through the living and abiding word of God.}

In the above verse, we have two seeds, two births, and two natures.

(1) The corruptible seed issues a corruptible nature: (Page 1082-Rom.1:23). {And exchange the glory of the incorruptible God for an image in the form of corruptible man and of birds and four footed animals and crawling creatures.} The seed of man became

depraved in the seed of Adam when he sinned in the garden or Eden: (Page 3-Gen.3:6-10 OT}. {When the woman saw that the tree was good for food, and that it was a delight to the eyes, and that the tree was desirable to make one wise, she took from its fruit and ate; and she gave also to her husband with her, and he ate. Then the eyes of both of them were opened, and they knew they were naked; and they sewed fig leaves together and made themselves loin coverings. And they heard the sound of the Lord God walking in the garden in the cool of the day, and the man and his wife hid themselves from the presence of the Lord God among the trees of the garden. Then the Lord called to the man, and said to him, "Where are you?" And He said, "I heard the sound of Thee in the garden, and I was afraid because I was naked; so I hid my self."} Corruptible man can produce only corruptible seed: (Page 919-Matt. 7:18). {A good tree cannot produce bad fruit, nor can a bad tree produce good fruit.} "All have sinned…": (Page1084-Rom. 3:23). {for all have sinned and fall short of the glory of God.} Because all are born in sin: (Page 529- Ps. 51:5 OT). {Behold, I was brought forth in iniquity, And in sin my mother conceived me.} You are not a sinner because of sin- you sin because you are a sinner.

(2) The incorruptible seed issues an incorruptible nature: (Page 1194-2Pet. 1:4). {For by these He has granted to us His precious and magnificent promises, in order that by them you might become partakers of the divine nature, having escaped the corruption that is in the world by lust.} You cannot corrupt that which is incorruptible; therefore the incorruptible seed of God issues a new nature that cannot be corrupted at any time, or in any way. The new birth produces the life of Christ, and this life is made living in man by the indwelling of Holy Spirit: (Page 1088—Rom. 8:8.9).

{and those who are in the flesh cannot please God. However, you are not in the flesh but in the Spirit, if indeed the Spirit of God dwells in you. But if anyone does not have the Spirit of Christ, he does not belong to Him.}

The seed of man is corruptible; the birth of man is natural. Therefore, the nature of man is sinful. The seed of God is incorruptible; the new birth is spiritual. Therefore, the new nature is sinless.

THE NEW BIRTH-ITS MEANS

(Page 1015-John 3:14-18). {And as Moses lifted up the serpent in the wilderness, even so must the Son of Man be lifted up; that whoever believes may in Him have eternal life.}

"Moses lifted up the serpent in the wilderness": (Page147 Num.-21:5-9 OT). {And the Lord sent fiery serpents among the people and they bit the people, so that many people of Israel died. So the people came to Moses and said, "We have sinned, because we have spoken against the Lord and you; intercede with the Lord, that He may remove the serpents from us." And Moses interceded for the people. Then the Lord said to Moses, "Make a fiery serpent, and set it on a standard; and it shall come about, that everyone who is bitten, when he looks at it, he shall live." And Moses made a bronze serpent and set it on a standard; and it came about, that if a serpent bit any man, when he looked to the bronze serpent, he lived.}

He lifted up the serpent for a sinful, disobedient people. When anyone was bitten by a serpent, he a choice: He could humble himself and by a simple act of faith look and live: (Page 667-Is.45:22 OT). {Turn to Me, and be saved, all the ends of the earth; For I am God, and there is no other.} Or he could refuse to look upon the serpent of bronze and die. Even see the Son of Man be lifted up. Just as the serpent in the wilderness was the only means for the healing of Israel, so the death of Jesus Christ is the only means for new birth. And the only way to appropriate the regenerating power of God is by faith in the vicarious death, burial, and resurrection of Jesus Christ: (Page 1109-1Cor. 15:1-4). {Now I make known to you, brethren, the gospel which I preached to you, which also you received, in which also you stand, by which also you are saved, if you hold fast the word which I preached to you, unless you believed in vain. For I delivered to you as of first importance what I also received, that Christ died for our sins according to the Scriptures, and that He was buried, and that He was raised on the third day according to the Scriptures.}

The sinner must come to Christ by faith, believing:

   (1) That Christ died for sins according to the Scriptures: (Page 673-Is.53:1-12 OT). {Who has believed our message? And to whom has the arm of the Lord been revealed? For He grew before Him like a tender shoot. And like a root out of parched ground; He has no stately form or majesty That we should look upon Him, Nor appearance that we should be attracted to Him. He was despised and forsaken of men, A man of sorrows, and acquainted with grief; And like one form whom men hide their face, He was despised, and we did not esteem Him. Surely our griefs He Himself bore, And our sorrows He carried; Yet we ourselves esteemed Him stricken, Smitten of God, and afflicted. But He was pierced through for our transgressions, He was crushed for out iniquities; The chastening for our well-being fell upon Him. And by His scourging we are healed. All of us like sheep have gone astray. Each of us has turned to his own way; but the Lord has caused the iniquity of us all To fall on Him. He was oppressed and He was afflicted, Yet He did not open His mouth; Like a lamb that is led to the slaughter, And like a sheep that is silent before its shearers, So He did not open His mouth. By oppression and judgment He was taken away; And as for His generation, who considered That He was cut off out of the land of the living, For the transgression of my people to whom the stroke was

due? His grave was assigned with wicked men, Yet He was a rich man in His death, Because He had done no violence, Nor was there any deceit in His mouth. But the Lord was pleased To crush Him, putting Him to grief; If He would render Himself as a guilt offering, He will see His offspring, He will prolong His days, And good pleasure of the Lord will prosper in His hand. As a result of the His anguish of His soul, He will see it and be satisfied; By His knowledge the Righteous one, My servant, will justify the many, As He will bear their iniquities, Therefore I will allot Him a portion with the great, And He will divide the booty with the strong; Because He poured out Himself to death, And was numbered with the transgressors; Yet He Himself bore the sin of many, And interceded for the transgressors.} Also: (Page 876-Zech.13:6 OT). {"And no one will say to him, 'What are these wounds between you arms?' Then he will say, 'Those with which I was wounded in the house of my friends.'}

(2) And He that was buried. This is the proof of His death. He was in the grave three days and nights.

(3) And that He rose again the third day according to the Scriptures. This is the gospel that saves-but it is powerless to save until the sinner believes it: (Page 1081-Rom 1:16). {For I am not ashamed of the gospel, for it is the power of God for salvation to every one who believes, to the Jew first and also to the Greek.}

The means of the new birth is found in that:

(1) "God so loved the world, that He gave His only begotten Son":- (Page 1015-John 3:16). {"For God so loved the world, that He gave His only begotten Son, that whoever believes in Him should not perish, but have eternal life.} To be the only means of the new birth. Also: (Page 1046- Acts 4:12). {"And there is salvation in no one else; for there is no other name under heaven that has been given among men, by

which we must be saved."}
(2) Jesus Christ gladly came into the world to become the only means of the new birth: (Page 1029-John 12:27). {"Now my soul has become troubled; and what shall I say, 'Father, save Me from this hour'? But for this purpose I came to this hour.} Also: (Page 1034-John17:1-5). {These things Jesus spoke; and lifting up His eyes to heaven, He said, "Father, the hour has come; glorify Thy Son, that the Son may glorify Thee, even as Thou gavest Him authority over all mankind, that to all whom Thou hast given Him, He may give eternal life. And this is eternal life, that they may know Thee, the only true God, and Jesus Christ, whom Thou hast sent. I glorified Thee on the earth, having accomplished the work which Thou hast given Me to do. And now, glorify Thou Me together with Thyself, Father, with the glory which I had with Thee before the world was."}
(3) The Holy Spirit came into the world on the day of Pentecost to convince men of their need of the new birth: (Page 1033-John 16:7-11). {"But I tell you the truth, it is to your advantage that I go away; for if I do not go away, the helper shall not come to you; but if I go, I will send Him to you. And He, when He comes, will convict the world concerning sin, and righteousness and judgment; concerning sin, because they do not believe in Me; and concerning righteousness, because I go to the Father, and you no longer behold Me; and concerning judgment, because the ruler of this world has been judged.}

A personal faith in the death, burial, and resurrection of Jesus Christ is the only means of the new birth.

THE NEW BIRTH-ITS THREEFOLD PROOF

(Page 1203-1John 5:1). {Whoever believes that Jesus is the Christ is born of God; and whoever loves the Father loves the child born of Him.}

Every "born again" child of God has the threefold proof of the new birth-proof that he is a child of God. This threefold proof is: first, inward proof; Second, outgoing proof; and third, outward proof.

(1) "Whoever believes that Jesus is the Son of God" (above in verse 1). My faith in Christ-that He is God-is personal evidence that I am a child of God. (Page 1203-1John 5:10-13). {The one who believes in the Son of God has the witness in himself; the one who does not believe God has made Him a liar, because he has not believed in the witness that God has borne concerning His Son. And the witness is this, that God has given us eternal life, and this life is in His Son. He who has the Son has the life; he who does not have the Son of God does not have life. These things I have written to you who believe in the name of the Son of God, in order that you may know that you have eternal life.} This in inward proof of the new birth.

(2)"Everyone who loves God is born of God": (Page 1202-1 John 4:7-11). {Beloved, let us love one another, for love is from; and everyone who loves is born of God. The one who does not love does not know God, for God is love. By this the love of God was manifested in us, that God has sent His only begotten son into the world so that we might live through Him. In this is love, not that we loved God, but that He loved us and sent His Son to be the propitiation for our sins. Beloved, if God so loved us, we also ought to love one another.} We are to love our fellow man with the love of God. This we are not capable of doing in the flesh; we must let God love man through us: (Page 1085-Rom. 5:5). {and hope does not disappoint, because the love of God has been poured out within our hearts through the Holy Spirit who was given to us.} This is outgoing proof of the new birth.

(3) "Everyone also who practices righteousness is born of Him": (Page 1200-1John 2:29). {If you know that He is righteous, you know that everyone also who practices righteousness is born of Him.} If you are born of God, you will make it a practice of doing right at all times and at all cost: (Page 1116-2Cor.5:17). {Therefore in any man is in Christ, he is a new creature; the old things passed away; behold, new things have come.} This is outward of the new birth.

If you do not have the threefold proof of the new birth, now is the time to get on your knees and accept Jesus Christ as your personal Savior-by faith in His vicarious death, burial, and resurrection.

MASTER OUTLINE NUMBER FOURTEEN

GOD'S PLAN OF SALVATION

There are seven facts revealed in God's plan of salvation, and as you study them, keep in mind that this is God's plan-not man's-it is God's. There is no other plan that can save your lost soul and make you a child of God: (Page 1046-Acts 4:12). {"And there is salvation in no one else; for there is no other name under heaven that has been given among men, by which we are saved."}

All roads lead to Rome, but all religions do not lead to God and salvation. There is only one way, and that is God's way; and God's way is a person, and that person is His Son the Lord Jesus Christ: (Page 1031-John 14:6). {Jesus said to him, "I am the way, and the truth, and the life; no one comes to the Father, but through Me.}

God's salvation is threefold:

First, Christ appeared on this earth to save you from the penalty of sin, by putting away sin by the sacrifice of Himself on the cross: (Page 1178- Heb. 9:26). {Otherwise, He would have needed to suffer often since the foundation of the world; but now once at the consummation of the ages He has been manifested to put away sin by the sacrifice of Himself.}

Second, He appeared in heaven, in the presence of God, after His resurrection, to save you from the power of sin: (Page 1177-Heb. 9:24). {For Christ did not enter a holy place made with hands, a mere copy of the true one, but into heaven itself, now to appear in the presence of God for us;} Also: (Page 1199-1John 2:1.2). {My little children, I am writing these things to you that you may not sin. And if anyone sins, we have an advocate with the Father, Jesus Christ the righteous; and He himself is the propitiation for our sins; and not for ours only, but also for those of the whole world.}

Third, He will appear again on this earth, the second time, as "Lord of lords and King of kings" to save you from the very presence of sin: (Page 1178-Heb. 9:28). {so Christ also, having been offered once to bear the sins of many, shall appear a second time for salvation without reference to sin, to those who eagerly await Him.}

Now come the seven facts of salvation with an open mind and a receptive heart, that God may bring salvation to your soul.

IT IS A FACT THAT GOD LOVES YOU

(Page 1015- John 3:16). {:For God so love the world, that He gave His only begotten Son, that whoever believes in Him should not perish, but have eternal life.}

It is an eternal fact that God loves you with an everlasting love that cannot be fathomed; it is so boundless that it can only be known by faith. The little word "so" in the above verse is most expressive. It gives you some concept of the magnitude of God's love. God so loved you, that He gave His only begotten Son, to be made sin for you, that you might become the righteousness of God in Him: (Page 1116-2Cor. 5:21). {He made Him who knew no sin to be sin on our behalf, that we might become the righteousness of God in Him.}

Jesus Christ was made that which God hates: sin-that you might become that which God loves: righteousness. Because God so loves you, you can exchange your sins for His righteousness. Could you ask for greater evidence of love? Calvary is proof that God loves you, and longs to save you.

Before turning to the next fact, admit to yourself that: "God loves me."

IT IS A FACT THAT YOU ARE A SINNER

(Page 1084-Rom. 3:23). {For all have sinned and fall short of the glory of God.}

What is sin?

Sin is lawlessness: (Page 1201-1John 3:4). {Everyone who practices sin also practices lawlessness; and sin is lawlessness.}

Sin is unbelief; It calls God a liar: (Page 1203- 1John 5:10). {The one who believes in the Son of God has the witness in himself; the one who does not believe God has made Him a liar, because he has not believed in the witness that God has borne concerning His Son.}

Sin is active rebellion against God: (Page 270-1Sam.15:23 OT). {"For rebellion is as the sin of divination, And insubordination is as iniquity and idolatry. Because you have rejected the word of the Lord, He has also rejected you from being king."}

Sin is passive rebellion against God: (Page 627-Is.1:2 OT). {Listen, O heavens, and hear, O earth; For the Lord speaks, "Sons I have reared and brought up, But they have revolted against Me."}

All unrighteousness is sin: (Page 1203-1John 5:17). {All unrighteousness is sin, and there is a sin not leading to death.}

God who cannot lie, said: "All have sinned." All includes you. You have sinned against God by thought, word, and deed. You have committed sins of commission and sins of omission. In the sight of God, you are a lost sinner.

Before turning to the next fact, admit to yourself: I am a lost sinner,because I have sinned.

IT IS A FACT THAT YOU ARE DEAD IN SIN

(Page 1087-Rom. 6:23). {For the wages of sin is death, but the free gift of God is eternal life in Christ Jesus our Lord.}

You have already confessed and admitted that you are a sinner. Now God would have you know that "…the wages of sin is death." You are dead in sin until you accept Christ as personal Savior. The Apostle Paul said: (Page 1131-Eph. 2:1). {And you were dead in your trespasses and sins.} To be saved is to be spiritually alive in Christ.

What is death?
- (1) Death is spiritual separation. Your sins have separated you from God; you are dead in your sins.
- (2) Death is physical separation. It separates the spirit and soul from the body.

(3) Death is eternal separation. If you remain lost in your sins, you will stand before God at the great white throne judgment. And there your sins will separate you from the mercy of God forever; this is Hades: (Page 1224-Rev. 20:11-15). {And I saw a great white throne and Him who sat upon it, from whose presence earth and heaven fled away, and no place was found for them. And I saw the dead, the great and the small, standing before the throne, and books were opened; and another book was opened, which is the book of life; and the dead were judged from the things which were written in the books, according to their deeds. And the sea gave up the dead which were in it, and death and Hades gave up the dead which were in them; and they were judged, everyone of them according to their deeds. And death and Hades were thrown into the lake of fire. This is the second death, the lake of fire. And if anyone's name was not found written in the book of life, he was thrown into the lake of fire.} You know that God loves you, and that you are a sinner-dead in sins.

Before turning to the next fact, admit to your self: "I am dead in sins."

IT IS A FACT THAT CHRIST DIED FOR YOU

(Page 1085-Rom.5:6-8). {For while we were still helpless, at the right time Christ died for the ungodly. For one will hardly die for a righteous man; though perhaps for the good man some one would dare even to die. But God demonstrates His love toward us, in that while we were yet sinners, Christ died for us. Much more then, having now been justified by His blood, we shall be saved from the wrath of God through Him.}

He died for those who are unlike God; this includes you. "While we were yet sinners, Christ died for us" (above verse 8). (Page 1116-2Cor.5:21). {He made Him who knew no sin to be sin on our behalf, that we might become the righteousness of

God in Him.} "Knowing that you were redeemed with perishable things like silver or gold…but with precious blood, as a lamb unblemished and spotless, the blood of Christ": (Page 1189- 1 Pet.1:18.19). {Knowing that you were not redeemed with perishable things like silver or gold from your futile way of life inherited from your forefathers, but with the precious blood of the lamb unblemished and spotless, the blood of Christ.}

(Page1192-1 Pet. 3:18). "For Christ died for our sins once and for all, the just and the unjust, in order that He might bring us to God, having been put to death in the flesh, but made alive in the spirit."

"Christ died for our sins according to the Scriptures": (Page 1109-1Cor. 15:3). {For I delivered to you as of first importance what I also received, that Christ died for our sins according to the Scriptures.}

In light of these wonderful Scriptures, will you now thank God for His great love in sending His Son to bear your sins in His own body on the cross, and admit to yourself that: "Christ died on Calvary for me."

IT IS A FACT THAT YOU CAN BE SAVED BY FAITH IN THE LORD JESUS CHRIST

(Page 1063-Acts 16:30.31). {And after he had brought them out, he said, "Sirs, what must I do to be saved?" And they said, "Believe in the Lord Jesus and you shall be saved, you and your household."}

The Philippian jailer asked Paul and Silas: "Sirs, what must I do to be saved?" The answer was a quick response, and positive in content: "Believe in the Lord Jesus, and you shall be saved, you and your household." Paul and Silas preached the gospel to the jailer and those in his house; they believed and were saved.

What is this gospel that saves when believed?
First, it is: "that Christ died for our sins."
Second: "that He was buried."
Third: "that He was raised on the third day"

(Page 1109-1Cor. 15:3.4). {For I delivered to you as of first importance what I also received, that Christ died for our sins according to the Scriptures, and that he was buried, and that He was raised up on the third day according to the Scriptures.}

Jesus Christ the God-Man died for you, was buried for you, and rose from the dead for you; and is now at the right hand of the Father interceding for you: (Page 1199-1John 2:1). {My little children, I am writing these things to you that you may not sin. And if anyone sins, we have an advocate with the Father, Jesus Christ the righteous.}

"For I am not ashamed of the gospel, for it is the power of God for salvation to everyone who believes": (Page 1081-Rom. 1:16). {For I am not ashamed of the gospel, for it is the power of God for salvation to everyone who believes, to the Jew first and also to the Greek.}

The gospel is the power of God for salvation only when you believe. Your faith in Jesus Christ releases the power of God that saves your soul. The man born blind received physical sight by a miracle; but spiritual sight came when Jesus asked, "Do you believe in the Son of Man?" He answered, "Lord, I believe": (Page 1025-John 9:35-38). {Jesus heard that they had put him out; and finding him, He said, "Do you believe in the Son of Man?" He answered and said, "And who is He, Lord, that I May believe in Him?" Jesus said to him, "You have both seen Him, and He is the one who is talking with you." And he said, "Lord I believe." And he worshiped Him.}

Salvation came to Thomas when he believed and confessed, "My Lord and My God": (Page 1038-John 20:24-29). {But Thomas, one of the twelve, called Didymus, was not with them when Jesus came. The other disciples therefore were saying to him, "We have seen the Lord!" But he said to them, "Unless I shall see in His hands the imprint of the nails, and put my finger into the place of the nails, and put my hand into His side, I will not believe." And after eight days again His disciples were inside, and Thomas with them. Jesus came, the doors having been shut, and stood in their midst, and said, "Peace be with you." Then He said to Thomas, "Reach here your finger, and see My hands; and reach here your hand, and put it into My side; and be not unbelieving, bur believing." Thomas answered and said to Him, "My Lord and my God!" Jesus said to him, "Because you have seen Me, have you believed? Blessed are they who did not see, and yet believed."}

When you confess with your mouth the Lord Jesus Christ, and believe in your heart that God raised Him from the dead, you will be saved: (Page 1090-Rom.10:9.10). {that if you confess with your mouth Jesus as Lord, and believe in your heart that God raised Him from the dead, you shall be saved; for with the heart the man believes, resulting in righteousness, and with the mouth he confesses, resulting in salvation.}

Accept Him now by faith, and pray this prayer: "Lord Jesus, I know You love me, because You died on the cross bearing my sins. Thank you, Lord, for revealing to me my lost, sinful condition. I confess that I am a sinner, dead in sin, and cannot save myself. I do now by faith, gladly accept You as my personal Savior, and thank You, Lord, for eternal salvation. Amen."

IT IS A FACT YOU CAN BE SAVED AND KNOW IT

(Page 1203-1 John 5:10-13). {The one who believes in the Son of God has the witness in himself; the one who does not believe God has made Him a liar, because he has not believed in the witness that God has borne concerning His Son. And the witness is this, that God has given us eternal life, and this life is in His Son. He who has the Son has the life; he who does not have the Son of God does not have the life. These things I have written to you who believe in the name of the Son of God, in order that you may know that you have eternal life.}

"…that you may know that you have eternal life…." (above verse 13). Upon the authority of God's Word, you can be saved and know it. Your faith in God's infallible Word is your assurance of salvation. "He who believes in the Son has (present tense) eternal life": (Page 1016- John 3:36). {"He who believes in the Son has eternal life; but he who does not obey the Son shall not see life, but the wrath of God abides on him."}

The Bible is a book of certainties. It strengthens convictions, and establishes beliefs. God would have you know:

(1) That you are now a child of God: (Page 1200- 1John 3:2). {Beloved, now we are children of God, and it has not appeared as yet what we shall be. We know that, when He appears, we shall be like Him, because we shall see Him just as He is.}

(2) That you have been made the righteousness of God in Christ: (Page 1116-2Cor. 5:21). {He made Him who knew no sin to be sin on our behalf, that we might become the righteousness of God in Him.} Also: (Page1090-Rom. 10:1-4). {Brethren, my hearts desire and my prayer to God for them is for their salvation. For I bear witness that they have a zeal for God, but not in accordance with knowledge. For not knowing about God's righteousness, and seeking to establish their own, they did not subject themselves to the righteousness of God. For Christ is the end of the law for righteousness to everyone who believes.}

(3) You are a new creature in Christ: (Page 1116-2Cor. 5:7). {for we walk by faith, not by sight-}

(4)That you are now a son and heir of God: (Page 1126-Gal. 4:7). {Therefore you are no longer a slave, but a son; and if a son, then an heir through God.}

Could you have greater assurance than is found in God's infallible Word? (Page 941-Matt. 24:35). {Heaven and earth will pass away, but My words shall not pass away.}

IT IS A FACT THAT GOD SAVED YOU TO OBEY HIM

(Page 1048-Acts5:29). {But Peter and the apostles answered and said, "We must obey God rather than Men.}

"We must obey God rather than men" (Above verse). You now belong to Jesus Christ. He is your Lord and Master, and "no one can serve two masters": (Page 918-Matt 6:24). {"No one can serve two masters; for either he will hate the one and love the other, or he will hold to one and despise the other. You cannot serve God and mammon.}

Determine now to obey your Lord and Master, Jesus Christ, in all things:

(1) Unite with a New Testament church. "And the Lord adding to their number day by day those who were being saved": (Page 1044-Acts 2:47). {praising God, and having favor with all the people. And the Lord was adding to their number day by day those who were being saved.}

(2) Follow Him in the ordinance of baptism: (Page 1044-Acts 2:41). {So then, those who had received his word were baptized; and there were added that day about three thousands souls.} Baptism does not save; it is a witness of your faith in the death, burial, and resurrection of Christ: (Page 1086- Rom. 6:4). {Therefore we have been buried with Him through baptism into death, in order that as Christ was raised from the dead through the glory of the Father, so we too might walk in newness of life.}

(3) Join a Sunday school class, and study the Word of God children: (Page 1160-2Tim 2:15). {Be diligent to present yourself approved to God as a workman who does not need to be ashamed, handling accurately the word of truth.}

(4) Attend the worship services of your church: (Page 1178-Heb. 10:25). {not forsaking our own assembling together, as a habit of some, but encouraging one another, and all the more, as you see the day drawing near.} You need the preaching of God's Word and Christian fellowship.

(5) Be a faithful steward: (Page 1100-1Cor. 4:2). {In this case, moreover, it is required of stewards that one be found trustworthy.} All that you are and have belong

to God. "…you are not your own. For you are bought with a price…": (Page 1102-1Cor. 6:19.20). {Or do you not know that your body is a temple of the Holy Spirit who is in you, whom you have from God, and that you are not your own? For you have been bought with a price: therefore glorify God in your body.} As a faithful steward, you will pay God His tithe: (Page 880-Mal. 3:10 OT). {"Bring the whole tithe into the storehouse, so that there may be food in My house, and test Me now in this," says the Lord of hosts, "If I will not open the store windows of heaven, and pour out for you a blessing until it (there is not room enough) overflows."} The tithe is one tenth of your income, and it is the Lord's: (Page 121-Lev. 27:30 OT). {Thus all the tithe of the land, of the seed of the land or the fruit of the tree, is the Lord's; it is holy to the Lord.}

(6) Make time in your daily life to pray and read God's Word, that you may grow in the grace and knowledge of the Lord Jesus Christ.

MASTER OUTLINE NUMBER FIFTEEN

HOW TO WITNESS EFFECTIVELY

One day as Jesus walked by the sea of Galilee He saw two men, Simon, called Peter and Andrew, his brother. They were fishermen: (Page 915-Matt. 4:19). {And He said to them, "Follow Me and I will make you fishers of men."}

Soul winners are not born. Therefore to be an effective witness, you must be taught, trained, and motivated by the power of the Holy Spirit. Jesus took three years to teach and train His disciples in the art of soul winning. After His resurrection He instructed them to stay in Jerusalem and, "wait for what the Father had promised": (Page 1041-Acts 1:4-8). {And gathering them together, He commanded them not to leave Jerusalem, but to wait for what the Father had promised, "Which," He said, "You heard of from Me; for John baptized with water, but you shall be baptized with the Holy Spirit not many days from now." And so when they had come together, they were asking Him, saying, "Lord, is it at this time You are restoring the kingdom to Israel?" He said to them, "It is not for you to know times and epochs which the Father has fixed by His own authority; but you shall receive power when the Holy Spirit has come upon you; and you shall be My witnesses both in Jerusalem, and in all Judea and Samaria, and even to the remotest part of the earth."}

When the disciples asked Jesus if the time had come for Him to restore the kingdom of Israel, He answered, "It is not for you to know times or epochs which the Father has fixed by His own authority; but you shall receive power when the Holy Spirit has come upon you; and you shall be My witnesses..."

On the day of Pentecost, the hundred and twenty received power to witness; and any believer who will acquire the know-how can be an effective soul winner.

He can know that he and the Holy Spirit are a witnessing team. Peter said, "And we are witnesses of these things; and so is the Holy Spirit, whom God has given to those who obey Him": (Page 1049-Acts 5:32). {"And we are witnesses (In Him or Of Him) of these things; and so is the Holy Spirit, whom God has given to those who obey Him."}

Therefore, when you witness remember that "your body is a temple of the Holy Spirit who is in you": (Page 1102-1Cor. 6:19.20). {Or do you not know that your body is a temple (sanctuary) of the Holy Spirit who is in you, whom you have from God, and that you are not your own? For you have been bought with a price; therefore glorify God in your body.}

When you witness, trust the Holy Spirit to do three things:
(1) Illuminate the mind of the believer. All lost souls are in spiritual darkness: (Page 1115-2Cor. 4:3.4). {And even if our gospel is veiled, it is veiled to those who are perishing, in whose case the god of this world has blinded the minds of the unbelieving, that they might not see the light of the gospel of the glory of Christ, who is the image of God.}
(2) Stir the heart of the unbeliever: As Peter preached Christ the listeners, "were pierced to the heart": (Page 1044-Acts 2:37). {Now when they heard this, they were pierced (smitten in conscious) to the heart, and said to Peter and the rest of the apostles, "Brethren, what shall we do?"}
(3) Move the will of the unbeliever. The prodigal returned home when he came to his senses and said, "I will get up and go to my father": (Page 997-Luke 15:18). {'I will get up and go to my father, and will say to him, "Father, I have sinned against heaven, and in (before you) your sight.}

You may be up to-date in all modern techniques of soul winning and able to quote the necessary Scriptures without a flaw; but if you do not evangelize in the power of the Holy Spirit, you soul winning efforts will be ineffective. Approach this Master Outline with an open heart and receptive mind, willing to be made fishers of men.

THE IMPORTANCE OF WITNESSING

(Page 1090-Rom. 10:13-17.). {For "Whoever will call upon the name of the Lord will be saved." How then shall they call upon Him in whom they have not believed? And how shall they believe in Him whom they have not heard? And how shall they hear without a preacher? And how shall they preach, unless they are sent? Just as it is written, "How beautiful are the feet of those who bring (preach the gospel) glad tidings of good things!" However, they did not all heed the glad tidings; for Isaiah says, "Lord, who has believed our report?" So faith comes from hearing, and hearing by the word of Christ.}

"For Whoever will call upon the name of the Lord will be saved." (above verse 13). Do not lift this text out of context. There are three questions in verse 14 that must be considered along with verse 13, they are:

First question, "How then shall they call upon Him in whom they have not believed?" The answer is, the lost cannot call upon the name of the Lord to be saved until they believe;

> (1) "That Christ died for our sins according to the Scriptures,
> (2) And that He was buried,
> (3) And that He was raised on the third day according to the Scriptures": (Page 1109-1Cor. 15:1-4). {Now I make known to you, brethren, the gospel which I preached to you, which also you received, in which also you stand, by which also you are saved, if you hold fast the word which I preached to you, unless you believed in vain. For I delivered to you as of first importance what I also received, that Christ died for our sins according to the Scriptures, and that He was buried, and that He was raised on the third day according to the Scriptures.}

Second question, "And how shall they believe in Him whom they have not heard?" The answer is, the lost cannot believe in Him until they hear the good news of salvation.

(1) The eunuch had to hear to believe: (Page 1052-Acts 8:26-39). {But an angel of the Lord spoke to Philip saying, "Arise and go south to the road that descends from Jerusalem to Gaza." (This is a desert road.) And he arose and went; and behold, there was an Ethiopian eunuch, a court official of Candace, queen of the Ethiopians, who was in charge of all her treasure; and he had come to Jerusalem to worship. And he was returning and sitting in his chariot, and was reading the prophet Isaiah. And the Spirit said to Philip, "Go up and join this chariot." And Philip had run up, he heard him reading Isaiah the prophet, and said, "Do you understand what you are reading?" And he said, "Well how could I, unless someone guides me?" And he invited Philip to come up and sit with him. Now this passage of Scripture which he was reading was this: "He was led as a sheep to the slaughter; And as a lamb before its shearer is silent, So He does not open His mouth. In humiliation His judgment was taken away; Who shall relate His generation? For His life is removed from the earth." And the eunuch answered Philip and said, "Please tell me, of whom does the prophet say this? Of himself, or of someone else?" And Philip opened his mouth, and beginning from this Scripture he preached Jesus to him. And as they went along the road they came to some water; and the eunuch said, "Look! Water! What prevents me from being baptized?" And Philip said, "If you believe with all your heart, you may." And he answered and said, "I believe that Jesus Christ is the Son of God." And he ordered the chariot to stop; and they both went down into the water, Philip as well as the eunuch; and he baptized him. And when they came up out of the water, the Spirit of the Lord snatched Philip away; and the eunuch saw him no more, but went on his was rejoicing.}

(2) Paul had to hear to believe: (Page1053-Acts 9:1-18). {Now Silas was still breathing threats and murder against the disciples of the Lord, went to the high priest, and asked for letters from him to the synagogues as Damascus, so that if he found any belonging to the way, both men and women, he might bring them bound to Jerusalem. And it came about that as he journeyed, he was approaching Damascus, and suddenly a light from heaven flashed around Him; and he fell to the ground, and heard a voice saying to him, "Saul, Saul, why are you persecuting Me?" And he said, "Who art Thou, Lord?" And He said, "I am Jesus whom you are persecuting, but rise, and enter the city, and it shall be told you what you must do." And the men who traveled with him stood speechless, hearing the voice, but seeing no one. And Saul got up from the ground, and though his eyes were opened, he could see nothing; and leading him by the hand, they brought him into Damascus. And he was three days without sight, and neither ate nor drank. Now there was a certain disciple at Damascus, named Ananias; and the Lord said to him in a vision, "Ananias." And he said, "Behold here am I, Lord." And the Lord said to him, "Arise and go to the street called straight, and inquire at the house of Judas for a man from Tarsus named Saul, for behold, he is praying, and he has seen in a vision a man named Ananias come in and lay his hands on him, so that he might regain his sight." But Ananias answered, "Lord, I have heard from many about this man, how much harm he did to Thy saints at Jerusalem; and he has authority from the chief priests to bind all who call upon Thy name." But the Lord said to him, "Go, for he is a chosen instrument of Mine, to bear My name before the Gentiles and kings and the sons of Israel; for I will show him how much he must suffer for My names sake." And Ananias departed and

entered the house, and after laying his hands on him said, "Brother Saul, the Lord Jesus, who appeared to you on the road by which you coming, has sent me so that you may regain your sight, and be filled with the Holy Spirit." And immediately there fell from his eyes something like scales, and he regained his sight, and he arose and was baptized.}

(3) Cornelius had to hear to believe: (Page 1054-Acts10:1-48). {Now there was a certain man at Caesarea named Cornelius, a centurion of what was called the Italian (battalion) cohort, a devout man, and one who feared God with all his household, and gave many alms to the Jewish people, and prayed to God continually. About the ninth hour of the day he clearly saw in a vision an angel of God who had just come to him, and said to him, "Cornelius!" And fixing his gaze upon him and being much alarmed, he said, "What is it, Lord?" And he said to him, "Your prayers and alms have ascended as a memorial before God. And now dispatch some men to Joppa, and send for a man named Simon, who is also called Peter; he is staying with a certain tanner named Simon, whose house is by the sea." And when the angel who was speaking to him departed, he summoned two of his servants and a devout soldier of those who were in constant attendance upon him, and after he had explained everything to them, he sent them to Joppa. And the next day, as they were on their way, and approaching the city, Peter went up on the housetop about the sixth hour to pray. And he became hungry, and was desiring to eat; but while they were making preparations, he fell into a trance; and he beheld the great sky (heaven) opened up, and a certain object (vessel) like a great sheet coming down, lowered by four corners to the ground, and there were all kinds of four footed animals and crawling (Or possibly reptiles) creatures of the earth and birds of the

air (Heaven). And a voice came to him, "Arise, Peter, kill (sacrifice) and eat!" But Peter said, "By no means, Lord for I have never eaten anything unholy and unclean." And again a voice came to him a second time, "What God has cleansed, no longer consider unholy." And this happened three times; and immediately the object (vessel) was taken up into the sky (heaven). Now while Peter was greatly perplexed in mind as to what the vision which he had seen might be, behold, the men who had been sent by Cornelius, having asked directions for Simon's house, appeared at the gate. And calling out, they were asking whether Simon, called Peter, was staying there. And while Peter was reflecting on the vision, the Spirit said to him, "Behold, three men are looking for you. But arise, go downstairs, and accompany them without misgivings; for I have sent them Myself." And Peter sent down to the men and said, "Behold, I am the one you are looking for; what is the reason for which you have come?" "Cornelius, a centurion, a righteous and God-fearing man well spoken of by the entire nation of the Jews, was divinely directed by a holy angel to send for you to come to his house and hear a message from you." And so he invited them in and gave them lodging. And the next day he arose and went away with them, and some of the brethren from Joppa accompanied him. And on the following day he entered Caesarea. Now Cornelius was waiting for them, and called together his relatives and close friends. And when it came about that Peter entered, Cornelius met him, and fell at his feet and worshipped him But Peter raised him up, saying "Stand up; I too am just a man." And as he talked with him, he entered, and found many people assembled. And he said to them, "You yourselves know how unlawful it is for a man who is a Jew to associate with a foreigner or to visit him; and yet God has shown me that I should not call any man unholy or unclean. That is why I came without even raising any objection when I was sent for. And so I ask for what reason you have sent for me?" And Cornelius said, "Four days age to this hour, I was praying in my house during the ninth hour; and behold, a man stood before me in shining garments, and he said, 'Cornelius, your prayer has been heard and your alms have been remembered before God. Send therefore to Joppa, and invite Simon, who is called Peter, to come to you; he is staying at the house of Simon the tanner by the sea.' And so I sent to you immediately, and you have been kind enough to come. Now then, we are all present before God to hear all that you have been commanded by the Lord." And opening his mouth, Peter said: "I must certainly understand now that God is not one to show partiality, but in every nation the man who fears (reverences) Him and does what is right, is welcome to Him. The word which He sent to the sons of Israel, preaching peace through Jesus Christ (He is Lord of all)- you yourselves know the thing which took place throughout all Judea, starting from Galilee, after the baptism which John proclaimed. You know of Jesus of Nazareth, how God anointed Him with the Holy Spirit and with power, and how He went about doing good, and healing all who were oppressed by the devil; for God was with Him. And we are witnesses of all the things He did both in the land of the Jews and in Jerusalem. And they also put Him to death by hanging Him on a (wood) cross. "God raised Him up on the third day, and granted that He should become visible, not to all people, but to witnesses who were chosen beforehand by God, that is, to us, who ate and drank with Him after He arose from the dead. And He ordered us to preach (Proclaim) to the people, and solemnly to testify that this is the One who has been appointed by God as Judge of the living and the dead. Of Him all the prophets bear witness that through His name everyone who believes in Him receives forgiveness of sins." While Peter was still speaking these words, the Holy Spirit fell upon all those who were listening to the message. And all the circumcised believers who had come with Peter were amazed, because the gift of the Holy Spirit had been poured out upon the Gentiles also. For they were hearing them speaking with tongues and exalting God. Then Peter answered, "Surely no one can refuse the water for these to be baptized who have received the Holy Spirit just as we did, can he?" And He ordered them to be baptized in the name of Jesus Christ. Then they asked him to stay on for a few days.}

(4) The Philipplian jailer had to hear to believe: (Page 1062-Acts 16:25-40). {But about midnight Paul and Silas were praying and singing hymns of praise to God, and the prisoners were listening to them: and suddenly there came a great earthquake, so that the foundations of the prison were shaken; and immediately all the doors were opened, and everyone's chains were unfastened. And when the jailer had been roused out of his sleep and had seen the prison doors opened, he drew his sword and was about to kill himself, supposing that the prisoners had escaped. But Paul cried with a loud voice, saying, "Do yourself no harm, for we are all here!" And he called for lights and rushed in and, trembling with fear, he fell down before Paul and Silas, and after he brought them out, he said, "Sirs what must I do to be saved?" And they said, "Believe in the Lord Jesus, and you shall be saved, you and your household." And they spoke the word of the Lord to him together with all who were in the house. And he took them that very hour of the night and washed their wounds, and immediately he was

baptized, he and all his household. And he brought them into his house and set food before them, and rejoiced greatly, having believed in God with his whole household. Now when they came, the chief magistrates sent policemen, saying, "Release those men." And the jailer reported these words to Paul, saying, "The chief magistrates have sent to release you. Now therefore, come out and go in peace." But Paul said to them, "They have beaten us in public without trial, men who are Romans, and have thrown us into prison; and now they are sending us away secretly? No indeed! But let them come themselves and bring us out." And the policemen reported these words to the chief magistrates. And they were afraid when they heard that they were Romans. And they came and appealed to them, and when they had brought them out, they kept begging them to leave the city. And they went out of prison and entered the house of Lydia, and when they saw the brethren, they encouraged them and departed.}

Third question, "And how shall they hear without a preacher (witness)?" The answer is, they cannot hear the good news of salvation without a witness.

   (1) Three thousand were saved at Pentecost because the 120 witnessed.
   (2) The eunuch was saved because Philip witnessed.
   (3) Paul was saved because Stephen witnessed: (Page 1051-Acts 7:54-60). {Now when they heard this, they were cut to the quick, and they began gnashing their teeth at him. But being full of the Holy Spirit, he gazed intently into heaven and saw the glory of God, and Jesus standing at the right of God; and he said, "Behold, I see the heavens opened up and the Son of Man standing at the right hand of God." But they cried with a loud voice, and covered their ears, and they rushed upon him with one impulse. And when they had

driven him out of the city, they began stoning him and the witnesses laid aside their robes at the feet of a young man named Saul. And they went on stoning Stephen as he called upon the Lord and said, "Lord Jesus, receive my spirit!" And falling on his knees, he cried out with a loud voice, "Lord, do not hold this sin against them!" And having said this, he fell asleep.} Jesus the God-man witnessed, and Ananias witnessed: (Page 1053-Acts 9:1-18). {Now Saul, still breathing threats and murder against the disciples of the Lord, went to the high priest, and asked for letters from him to the synagogues at Damascus, so that if he found any belonging to the way, both men and women, he might bring them bound to Jerusalem. And it came about that as he journeyed, he was approaching Damascus, and suddenly a light from heaven flashed around him; and he fell to the ground, and heard a voice saying to him, "Saul, Saul, why are you persecuting Me?" And he said, "Who art Thou, Lord?" And He said, "I am Jesus whom you are persecuting, but rise, and enter the city, and it shall be told you what you must do." And the men who traveled with him stood speechless, hearing the voice, but seeing no one. And Saul got up from the ground, and though his eyes were opened, he could not see nothing; and leading him by the hand, they brought him to Damascus. And he was three days without sight, and neither ate nor drank. Now there was a certain disciple at Damascus, named Ananias; and the Lord said to him in a vision, "Ananias" And he said, "Behold, here am I, Lord." And the Lord said to him, "Arise and go to the street called Straight, and inquire at the house of Judas for a man from Tarsus named Saul, for behold, he is praying, and he has seen in a vision a man named Ananias come in and lay his hands on him, so that he might regain his sight." But Ananias answered, "Lord, I have heard from many about this man, how much harm he did to Thy saints at Jerusalem; and here he has authority from the chief priests to bind all who call upon Thy name." But the Lord said to him, "Go, for he is a chosen instrument of Mine, to bear My name before the Gentiles and kings and the sons of Israel; for I will show him how much he must suffer for My names sake." And Ananias departed and entered the house, and after laying his hands on him said, "Brother Saul, the Lord Jesus, who appeared to you on the road by which you were coming, has sent me so that you may regain your sight, and be filled with the Holy spirit." And immediately there fell from his eyes something like scales and he regained his sight, and he arose and was baptized.}

(4) Cornelius and his household were saved because Peter witnessed.

(5) The Philippian jailer and his household were saved because Paul and Silas witnessed.

(6) You were saved because someone witnessed to you.

According to the word of God, the lost cannot be saved without a witness. They must have a witness to hear, they must hear to believe, they must believe to call, and they must call to be saved. But they cannot call until they believe and they cannot believe until they hear and they cannot hear without a witness. "So faith (saving faith) comes from hearing" (above verse 17). We are not born with saving faith; it comes only when we hear the gospel. Therefore, it is of utmost importance that every born again child of God obey the great commission to evangelize, to go with the gospel.

THE QUALIFICATIONS OF A WITNESS

(Page 1143-Col. 2:6.7). {As you therefore have received Christ Jesus the Lord, so walk in Him, having been firmly rooted and now being built up in you faith, just as you were instructed, and overflowing with gratitude.}

A qualified witness is one who is:

(1) Established in the faith. To be established in the faith is to be rooted and grounded in God's Word. Peter said: (Page 1192-1Pet. 3:15). {But sanctify Christ as Lord in your hearts, always being ready to make a defense to everyone who ask you to give an account for the hope that is in you, yet with gentleness and reverence."} The fifteen Master Outline studies in the Christian Life New Testament were prepared to help establish you in the faith. Study them, carry your Bible with you and take advantage of every opportunity to ponder a portion of one of the great doctrines. They will give you a foundation on which to build a strong faith: (Page 1161-2Tim. 3:16.17). {All Scripture is inspired by God and profitable for teaching, for reproof, for correction, for training in righteousness; that the man of God may be adequate, equipped for every good work.}

(2) Saved and knows it. I know that I am saved because God tells me so in His word and God cannot lie. We have the:

(a) Witness of the Spirit: (Page 1088-Rom. 8:16). {The Spirit itself bears witness with our spirit that we are children of God.}

(b) The witness of the Word: (Page 1203-1 John 5:13). {These things I have written to you who believe in the name of the Son of God, in order that you may know that you have eternal life.}

(c) The witness of faith. "The one who believes in the Son of God has the witness in himself": (Page 1203-1John 5:9.10). {If we receive the witness of men, the witness of God is greater; for the witness of God is this, that He has borne witness concerning His Son. The one who believes in the Son of God has the witness in himself; the one who does not believe God has made Him a liar, because he has not believed in the witness that God has borne concerning His Son.}

(3) Separated. Paul said that he was "set apart for the gospel of God": (Page 1081-Rom. 1:1-16). {Paul, a bond-servant of Christ Jesus, called as an apostle, set apart for the gospel of God. Which He promised beforehand through the Scriptures, concerning His Son, who was born of a descendant of David according to the flesh, who was declared the Son of God with power by the resurrection from the dead, according to the spirit of holiness, Jesus Christ our Lord, through whom we have received grace and apostleship to bring about the obedience of faith among all the Gentiles, for His name's sake, among whom you also are the called of Jesus Christ; to all who are beloved of God in Rome, called as saints: Grace to you and peace from God our Father and the Lord Jesus Christ. First, I thank my God through Jesus Christ for you all, because your faith is being proclaimed throughout the whole world. For God, whom I serve in my spirit in the preaching of the gospel of His Son, is my witness as to how unceasingly I make mention of you, always in my prayers making request, if perhaps now at last by the will of God I may succeed in coming to you. For I long to see you in order that I may impart some spiritual gift to you, that you may be established; that is, that I may be encouraged together with you while among you, each of us by the other's faith, both yours and mine. And I do not want you to be unaware, brethren, that often I have planned to come to you (and have been prevented thus far) in order that I might obtain some fruit among you also, even as among the rest of the Gentiles. I am under obligation both to Greeks and to barbarians, both to the wise and to the foolish. Thus, for my part, I am eager to preach the gospel to you also who are in Rome. For I am not ashamed of the gospel, for it is the power of God for salvation to everyone who believes, to the Jew first and also to the Greek.}

This is positive separation and Paul analyzed it as:
(a) A holy desire to share spiritual gifts (verse11).
(b) A holy purpose to bear fruit (verse 13).
(c) A holy obligation to pay a spiritual dept (verse14).
(d) A holy eagerness to share the gospel (verse 15).
(e) A holy boldness to exalt the cross (verse 16).
To be separated unto the gospel is to share the Good News with the lost.
(4) Filled with the Holy Spirit. "Be filled with the Spirit": (Page 1135-Eph 5:18). {And do not get drunk with wine, for that is dissipation, but be filled with the Spirit.} We are commanded to be filled with the Holy Spirit. Evidence of the Spirit-filled life as seen in the early Christians:
(a) They spoke the word of God with boldness: (Page 1047-Acts 4:31). {And when they had prayed, the place were they had gathered together was shaken, and they were all filled with the Holy Spirit, and began to speak the word of God with boldness.}
(b) They witnessed with great power: (Page 1047-Acts 4:33). {And with great power the apostles were giving witness to the resurrection of the Lord Jesus, and abundant grace was upon them all.}
(c) They answered with grace: (Page 1047-Acts 4:33). {And with great power the apostles were giving witness to the resurrection of the Lord Jesus Christ, and abundant grace was upon them all.}
(d) They shared their wealth: (Page 1047-Acts 4:34-37). {For there was not a needy person among them, for all who were owners of land or houses would sell them and bring the proceeds of the sales, and lay them at the apostles feet; and they would be distributed to each, as any had need. And Joseph, a Levite of Cyprian birth, who was also called Barnabas by the apostles (which translated means, Son of encouragement), and who had a tract of land,

sold it and brought the money and laid it at the apostles feet.}

(e) They worshiped in unity: (Page 1044-Acts 2:42-47). {And they were continually devoting themselves to the apostles teaching and to fellowship, to the breaking of bread and prayer. And everyone kept feeling a sense of awe; and many wonders and signs were taking place through the apostles. And all those who had believed were together, and had all things in common; and they began selling their property and possessions, and were sharing them with all, as anyone who had need. And day by day continuing with each one mind in the temple, and breaking bread from house to house, they were taking their meals together with gladness and sincerity of heart, praising God, and having favor with all the people. And the Lord was adding to their number day by day those who were being saved.}

(f) They suffered persecution: (Page 1052-Acts 8:1-4). {And Saul was in hearty agreement with putting them to death. And on that day a great persecution arose against the church in Jerusalem; and they were all scattered throughout the regions of Judea and Samaria, except the apostles. And some devout men buried Stephen, and made loud lamentation over him. But Saul began ravaging the church, entering house after house; and dragging off men and women, he would put them in prison.}

(g) They gloried in tribulations: (Page 1085-Rom. 5:3). {and not only this, but we also exult in our tribulations, knowing that tribulation brings about perseverance.}

(h) They sang in prison: (Page 1062-Acts 16:25). {But about midnight Paul and Silas were praying and singing hymns of praise to God, and the prisoners were listening to them.}

(i) They loved and prayed for their executioners: (Page 1051-Acts 7:54-60). {Now when they heard this, they were cut to the quick, and they began gnashing their teeth at him. But being full of the Holy Spirit, he gazed intently into heaven and saw the glory of God, and Jesus standing at the right hand of God; and he said, "Behold, I see the heavens open up and the Son of Man standing at the right Hand of God." But they cried out with a loud voice, and covered their ears, and they rushed upon him with one impulse. And when they had driven him out of the city, they began stoning him, and the witnesses laid aside their robes at the feet of a young man named Saul. And they went on stoning Stephen as he called upon the Lord and said, "Lord Jesus, receive my spirit!" And falling on his knees, he cried out with a loud voice, "Lord, do not hold this sin against them!" And having said this, he fell asleep.}

(i) They rejoiced to suffer shame for His name: (Page 1049- Acts 5:41). {So they went on their way from the presence of the council, rejoicing that they had been considered worthy to suffer shame for His name.}

They were accused of:
(1) Filling Jerusalem with the gospel: (Page 1048-Acts 5:28). {saying, "We gave you strict orders not to continue teaching in His name, and behold, you have filled Jerusalem with your teaching, and intend to bring this man's blood upon us."}
(2) Upsetting the world: (Page 1063-Acts 17:6). {And they did not find them, they began dragging Jason and some brethren before the city authorities, shouting, "These men who have upset the world have come here also.}

The 120 Spirit-filled Christians witnessed on the day of Pentecost and the people were:

(1) Bewildered, that is, they were mentally arrested: (Page 1043- Acts 2:6). {And when this sound occurred, the multitude came together, and were bewildered, because they were each one hearing them speak in his own language (dialect).}

(2) Amazed, that is, they were mentally frustrated: (Page 1043- Acts 2:7). {And they were amazed and marveled, saying, "Why, are not all these who are speaking Galileans"?}

(3) Marveling, that is, they stood in mental awe: (Page 1043- Acts 2:7). {And they were amazed and marveled, saying, "Why, are not all these who were speaking Galileans"?}

(4) Mocking, that is, some mentally reacted: (Page 1043- Acts 2:13). {But others were mocking and saying, "They are full of sweet wine."}

(5) Inquiring, that is, some mentally acted: (Page 1044- Acts 2:37). {Now when they heard this, they were pierced to the heart, and said to Peter and the rest of the apostles, "Brethren, what shall we do?"}

The gospel proclaimed in the power of the Holy Spirit will motivate the healer to act or react. On the day of Pentecost three thousand acted as evidence by repentance and baptism, while others reacted with mocking. No one, but no one, ignored the witness of those Spirit-filled believers.

THE APPROACH

(Page 1013- John 1:40-42). {One of the two who heard John speak, and followed Him, was Andrew, Simon Peter's brother. He found first his own brother Simon, and said to him, "We have found the Messiah" (which translated means Christ). He brought him to Jesus. Jesus looked at him, and said, "You are Simon the son of John; you shall be called Cephas" (which translated means Peter).}

There are two ways to approach the prospect. The first is:

(1) The direct approach. This approach can be used when witnessing to:
   (a) A relative. Andrew used the direct approach to bring his brother Simon Peter to Christ (above verses 40-42).
   (b) A friend. Philip the apostle used the direct approach to bring Nathanael to Jesus: (Page 1013- John 1:45.46). {Philip found Nathanael and said to him, "We have found Him of whom Moses in the law and also the prophets wrote, Jesus of Nazareth, the son of Joseph," And Nathatael said to him, "Can any good thing come out of Nazareth?" Philip said to him, "Come and see."}
   (c) The concerned. Jesus used the direct approach to win Nicodemus: (Page 1014- John 3:1-21). {Now there was a man of the Pharisees, named Nicodemus, a ruler of the Jews; this man came to Him by night, and said to Him, "Rabbi, we know that You have come from God as a teacher; for no one can do these signs that You do unless God is with him." Jesus answered and said to him, "Truly, truly, I say to you, unless one is born again, he cannot see the kingdom of God." Nicodemus said to Him, "How can a man be born when he is old? He cannot enter a second time into his mother's womb and be born, can he?" Jesus answered, "Truly, truly, I say to you, unless one is born of water and the Spirit, he cannot enter into the kingdom of God. That which is born of flesh is flesh, and that which is born of the Spirit is spirit. Do not marvel that I said to you, 'You must be born again.'" The wind blows where it wishes and you hear the sound of it, but do not know where it comes from and where it is going; so is everyone who is born of the Spirit." Nicodemus answered and said to Him, "How can these things be?" Jesus answered and said to him, "Are you the teacher of Israel, and do

not understand these things? Truly, truly I say to you, we speak that which we know, and bear witness of that which we have seen; and you do not receive our witness. If I told you earthly things and you do not believe, how shall you believe if I tell you heavenly things? And no one has ascended into heaven, but He who descended from heaven, even the Son of Man. And as Moses lifted up the serpent in the wilderness, even so the Son of Man be lifted up; that whoever believes may in Him have eternal life. For God so loved the world, that He gave His only begotten Son, that whosoever believes in Him should not perish, but have eternal life. For God did not sent the Son into the world to judge the world, but that the world should be saved through Him. He who believes in Him is not judged; he who does not believe has been judged already, because he has not believed in the name of the only begotten Son of God. And this is the judgment, that the light is come into the world, and men loved the darkness rather than the light; for their deeds were evil. For everyone who does evil hates the light, and does not come to the light, lest his deeds should be exposed. But he who practices the truth comes to the light, that his deeds may be manifested as having been wrought in God."}

(d) The seeker: Paul and Silas used the direct approach to lead the Philippian jailer to Jesus: (Page 1062-John 16:19-34). {But when her masters saw that their hope of profit was gone, they seized Paul and Silas and dragged them into the market place before the authorities, and when they had brought them to the chief magistrates, they said, "These men are throwing our city into confusion, being Jews, and are proclaiming customs which it is not lawful for us to accept or to observe, being Romans." And the crowd rose up together against them, and the chief magistrates tore their robes off them, and proceeded to order them to be beaten with rods. And when they had inflicted them many blows upon them, they threw them into prison, commanded the jailer to guard them securely; and he, having received such a command, threw them into the inner prison, and fastened their feet in the stocks. But about midnight Paul and Silas were praying and singing hymns of praise to God, and the prisoners were listening to them: and suddenly there came a great earthquake, so that the foundations of the prison house were shaken; and immediately all the doors were opened, and everyone's chains were unfastened. And when the jailer had been roused out of sleep and had seen the prison doors opened, he drew his sword and was about to kill himself, supposing that the prisoners had escaped. But Paul cried out with a loud voice, saying, "Do yourself no harm, for we are all here!" And he called for lights and rushed in and, trembling with fear, he fell down before Paul and Silas, and after he had brought them out, he said, "Sirs, what must I do to be saved?" And they said, "Believe in the Lord Jesus, and you shall be saved, you and your household." And they spoke the word of the Lord to him together with all who were in his house. And he took them that very hour of the night and washed their wounds, and immediately he was baptized, he and all his household. And he brought them into his house and set food before them, and rejoiced greatly, having believed in God with his whole household.}

The second is:

(2) The indirect approach. This approach can be used when witnessing to:

   (a) A stranger. Jesus used the indirect approach to the Samaritan woman: (Page 1016- John 4:7-26). {There came a woman of Samaria to draw water. Jesus said to her, "Give Me a drink." For His disciples had gone into the city to buy food. The Samaritan woman therefore said to Him, "How is it that You, being a Jew, ask me for a drink since I am a Samaritan woman?" (For Jews had no dealings with Samaritans.) Jesus answered and said to her, "If you knew the gift of God, and who it is who says to you, 'Give Me a drink,' you would have asked Him, and He would have given you living water." She said to Him, "Sir, (Lord) You have nothing to draw with and the well is deep; where do You get that living water? You are not greater than our father, Jacob, are You, who gave us the well, and drank of it himself, and his sons, and his cattle?" Jesus answered and said to her, "Everyone who drinks of this living water shall thirst again; but whoever drinks of the water that I shall give him shall never thirst; but the water that I shall give him shall become in him a living well of water springing up to eternal life." The woman said to him, "Sir, give me this water, so I will not be thirsty, nor come all the way here to draw." He said to her, "Go call your husband, and come here. For you have had five husbands, and the one whom you now have is not your husband; this you have said truly." The woman said to Him, "Sir, I perceive you are a prophet. Our fathers worshiped in this mountain, and you people say that in Jerusalem is the place where men ought to worship." Jesus said to her, "Woman, believe Me, an hour is coming when neither in this mountain, nor in Jerusalem, shall you worship the Father. You worship that which you do not know; we worship that which we know, for salvation is from the Jews. But an hour is coming, and now is, when true worshipers shall worship the Father in spirit and truth; for such people the Father seeks to be His worshipers. God is spirit, and those who worship

Him must worship in spirit and truth." The woman said to Him, "I know that Messiah is coming (He who is called Christ); when that One comes, He will declare all things to us." Jesus said to her, "I who speak to you am He."}

(b) The religious. Philip the evangelist used the indirect approach to lead the Ethiopian eunuch to Christ: (Page 1052-Acts 8:26-39). {And an angel of the Lord spoke to Philip saying, "Arise and go south to the road that descends from Jerusalem to Gaza." And he arose and went; and behold, there was an Ethiopian eunuch, a court official of Candace, queen of the Ethiopians, who was in charge if all her treasure; and who had come to Jerusalem to worship. And he was returning and sitting in his chariot, and was reading the Prophet Isaiah. And the Spirit said to Philip, "Go up and join this chariot." And when Philip had run up, he heard him reading Isaiah the prophet, and said, "Do you understand what you are reading?" And he said, "Well, how could I, unless someone guides me?" And he invited Philip to come up and sit with Him. Now the passage of Scripture which he was reading was this: "He was led as a sheep to slaughter; And as a lamb before its shearer is silent, So He does not open His mouth. In humiliation His judgment was taken away; Who shall relate His generation? For His life is removed from the earth." And the eunuch answered Philip and said, "Please tell me, of whom does the prophet say this? Of himself or of someone else?" And Philip opened his mouth, and beginning from this Scripture, he preached Jesus to him. And as they went along the road they came to some water; and the eunuch said, "Look! Water! What prevents me from being baptized?" And Philip said, "If you believe with all you heart, you may." And he answered and said, "I believe that Jesus

Christ is the Son of God." And he ordered the chariot to stop; and they both went down into the water, Philip as well as the eunuch; and he baptized him. And when they came out of the water, the Spirit of the Lord snatched Philip away; and the eunuch saw him no more, but went on his way rejoicing.}

The method in either case will vary according to the leading of the Holy Spirit. Whether you use the direct or the indirect approach, be sure to follow through until you have presented God's plan of salvation and invited them to accept Christ as their personal Savior.

THE FOLLOW-THROUGH

(Page 926- Matt. 13:3-8, 18-30). {And He spoke many things to them in parables, saying, "Behold, the sower went out to sow; and as he sowed, some seeds fell beside the road, and the birds came and ate them up. And others fell upon rocky place, where they did not have much soil; and immediately they sprang up, because they had no depth of soil. But when the sun had risen, they were scorched; and because they had no root, they withered away. And others fell among thorns, and, the thorns came up and choked them out. And others fell on the good soil, and yielded a crop, some a hundredfold, some sixty, and some thirty. He who has ears , let him hear. Hear again the parable of the sower. When anyone hears the word of the kingdom, and does not understand it, the evil one comes and snatches away what has been sown in his heart. This is the one of whom the seed was sown beside the road. And the evil one on whom seed was sown on the rocky places, this is the man who hears the word, and immediately receives it with joy. Yet he has no firm root in himself, but is only temporary, and when affliction or persecution arises because of the word, immediately he falls away. And the one on whom seed was sown among thorns, this is the man who hears the word, and the worry of the world, and the deceitfulness of riches choke the word, and it becomes unfruitful. And the one on whom seed was sown on the good soil, this is the man who hears the word and understands it; who indeed bears fruit, and brings forth, some a hundredfold, some sixty, and some thirty." He presented another to them, saying, "The kingdom of heaven may be compared to a man who sowed good seed in his field. But when men were sleeping, his enemy came and sowed tares also among the wheat and went away. "But the wheat sprang up and bore grain, then the tares became evident also. And the slaves of the landowner came and said to him, 'Sir, did you not sow good seed in your field? How then does it have tares?' And he said to them, 'An enemy has done this!' And the slaves said to him, 'Do you want us, then, to go and gather them up?' But he said, 'No, lest while you are gathering up the tares, you may root up the wheat with them. Allow them both to grow together until the harvest; and in the time of the harvest I will say to the reapers, "First gather up the tares and bind them in bundles to burn them up; but gather the wheat into my barn.""'}

The parable of the sower illustrates the importance of the followthrough. Only one fourth of the soil was ready for the seed, so only one fourth of the seed brought forth fruit. Jesus explains the parable in (verses 18-23), and we learn that:

(1) The sower is the witness.
(2) The seed is the word of God.
(3) The soil is the heart.
  We also learn that there are four types of hearts. They are:
(1) The hard heart; this is the wayside of the soil, fertile but hard.
(2) The shallow heart; this is the stony soil, fertile but depthless.
(3) The worldly heart; this is the thorny soil, fertile but possessed.
(4) The understanding heart; this is good soil, fertile and prepared.

The lesson is a simple one if we expect the seed, the word of God to bear fruit, the heart must be made ready. The hard heart must be broken; the shallow heart must be given depth; and the worldly heart must be taught that the things of this world are temporal: (Page 961-Mark 8:36.37). {For what does it profit a man to gain the whole world, and forfeit his soul? For what shall a man give in exchanges for his soul?}

This requires time, work, and patience.

HOW TO SHARE GOD'S PLAN OF SALVATION.

(Page 1046-Acts 4:12). {"And there is salvation in no one else; for there is no other name under heaven that has been given among men, by which we must be saved."}

There are seven simple steps to take in sharing God's plan of salvation.

    (1) Share your personal experience of salvation. Don't give your life story. It should not take more than a few minutes to tell how the Lord saved you. As you come to close of your testimony, bring out your Bible and say, "May I share with you God's plan of salvation that changed my life?"

    (2) Now share fact number one on Page 1015. It is a fact that God loves you. Read John 3:16 and the notes that are with it and on the love of God. When you come to the close, say something like this: Tom, will you now admit that God loves you?" Lead him to admit it if you can. This will get him involved in the plan of salvation.

    (3) Now share the fact number two on page 1084. It is a fact that you are a sinner. Read the Scripture, and the notes that come with it; and ask them to admit that he is a lost sinner. When he admits that he is a lost sinner, you say something like this: "Tom, isn't it wonderful? God loves you even though you are a lost sinner."

    (4) Now share fact number three on page 1087. It is a fact that you are dead in sin. Read the Scripture and the notes that come with it; and as you come to a close, ask him to admit that he is dead in sin. When he admits that he dead in sin, say something like this: "Tom, isn't

it great? Even though you are a lost sinner dead in sin, God loves you."

(5) Now share the fact on page 1085. It is a fact that Christ died for you. Read the Scripture and the notes that come with it; and, as you come to the close, ask him to admit that Christ died on Calvary for him. Say something like this, "Tom, isn't it wonderful? Isn't it great that God loves you so much that He died on Calvary bearing your sins?"

(6) Now share with him fact number five on page 1063. It is a fact that you can be saved by faith in the Lord Jesus Christ. Read the Scripture and the notes that come with it; and, as you come to the close, be ready to ask him to accept Christ as his personal Savior.

(7) Now lead him to call upon the name of the Lord in prayer: (Page 1090- Rom.10:13). {"for whoever will call upon the name of the Lord will be saved."}

HOW TO GIVE THE INVITATION

(Page 1226-Rev. 22:17). {And the Spirit and the bride say, "Come." And let the one who hears say, "Come." And let the one who is thirsty come; let the one who wishes take the water of life without cost.}

To give the invitation is to invite the person witnessed to, to by faith accept the Lord Jesus Christ as his personal Savior. As you finish reading the page 1063 on It is a fact that you can be saved by faith in the Lord Jesus Christ (Acts 16:30-40), say something like this: "Tom, will you kneel with me in prayer as I ask the Lord to save you, right here and now?" (Don't wait for him to get on his knees; you lead the way. If he will not kneel, don't force it; pray a short prayer that the Lord will convict him of sin and bring him to repentance. Get up and make an appointment to return for another witness session. If he does kneel with you, pray a brief prayer and ask the Lord to save him now.)

Now ask him to pray after you the prayer of acceptance. You pray, "Lord Jesus, I know you love me." Now he prays, "Lord Jesus, I know you love me." Continue in this manner until you have led him through the prayer. Now when you have finished leading him through the prayer stand up and say, "Tom, did you by faith accept the Lord Jesus Christ as your personal Savior as you Prayed, 'I do now by faith, gladly accept you as my personal Savior, and thank you Lord, for eternal salvation'?" When he answers yes, take him by the for "Whoever will call upon the name of the Lord will be saved."

HOW TO FOLLOW UP

(Page 1044-Acts 2:41-47). {So then, those who had received his word were baptized; and there were added that day about three thousand souls. And they were continually devoting themselves to the apostles teaching and to fellowship, to the breaking of bread and to prayer. And everyone kept feeling a sense of awe; and many wonders and signs were taking place through the apostles. And all those who had believed were together, and had all things in common; and they began selling their property and possessions, and were sharing them with all, as anyone might have need. And day by day continuing with one mind in the temple, and breaking bread from house to house, they were taking their meals together with gladness and sincerity of heart. Praising God, and having favor with all the people. And the Lord was adding to their number day by day those who were being saved.}

When you have led a soul to Christ your responsibility does not end. You have a spiritual baby, and that baby needs help if it is to grow in grace and knowledge of the Lord Jesus Christ. There are seven things that you can do that will help the new Christian to grow spiritually.

    (1) Give him your bible if he does not already have one.
    (2) Explain the Master Outline system of study. Show him all fifteen Master Study outlines. Then urge him to get his own personal Master Outline Study system. Then

explain to him how it works so he can also become an effective witness.

(3) Now show him how he can know that he saved. Turn to (Page 1203-1 John 5:10-12) It is a fact that you can be saved and know it. As you take him through the outlines, be sure to look up each scripture reference and point out that we have a "now salvation."

(4) Now to turn to (Page 1048-Acts5:29-32) It is a fact that you are now a child of God and you are to obey Him. Start him out right; the fact that we are to obey the Lord in all things.

(5) Lead him into a New Testament church. Say something like this: "Tom, I am a member of a New Testament church, and I want you to be my guest at the next service." Take him to church and sit with him; and, when the invitation is given, ask him to go forward with you to make his public profession of faith in Christ: (Page 923-Matt. 10:32). {Everyone therefore who shall confess Me before men, I will also confess him before My Father who is in heaven.}

(6) Encourage him to witness. "Let the redeemed of the Lord say so": (PagePs.107:2). {Let the redeemed of the Lord say so, Whom He has redeemed from the hand of the adversary.}

(7) Now help him through the Fifteen Master Outlines In the Bible.

When you have reached Master Outline Number Fifteen, he should be in the

church, with a doctrinal foundation on which to continue to grow spiritually.

And by now he should be involved in evangelism. He is ready to go with the

gospel. **AMEN!**

MORAL CHARACTER

All men are created equal. This means that all humans have the same abilities. We are all born into this existence with the same mind. We all have been born lost. We all have the same mind virus. All have dreams that we need to pursue. We all see the same world around us. There are no excuses for our failures. If you put your heart into it there is fortune to be found in every business if you make it fun. If you make it fun there will be no failure. Because there will be no burden. It is all learning.

The only dangerous brand of poverty that exists today is poverty of character. Poverty of character can be seen in every corner of the earth. Poverty of character springs from not knowing who you are or where you come from. You are not aware of your eternal worth. Poverty means poor quality. In short it means your stupidity, your dumbness. This is why you desperately need to know about your personality.

Your ultimate successful life will not come about as a result of chance, luck or by accident or even good fortune. Success is un-inheritable. Success is born out of applied knowledge. More accurately success is born out of knowledge and wisdom.

There is one thing given us all at birth which is reserved for all human beings alike and that is the power of choice. The power of choice is misapplied, miss understood. It is ignored. It is abused. The power of choice has been strictly for bidden in some places. For the most part it is controlled.

If you want to rise in this world then you must understand the power of leverage. You must understand the law of elevation, which is the law of lift. If you want to rise in the world then you must prepare your self for what you are about to receive. So what this is saying is that you must go through a period of preparing first. What is it your preparing for today. What ever it is, you will become tomorrow. Prepare your self for what you earnestly desire.

So start with your dreams. Always start with your desires and work outwardly. This way you are always centered. Quit looking at your environment. Your environment is the surroundings. Look at your own ideals. Your surroundings are the creation of someone else. You are a mini creator. Use the power of imagination. This is rising above your environment.

Know what the rules are only to know where you can break the rules. Rules are there to keep the stupid in there place. By the same token you must realize that you and you alone can change your circumstances. But first you must take full responsibility for all your activities, for everything in your life.

Don't spend precious mental energy on petty things like how others perceive you. Put your mental focus forward and march. People may not under stand what the hell you are doing, but no matter. What you want and when to pursue is written in your heart. If you do not know what the hell you are doing so what. It will all come together in time.

We only see today for today. We do not know what is off the radar screen. Through knowledge and understanding you can change your destiny. But this also takes intense will and focus. No one can confine the glorious mind that you possess. Confinement can only come through fear, worry, and doubt. These are the murders of success. They always retard, stop cold, turn you around. Rob you of all joy, love and ultimately your possessions and even your life.

It has been said that there is one thing that creditors cannot take away from you and that is your knowledge that you have accumulated. So, spend large amounts of time in private gaining knowledge. What ever you do privately you will be rewarded openly in due time.

I heard it once said long ago that progress is not in the moving forward but in the going backward. It is not fast forward, but in the slowing down. This explains why our trials are the most valuable things we have. Out of your adversity there can be found the seeds of an equal or greater opportunity. So out of every adversity there can be found within it seeds of greater knowledge, understanding, and ultimately opportunity. So, that's why there is really no such thing as a bad situation.

Yesterday is gone forever, tomorrow isn't here yet. The only day that we possess is today. So, live in the here and now all day every day. Today, go the extra mile by doing the little things. Put out a satisfaction guaranteed or your money back. Those little courtesies and little efforts pay off.

The three great essentials to success in mental and physical labor are practice, patience, and perseverance. The greatest of these three is perseverance, which means to persist. The things you want most in life are the hardest to get. Believe firmly that if you do not find a way you can make one. Then you will triumph.

You can never learn without your own efforts. All the teachers of the world cannot make a scholar of you if you do not apply your self with all your might.

It is useless to say I cannot do this thing. You can at least keep your eyes open to all of the possibilities. You have to cultivate your powers of I can do this thing. This is using the power of creative imagination to be open to what you can do. This "I can't" never accomplished any thing, and it never will. When you once see your opportunity, you are to think for it, plan for it, work for it, and live for it. If you throw your mind, might, heart and soul into it, then in due time success will crown you. It has to because of the law of attraction.

The successful people of today are people of one over mastering idea, people of a single and intense purpose.

The world is all gates. Opportunities are there for those who see them and use them. Opportunities are all around you. We live in a dreamer's paradise.

What is this life any way but to heighten, broaden, and deepen the God given talents within? You must round out your being into symmetry, harmony and beauty. The opportunity of service is the highest opportunity in life. Conversation enriches understanding.

Solitude is the nest of thought, school of geniuses. During our time of solitude our attitude is extremely important. It has to be positive. Important thing in prayer, ask and it is given, seek and you shall find, knock and it will be opened to you. For every one that asks he shall receive. He that does knock it will be opened. First one must believe in these great truths. Then they will work for you. Prayer need not be long if faith is strong. Prayer is the key that unlocks the throne room of Gods mercy.

As a man thinks so is he. As a man expects so is he. Let us think constantly about what we pray. Then constantly expect the fulfillment of what we prayed. We tend to become what we think about most of the time. As you can see our thoughts have every thing to do with our success or failure in life.

There is a law called the law of attraction. Like produces like. Plus thoughts build, minus or negative thoughts tear down. We build and grow as we think, move and talk. What ever we assert firmly believing, we will become. So, therefore one must hold successful thoughts in the mind before we can attain it. If we hold failure thoughts in the mind we are just as certain heading toward it as well.

Working for one thing is incompatible with expecting something else. This is not in harmony with the law of attraction. Therefore it will not work. When achievement is constantly held in the mind; It will soon become reality and we see success.

There are two curses of mankind. Humanity is plagued with fear and worry. They are the great destroyers of success and happiness. They are insidious enemies. Nothing else is so dreaded quite as much as these two hideous monsters. If we open the door to thoughts of fear, worry and doubt, we are committing mental suicide, whether we know it or not. Yet, never the less we do it anyway.

But the good news is we can control our minds. We are created to live a rich full life. Don't ever let the obstacles you face open the door of your mind to fear, worry, and doubt. We will feel discouragement at times, but this is only temporary. It is only a passing moment. All outward circumstances bend to the one with a resolute will. An iron will. Once they creep in antidote them at once. For, they are the great retardants of the human race. They are the insidious monsters of progress. In other words they hold back. This means there is no progress. They are the stranglers of aspirations, the murders of success. Always remember it is you and you alone who can open or close the door to your mind to these evils.

We were created to be triumphant, successful, glorious achievers. Everything that we need or desire is in our DNA. We must open our minds, our faith, and our confidence to its reality. Then back this with intelligent effort. To have power over these monsters you must understand who you are and who you are suppose to be. What you become is up to you. What lies within you is the field of all possibilities. You can be anything you put you mind to.

When you have a vision you must glorify it in your mind. Vision: meaning foresight. The idea that you enthrone in your heart, this you will build your life by. This is none other than a chief aim.

MAGNETIC PERSONALITY

Personality is the constitutional, mental, social, and emotional characteristic that gives personal identity to individuals. We are not born with a pleasing personality. A pleasing personality is an un-inheritable trait. It must be cultivated through social intercourse after we have learned the many traits that make up its being.

AFFABLE: Easy to talk to. Affability- an affable person is one who is not difficult to approach or talk to because of his polite and friendly being. He is down to earth. As the expression goes not aloof.

ALOOF: Indifferent and reserved, or beyond the normal means of communication. Antidote selfishness with a feeling of kindness and good will to all peoples. Affability is a very important trait. It will mean the difference to you between success and failure.

BENEVOLENCE: Kindly good will. Benevolence simply stated is the desire to good for others. Doing good is the only certain happy action of a persons life. The very consciousness of well being is in it self.

AMPLE: More than enough rewards for our efforts in this right direction. In a moral sense we know that it is more blessed to give than to receive. Jesus said, give and it will be given back to you, pressed down shaken together and running over one hundred fold. According to the measure that you give, it will be given back. Be good, do good. There is no success without it.

CHARACTER: The combination of all qualities. Character is to a man what the fly wheel is to an engine. By the force of its momentum it will carry you through time of temptation and trial and by putting character into action it makes a guiding and controlling influence over your life. When a person has lost his character he has lost everything. If he possess nothing but character he can still be of service to his community, and to society as a whole, and even to the world to his neighbor his friends and to him self. The difference between character and reputation is character is within, is what a person is. Character is always real. Reputation is what others thinks' he is. Reputation without it can sometimes be false. The secret of character building means an absolute surrender. Consecration ordained as sacred and devotion of all that is better and purer and truer. To grow in character is by a consuming zeal, eagerness, fervor passion for all that is noble, famous, lofty, superior and excellent.

CHARITY: Is another name for love not influenced by selfish motives. It takes a kind and unselfish personality to do good for others in any way within your power. This trait must be cultivated. The charity soil carries with it a charmed, fascinating, attractive atmosphere of peace and love. All who come within its favorable influence unfolds their famous lofty, superior qualities and develops their most good, natural, distinguished, personal mark, habit. One of the secrets of ones ultimate success will be found in this, if you have the determination and persistency to live constantly in the presence of your supreme ambition. When the conscious mind can see clearly the kind of power and mental forces required. You must impress that image upon the subconscious with its deepest and strongest desire for its realization. The impression thus made will call forth. In time the power and intelligence required will come forth. This is your genie in action. The law is this.

The subconscious will respond with the exact quantity and quality that you were conscious of, or that you mentally discerned at the time the impression was made. It is therefore extremely important to elevate the conscious mind into the largest and most superior state of thought and feeling possible before the effort is made to impress the subconscious. You must live constantly in the deep interior feeling of greater power, greater intelligence, greater personal worth and greater mental brilliantness. It is to constantly call upon the subconscious to produce these things in ever larger measure.

Energy of will is a self originating force. This is the soul of every great character. Where it is there is life. Where it is not there is faintness, helplessness, and despondency. We get out of life exactly what we put into it. The world has for us just what we have for it. It is a mirror which reflects the faces we make. Weak people wait for opportunities. Strong people make their opportunities. Where there is a will there is a way. To think we are able is almost to be so. To determine upon attainment is frequently attainment it self. He who intensely wills to do a thing will find a way. An intense desire itself transforms possibilities into reality. Our wishful prayers are but prophecies of the things we are capable of doing.

The sick, feeble willed person finds everything impossible because he believes it to be so. A will to succeed is a steadfast determination. It is a burning desire to attain the object of your wishes. A burning desire is no ordinary desire or wish. It is enthusiastic faith in the attainment of a goal, an object of ones desires.

Hope for the achievement of any thing must be backed by an unwavering, steadfast determination backed by faith until it is attained. A steadfast determination is desire plus expectation.

Plan on planning or plan on failing. Planning is the second step for the attainment of your wishes in life. We first must give before we can ever expect to receive. On the great clock of time there is but one word, NOW. A great action is always proceeded by a great purpose. There is an unyielding, inflexible law of nature that what ever is not used dies. Nothing for nothing is her maxim. If we are idle and shiftless by choice, we shall be nerveless and powerless by necessity.

CONSCIENTIOUS: Careful, dictated by conscious, the more brains that you mix with your muscle the greater the rewards. Be conscientious. Be dedicated. Be devoted to your task.

CHEERFUL DISPOSITION: Natural attitude towards things. Gloom and depression are contagious enemies of the soul. Cheerfulness is contagious too. A smiling person of good cheer spreads cheer. Cheerful is a big word. Its definition is that it is a state of mind derived from a state of being of in spirit from what you believe. It brings hope and courage to where it is needed naturally. It helps you grow. Cheerfulness is having or showing. In other words it means, it brings out the good and natural side of people. It is the bright and cheerful spirit that wins the final triumph. Cheerfulness will prevail over gloom and depression will fail. Being of good cheer puts you in tune with the very source of all things.

CONVERSATION: speech is the mirror of the soul. As a person speaks so is he. As a person thinks so is he. We facilitate communication when we learn to become good listeners.

COURAGE: Courage is the ability to conquer fear, and despair. Courage is valor, bravery. Courage is personal bravery and heroism, prowess and gallantry.

COURTEOUS: Marked by respect by others, politeness. Nothing will develop a spiritual heart of true politeness except a mind that is deeply penetrated with goodness, justice, generosity. True courtesy every where is the same.

DECISION: It has been truly said that the great moral victories and defeats of the world often turn in minutes. A hesitating, faltering, undecidedly policy will ruin the most brilliant genius. There is nothing to be more admired than a manly firmness and decision of character.

DIGNITY: True dignity is just the outward expression of inherent worth and character.

INHERENT: Established as an essential part of something. Like the nature of God. True dignity exists independent of studied gestures or well practiced smiles. It is a character of God.

EMOTIONAL CONTROL: Emotional control or the emotion of the self is said to be the highest form of courage. It is the base of all virtues. It is one of the most important but one of the most difficult things for a powerful mind to be its own master. This cannot be done except through awareness of feelings, backed by an unwavering faith.

ENTHUSIASM: Enthusiasm is faith in action. Enthusiasm is a Greek word meaning in God. Enthusiasm is the propellant we receive when we tap the power within. Enthusiasm is the solid faith in a first cause. It is a solid faith in ones self, and the rooted faith in our mission or calling. Enthusiasm is the force of character, it is our inward power. Enthusiasm knows of nothing but success. It will not hearken to the voice of discouragement. It never yields its purpose. Enthusiasm with a moderate degree of wisdom will carry a person farther than any amount of intellect without it. Enthusiasm will open doors when all others fail.

HONESTY/VERACITY: Veracity is the habitual observance of truth. No substitute has ever yet been discovered for honesty, or veracity. They are the most important virtues in character. It should be a living mainspring. Honesty and veracity are bright and shining qualities on the part of any one who strives to make the most of life's possibilities. Without these two virtues there is no reliance upon language. No confidence in friendship. No security in promises and oaths. Truth is always consistent with it self. Truth needs nothing to help it out. Truth is always near at hand and sits upon our lips. The love of truth and what is right is the mainspring source of integrity. Truth is the foundation of all knowledge and the cement of all society.

KINDNESS: Kindness is one of the most purest traits that find a place in the human heart. Its influence never ceases. It is done by little acts of a watchful eye. It is done by words, by tones, by gestures, by looks, that affection is won. Life is made up not of great sacrifices or duties, but of little things. The little unreserved acts of kindness and of love are the best portion of a good mans life. Little kindnesses are great ones. They drive away sadness and cheer up the soul beyond all common appreciation. When such kindnesses are administered in times of need, they are like rivers of flowing water that bring life to the soul. It brings health to the bones and quickens the spirit, and will be long remembered. A word of kindness in a desperate strait is as welcomed as the smile of an angel.

LOVE: Love is the crowning grace of humanity. Love is the sun of life. Love is the bond and cement of society. Love is the spirit and spring of the universe. Love is the holiest right of the soul. Love is the golden link that binds us to duty and truth. Love is the redeeming principle that chiefly reconciles the heart of life and its prophetic eternal good. Love purifies the heart from self. It strengthens and enables the character and gives higher motives and a nobler aim to every action of life. Love makes man and woman strong, noble, and courageous. We can serve only as long as we can love.

LOYALTY: Loyalty is the faithful constant exercise of and devotion to a duty or obligation owing to someone or something. Loyalty implies unswerving allegiance to something or someone. Loyalty, faithfulness and consistency are priceless ingredients, they are worth more than silver and gold. They are the jewels in the crown of life.

MODESTY/HUMILITY: True self reliance does not call on all men to witness its exploits. It displays it self in action. Modesty when put to the test by necessity, it so own powers. Humility is only anxious for the aid of others. Modesty is a beautiful setting to the diamond of talents and genius. The mark of a truly successful man is the absence of pretensions. It is always found that modesty accompanies great merit. Merit without modesty is generally proud and haughty, over bearing in expression.

HAUGHTY: Disdainfully proud.

DISDAIN: Feeling of contempt. All great developments complete themselves in the world, and modesty waits in silence, never praising them selves. They never announce themselves either. What so quickly commands our good wishes as modesty struggling under discouragement. What is our respect and love more than modesty ministering to the distress of others. There is no surer passport to the favor of others than modesty in action. Modesty has a rare virtue. It is the quality of being. In its own way it is true strength and beauty. The crimson glow of modesty will over spread your cheeks and give new luster to your charms. With modesty you are so rich within, so pure without, with modesty manners general appearance and soul virtue so rare.

OBSERVATION: He alone is a sharp observer who can observe minutely without being observed. The difference between people men and women, in a big way is in the intelligence of their observation. One of the greatest hindrances to advancement and promotion in life is the lack of observation and the unwillingness to take pains. A keen, cultivated observation will see a fortune and find it, is not an idle slogan. It is the mind that sees as well as the eye. Where unthinking gazers observe nothing, men of intelligence, vision, penetrate into the very fiber of the phenomena presented to them.

OBSERVATION: the action of habit of observing; the result of watching, examining, noting, attentive watchfulness.

PATIENCE: patience has been defined as the courage of virtue. He that has patience can have what he wills. There is no road to long to the man who advances deliberately and without undue haste. There is no honor to distant for the man who prepares himself for them with patience. Love is patient. Patience is needed to rebuke, reprove, and exhort. Without patience one cannot endure. If we do not have patience with others then others will not have patience with us. With all forgiveness patience will come. Patience is sorrows salve. Patience is sorrows healing, it sooths the conscious. Patience is alert. Patience is the quality of enduring with calmness; quite perseverance, bearing trials without murmuring, not easily made angry, calm not hasty.

PERSONAL APPEARANCE: Three tenths of good looks are due to nature. The rest is due to dress. First remember that the outward appearance is but secondary to the advancement of the soul with all noble and great qualities. A well poised body while expressing a well poised character reacts in turn on that character which in turn to help and enrich the whole personality. To bear one self with grace and kind dignity is to foster and breed graciousness and self respect, as well as to disseminate them.

DISSEMINATE: To sow as seed; to scatter abroad; to broadcast, to circulate.

PRAYER: Our wants are our prayers. What ever it is that you want, our wants are the very root of our achievement. Our prayers are behind all progress. All the great discoverers, scientists, explorers, inventors, and philosophers who have pushed the world forward and accomplished immeasurable service to mankind had their beginning in wants. They pictured their dreams as reality. They visualized themselves accomplishing the thing they were ambitious to do long before they were able to work them out in actual and make them realities. Our wants that have there source in the longings of the soul are really the expression of the divine within our soul. Longings are the kingdom within. They are worthy of our aspirations. They are worthy of our goals. Toward there fulfillment we should constantly struggle. Live for something definite and practical. Take hold of things with a will. They will yield to you and become ministers of your success. They will become your happiness, and the happiness of others. Happiness is a state of mind. This is a place where you have found peace and fulfillment. What is it that you want? What ever it is, include a full measure of happiness. Success without happiness is not true success. Happiness is the greatest paradox in nature.

PARADOX: A statement that seems contrary to common sense yet is perhaps true. It can grow in any soil, live under any conditions. Happiness consists not of having but of being. Not of possessing but of enjoying. We are the creator of our own circumstances; and we are the creator of our own happiness. Happiness or joy is the aroma of a life lived in harmony with our high ideals. What a person obtains in life he is. It rests with himself alone. What he obtains is but acquisition. These are but possessions. What he attains is growth. Happiness is the soul's joy in the possession of the intangible. This is not solid or material. We know that everything in the universe including our lives is based upon principle, following a divine law. We know that the law of prosperity and abundance is just as definite as the law of gravitation.

PRUDENCE: Care, wise, and sensible. Prudence is gained through the study of facts, knowledge of history, human nature, experience and logical thought. Prudence never over reacts in the face of short term failure. What ever you wish, that is what you are. For such is the force of the human will. Joined to God the divine that what ever we wish to be A seriously, and with a true intention we will become. Give it everything you've got. The quality of your work is your trade mark.

CONCENTRATION: Concentration of effort is an outstanding key to success. Concentration of purpose is a concentration which never scatters its forces. He who scatters his efforts in this intense concentrated age cannot hope to succeed.

INEVITABLE: Certain to occur, inescapable. Every act and every thought is like a seed. Give kindness and love and it will come back to you. Give hatred and indifference and scorn and it too will come back to you. You get what you deserve. You get what you got coming to you. You and you alone set in operation the causes that must follow by there inevitable results. This is the law of compensation.

COMPENSATION: Pay for. Make up for. The universe has a way of paying every body their dues. If you smile you are smiled upon. If you frown then you will be frowned upon. If you love the world and earnestly seek for the good therein; you will be surrounded by loving friends. Nature will then pour into your lap the treasure of the earth. The law of cause and effect means doing something for a result. Give from your self, from your being, your time, talents, energies and money to make your world a better place. Do everything with a satisfaction guaranteed, or your money back.

PERSERVANCE- First set your aim high with expectation and an upright heart within reality. Then you can cheerfully take up trials and burdens that life will throw at you along the way. But persevere and go forward. Only when you learn to work at something constantly carrying out the plan of work which an enlightened judgment decides is the best. Then you will force life to give, produce or surrender or yield to you its grandest triumph. Only when you carry something through in all its details by working at it constantly, then you have controlled or measure the secret to success.

PRACTICE: Way of doing, custom, habit, professional occupation. Patience is defined as courage of virtue. But to continue to work at something constantly, this is perseverance. It is the most important of the three. Remember that nothing within the possible can with stand the person intelligently bent on success. You have to drive straight forward. When you need to stop and get your second wind. Reevaluate your plans and then alternate as needed. There is no such thing as failure until you except it as such. Mental attitude is everything. Take on the attitude of upward, outward, and flamboyant cheerful soul. It is worth far more than diamonds, silver or gold. A person with such an attitude has clear sailing over life's difficulties and obstacles which tend to make others miserable and disagreeable.

Learn early in life not to depend on others. You are often tempted unknowingly. Blaze your own trail in life. What ever it is you want, there is always a price tag. The question is, are you willing to pay the price? The shifting habit of drifting of good for nothingness should be anti doted with ambitious thoughts.

There is weakness in the person that says that luck is against them. They are admitting their own weakness, and not master over their situation.

To succeed you must have a program, fix or plan your course and stick to it. Lay out your plans and execute them. Go straight to your goal. Don't be pushed aside one way or another, just because a difficulty is pushed your way. If you can't go over it, find a way to go thru it. Rise above your circumstance.

You cannot keep a determined person from success if that person has an over mastering purpose which dominates his soul. If you have determination and grit, you are sure to succeed.

Brains are second in importance to will. The person who is always changing their mind is the one who is always pushed aside in the race of life. You must have an iron will and have a determination that nothing will stop you. Nothing will shake you from it. No one fails if they do their best, for if the critical world ignores you, the universe won't. The universe says that in your weakness I will make you strong. The law of cause and effect steps in. Therefore there is no loss of energy in the world.

CONCIENTOUS: Carefully dictated by conscious of the inner moral self. Persistence cannot fail relating to the first most ultimate reward. Success is failure turned inside out. The danger is not in the fall, but in the failing to rise when knocked down. Difficulties call out great qualities and make greatness possible.

The person who has had victories over difficulties bears the signs of victory in his face and an aurora of triumph is seen in every movement.

The most essential factor is persistence. Persistence is the determination never to allow your energy or enthusiasm to become dampened by the discouragement that must inevitably come. Greater is the person that has determination and little talent, than the one who has great talent and little determination. The best tools receive their temper with fire, their edge from grinding. Hot fire makes good steel. The noblest of characters are developed in the same way. The harder the diamond the more brilliant the luster and the greater friction necessary to bring it out. Only its own dust is hard enough to make the precious stone reveal its own beauty. The hotter the fire, the greater the temperance. The more grinding the sharper the edge. All the friction was necessary to bring it out.

Your failures sharpen you edge. Your trials are the grinding. It is defeat that turned bone to flint, and gristle into muscle. The worlds' greatest victories have been born out of defeat. It required four centuries of martyrdom to establish Christianity. The wounded oyster mends his shell with pearl. No person is a failure who is upright and true. There is but one failure and that is not to be true to the best that is in us. Failure is in a sense the highway to success.

APPEARANCE: Brightness, radiance, light. The ass is still ass even though he wears a lion skin. A person may change their dress but still be the same person. The world has always and still is deceived by outward ornaments. If it be of a corrupt intention, its purpose is to entrap the wisest of men, to hide the corruptions within their soul. But, the enlighten one sees thru it.

CONTIUUM: First and foremost is attitude. You must get and then maintain a positive attitude. Progress starts by being progressive.

PROFRESSIVE: Move forward. Improve. So, be positively moving forward and become mentally aware of your instincts which will lead you to what you want. Moving forward means by calculated risks. This takes mental energy. Focus brings you to central point. As the old saying goes it takes as much energy to fail as it does to succeed. Wisdom and prudence is the giving of success. There are two things that over ride it and they are time and chance. So all in all success is never guaranteed, but its chances are greatly increased.

PRACTICE, PATIENCE, AND PERSERVENCE Out of these three perseverance is perhaps the greatest. All three are the greatest essentials for success. Perfect practice makes perfect. You can never learn without your own efforts. There is no such thing as I can't. Can't never accomplished anything. It is your weakness that says I cannot. It is your resistance that says I won't. It is your ego that listens to it. All three spells disaster. If you want it then look at what ever it takes to make it happen. Either way you choose to look at it your right. Look at what you can do not what you cannot do. As you enter this mind set your imagination will take over from there. As you let go your will then has its way. Your desire will make it come to pass.

PATIENCE: Once you know what it is that you want you are to think for it, plan for if, work for it, live for it, and then be patient in its coming.

PERSEVERANCE: Steady persistence in a course of action. Perseverance commonly suggests activity maintained in spite of difficulties. In other words, ride the wave all the way to shore. But, believe in your cause. Believe in it with all you have. If you do this you will soon be recognized. This is success in it self.

Is your mind a stem of thorns? If it is like mine then yes. The state of poverty is derived from a stem of thorns. This is the reason that poverty stricken areas are dangerous. Afflicted by disease, poverty of mind equals poverty of character equals a malfunction environment. It is an environment of lack. Poverty of character is described as a person who does not believe in their self worth. A person of poverty is a person who believes in and acts on the negative forces of life. They have not the will to pull them self up by their own boot straps.

Every human has the capabilities to accomplish all things, to become all things. All possibilities exist at the same time. Poverty is choosing the wrong thoughts. All beings are capable of enduring hardships under adverse conditions. You must come face to face with your present situation. Then tune your self into the powers that are yours. That is the power to create. The world is said to be all gates.

Poverty is a world full of bars. Poverty is a prison. The real prison is your mind. Your fears and worries thwart you at every turn. To open your mind to them is mental suicide. Fear is usually self induced worry and over what exactly, usually the unknown. Doubt comes from a lack of knowledge and experience. Time to get out of it is now.

Every human being has the ability to become anything they want to become. This is your God given talents and right. The capabilities are endless. You possess the field of all possibilities. You are able to endure extreme hardships under adverse conditions. You must come face to face with this early on.

Better said, you must learn this early in life, the sooner the better. You must be sensitive to the powers that be. The world is said to be all gates. This fact along with your natural born talents becomes a vehicle for purpose. You the watcher choose the direction. Fear, worry and doubt are killers of your success and happiness. This has held me back all my life. To open your mind to them is committing mental suicide. GOD- God is our creator. This is a supernatural fact as well as a natural fact. We are created in his image. The interpretation of this is simple. His image means to first conceive it. Then, the ability to believe we have the raw materials to make it, then the ability to create it, thus, having everything necessary to materialize it. Bring from incorporeal to corporeal.

In today's world what ever you decide to do somebody is already there doing it first. This is an easy trap to fall under. You must not let this stop you. Become the other alternative. No matter how insignificant this may seem it has been a huge problem for my self. I strive to be the first. There are always more educated, smarter and degreed professionals who seem more qualified. But they are only humans like you and I. Yet God has given us all something special. He has given us all something unique. All things created have an expression of the divine one within.

This doesn't have to sound mysterious. It simply means that the way you express yourself and do things are unique. To find out what your talents are lies within your self. But your ego can get in the way. If you think of something you love and it's important to you, you will get confirmation by experiencing resistance. This means you are on the right track. If you are scared of it, this is a good sign. Delve deep within it secretly. This is your ideal. This is your baby. Give birth to it.

    Some people take a life time to find this out. Always looking outside, All the while it lies within. This is why you must look to your own happiness. This is your true path. Follow the peace in your heart. This is a healthy choice. If it is good for your organism it is good for you. Become more attuned with your feelings and go find peace. When you find it cling to it, embrace it, covet it and you will find harmony, reason, and tranquility.

    For me and my house peace and tranquility is paramount. Along with our regular daily experience we have darts, insults, rocks and boulders thrown at us from all direction. We find our selves combating these forces just to keep our sanity. Sometimes it's best to retreat just to fight another day. Kind of sounds like warfare doesn't it. Well, if you think about it, it is warfare. Even love is war. All is fair in love and war. Start training your self for this warfare.

    Become instinctive in all your ways. Your intuition knows what is going on. Some call this intuition their little person inside. What ever you do your sanity is your most precious asset. Guard it with your life. This also means you must go to war sometimes. All of life comes down to war and peace.

    YOUR MINDS EYE. Your minds eye is your spiritual eye. This consists of your experiences, your wisdom, and all the emotion that comes with that. The minds eye comes out of the third mind. The third mind is the mind of the universe.

    After every experience you are different. This is more wisdom that you did not have before.

    All said and done you now should quit looking vertical for answers you should start looking horizontal, which is wide scope. The third minds eye is the culmination of all experiences. It is your intelligence. So the more in tune you are with your feelings and the more you are in tune with your direction and what it is you want the more you use your intelligence. The more you use your intelligence the greater you build your third mind. Then you will see the world more for what it really is. See the world from the cosmic view.

Don't be subject to your emotions. Subject your emotions to your iron will. Examine your self carefully. Do this every moment of every day.

Your thoughts are the battle ground. You fight you and yourself. You fight others. You fight the system. You fight everything about everybody. Stop already. Your killing you self. It's all wasted energy.

Direct your thoughts with purpose. Cherish your thinking and your thinking will cherish you. Thoughts create expression. Expression creates the lines on our faces.

What ever it is you want you first must visualize your self in possession of it. Then move toward it with style and grace. Then dare to carry this image around with you all the time where ever you go. Pretty soon the thoughts of your thinking it will drop into your spirit. Once it does, it becomes a part of you. Once it becomes a part of you then you now have your being in it. You are now one with your ideal.

Sometimes you have to live by faith. The opposite of living by faith is hope deferred, which actually makes the heart sick. So what this means is that to believe is healthier than to not to believe. Believe to the point to where you are a little bit embarrassed. This way you push the limits.

Faith is best defined as: to believe in something as though it is even though it's not. Sounds simple enough.

Always maintain quality of life. So, you have no money, have not the finer things in life. I believe strongly in maintaining a quality oriented life style. This means always being clean and orderly in everyway possible. I believe in standing up for what I believe in today. Tomorrow that may change. I also believe in being fair so that God may be fair with me, being firm when it is needed. Never deny a hungry stomach. No matter what it is being a human or beast.

Who are you, I don't know. Chances are you don't even know that either. Heck, I'm still discovering who I am on a daily basis. But I can tell you this. You can only find out by facing your maker. He will show you who you are. You are rich and poor. You are small and great. You are from heaven and yet live on earth. We are lowly yet from on high. We are dumb yet we are smart. We are lost yet we can be found. We are sick yet we can heal our selves. Your maker will show you who you are and who you are not. It you have the courage to do so. You will not be disappointed. You will only come out the wiser.

Personality can be special. I believe it takes every personality that has ever been created to make up the personality of God. Our experiences coupled with our convictions wrought our very own unique personality. There is none other like you in the whole galaxy. This alone makes you a great treasure, worthy of praise. He created the very essence of our being. Our personality is the combination of traits that are inherent within. Trait means: a distinguishing characteristic or quality. Character is a combination of qualities. In short, character is conviction in action.

INTENSE WILL: Once you are energized by good thinking; this is called energy of will. Energy of will is a self originating force. It is the soul of every great person, in other words, it breaths life back into you. Where it is there is life.

Where it is not there is non life, better yet life draining. There is faintness, helplessness, and confusion. The world has for us exactly what we have for it. The world is a mirror which reflects the faces we make. Weak people wait for opportunities. Strong people make opportunities. Like the old saying goes, "where there is a will there is a way".

If you intensely will to do something you will find a way. An intense desire itself transforms possibilities into reality. Our wishful prayers are but prophecy of the things we are capable of doing. The shy feeble willed person finds everything impossible because he believes it to be so. A will to succeed is a steadfast determination. It is a burning desire to attain the object of your wishes. A burning desire is no ordinary desire, or idle wish. It is enthusiastic faith in the attainment of the goal. A steadfast determination is desire plus expectation.

Plan on planning or plan on failing. Planning is the next step in the attainment of you desires. We first must give before we can expect to receive.

SITTING IDLE: On the great clock of time A great action is always proceeded by a great purpose. So, step forward and act with purpose. Nothing breeds nothing. If we are idle and shiftless by choice, we shall be nerveless and powerless by necessity.

CHARACTERISTICS OF PERSONALITY The most important characteristics of your personality are as follows: Be conscientious, cheerful, be of good courage. Be courteous. Be decisive. Have dignity. Exercise emotional control. Have enthusiasm. Be honest and have veracity. Be kind and love your fellow man. Have loyalty. Be modest. Be an observer and last have patience. Never react in the face of short term failure. Give it everything you've got. The quality of your work is your trade mark.

God using nature has a way of paying every person what is due to him after all this is a justly ordered universe. If you smile you will be smiled upon. If you frown you will be frowned upon. If you sing you will be invited into gay company. If you think you will be entertained by thinkers. If you love the world and earnestly seek for the good therein, you will be surrounded by loving friends, and nature will pour into your lap the treasures of the earth.

The law of cause and effect means doing something for a result. Give from your self and from your own being your time, talents, energies, and money, to make your world and this world a better place. Do everything with a satisfaction guaranteed or your money back.

About the Author

Dear Reader,

    My name is Ernest Johnson. If this letter reaches your eyes and ears, then pay attention to the details. Our galaxy is fully occupied by the unseen gods. All of them are positioning themselves to bring about the Judgment of End Times. All heavenly forces and wicked forces have their agenda. They are all active. They all have hardened positions and winner takes all. Where we are at on the great apocalypse time clock is alarming to say the least. I speak to all conscious beings, both dead and alive, to support anyone, anywhere who can bring you deep knowledge that will enlighten our understanding on the unforeseen forces.

    Deeply you know this subject I'm speaking of. You instinctively understand what is at stake. You know you heart beats to your dream. To be faceless is to be enlightened. Give up self to allow the energy of these forces to lead you to your destiny, whatever it is, for only you decide.

I have been from heaven to hell to bring to you the nasty facts of life. BS/No BS razor's edge, set on fire by the Holy Spirit. I can only be your friend by not becoming your friend. My material is not the light hearted. You may not be suited for my writings.

Duality is misleading if we judge from this place. Church is not what it seems. Hell is neither Christ or Satan! Truth is, your reality is only that, your own reality. I have brought to you Earth shattering, thunder thinking. You will learn by subjecting yourself to this new cutting edge, bone shattering thunder. Only then can you appreciate the spirit of man.

If you think this letter is either honest or deceptive, you are right either way. But do us both a favor, reread this letter. Act with love or hatred. Either one will work. Just educate yourself in any way you choose. But learn, you must do. We live in a world that doesn't understand deep inner things. But we all crave it. My material is my best that this hard-working man of iron can muster. Honesty and truth are not the same. The church is not what is seems. My material is designed to clear all the cobwebs, address the sin of man from a dual mind set, with quadruple points of view.

This is why nothing is as it seems. Learn why you're here. What your mission is. What your part is. Last but not least, where you'll end up.

This is how I present my audio. It's shut up, sit your ass down and listen to what the gods have to say to you. Period! But not all at once. Each subject is just that, one subject. But all combined, Yes! After continuing for a season you will understand this to be true!

Stand for something or fall for anything! The cosmic gates are about to swing wide. Support for this cause is paramount. Capture the energy, capture the matter. Live life on the run!

Whatever it is that you desire, first rule is to lock yourself into the energy of it. Look deeply into the subject and dive in. That's it. Secret revealed! All success is wrapped up in this key!

Ernest Johnson

www.ingramcontent.com/pod-product-compliance
Lightning Source LLC
Chambersburg PA
CBHW032038150426
43194CB00006B/333